Outcast

BY **KIRKMAN**
& **AZACETA**

VOLUME **1**: A DARKNESS SURROUNDS HIM

OUTCAST BY KIRKMAN & AZACETA
VOL. 1: A DARKNESS SURROUNDS HIM
January 2015
First printing

ISBN: 978-1-63215-053-0

Published by Image Comics, Inc.

Office of publication: 2001 Center Street, 6th Floor,
Berkeley, CA 94704.

For information regarding the CPSIA on this printed
material call: 203-595-3636 and provide reference #
RICH - 599211.

Robert Kirkman
Creator, Writer

Paul Azaceta
Artist

Elizabeth Breitweiser
Colorist

Rus Wooton
Letterer

Paul Azaceta
Elizabeth Breitweiser
Cover

Helen Leigh
Assistant Editor

Sean Mackiewicz
Editor

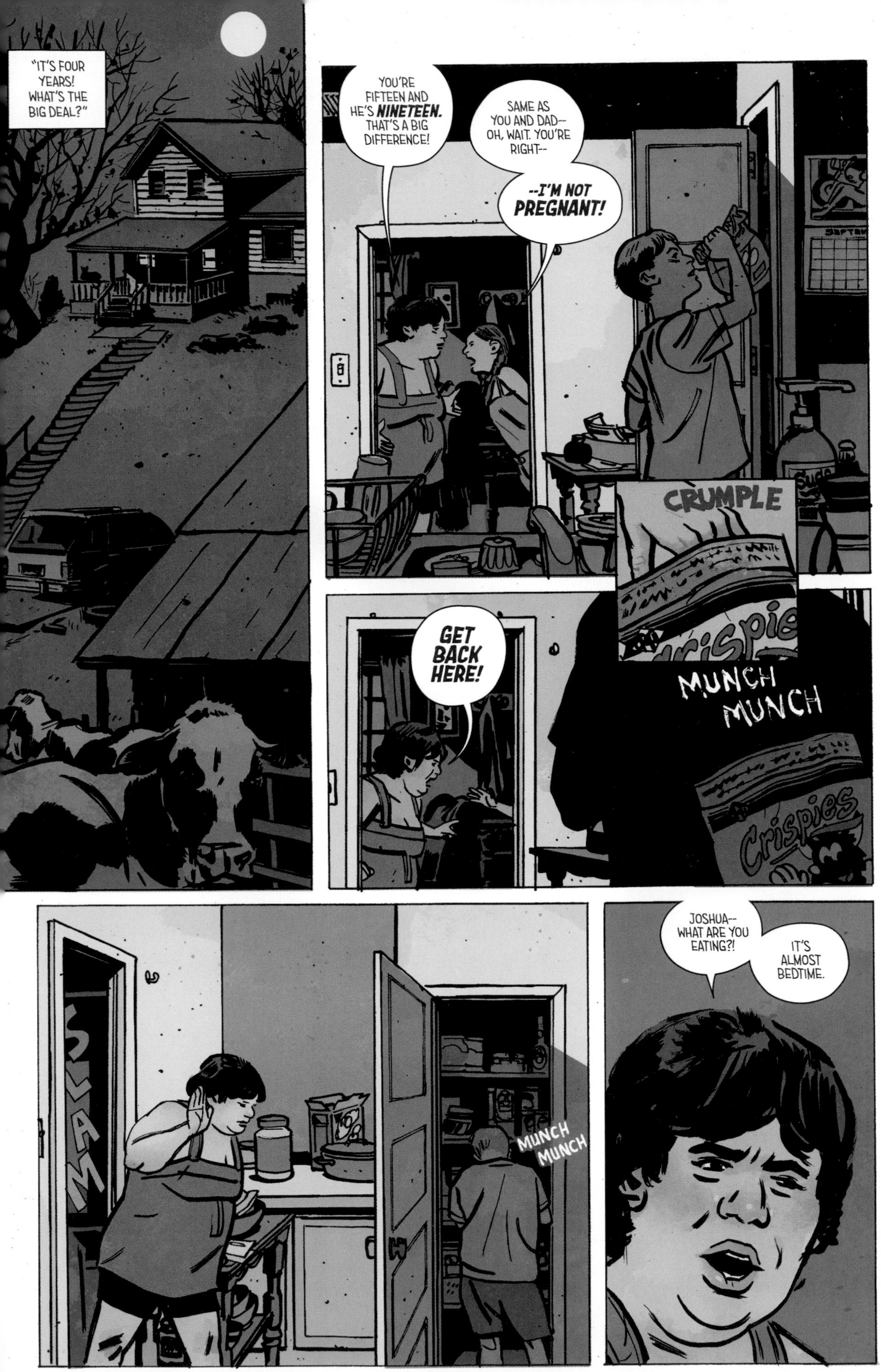
"IT'S FOUR YEARS! WHAT'S THE BIG DEAL?"
YOU'RE FIFTEEN AND HE'S **NINETEEN.** THAT'S A BIG DIFFERENCE!
SAME AS YOU AND DAD-- OH, WAIT. YOU'RE RIGHT--
--I'M NOT PREGNANT!
CRUMPLE
Crispies
GET BACK HERE!
MUNCH MUNCH
Crispies
SLAM
MUNCH MUNCH
JOSHUA-- WHAT ARE YOU EATING?!
IT'S ALMOST BEDTIME.

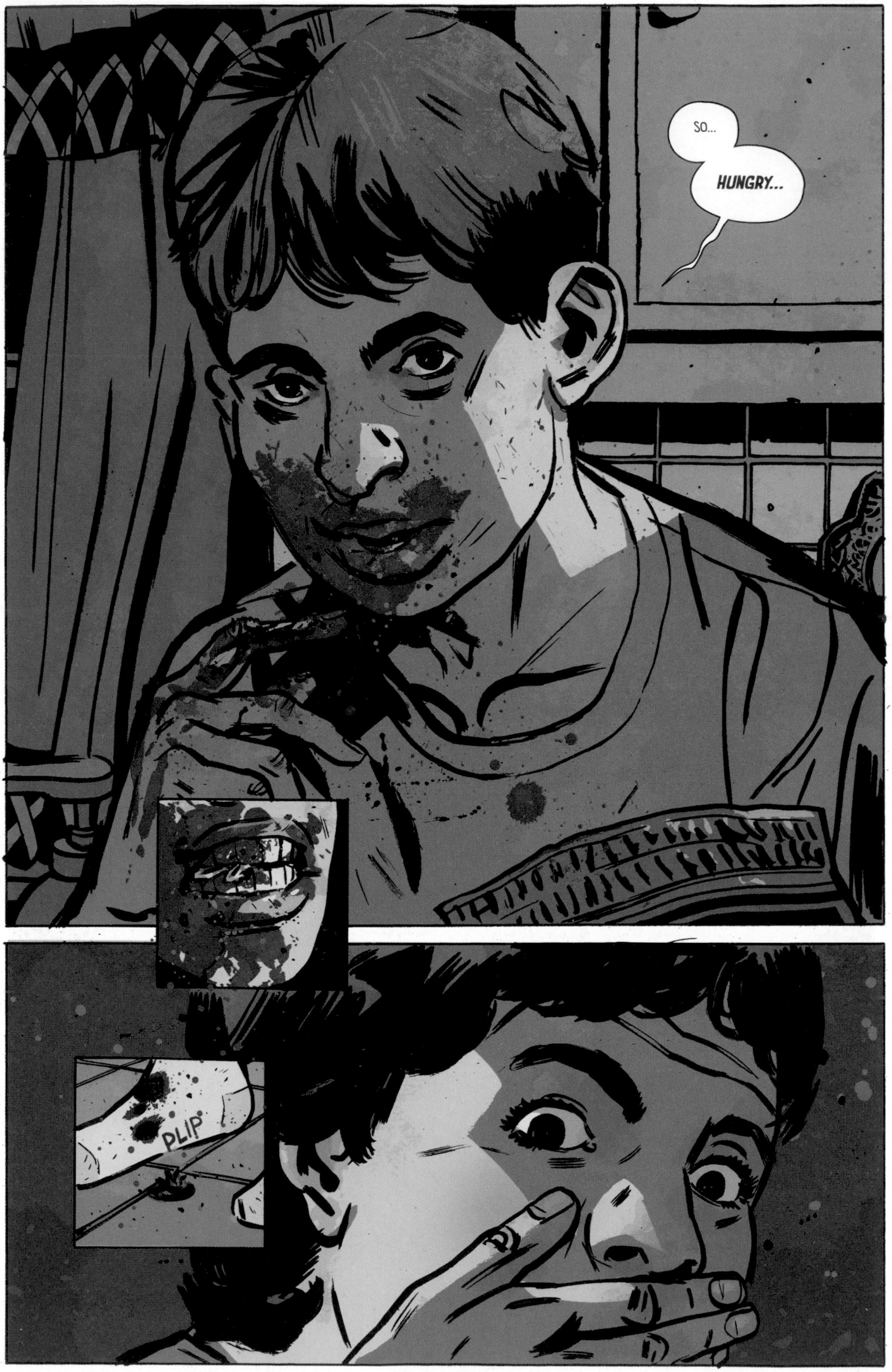
SO...
HUNGRY...
PLIP

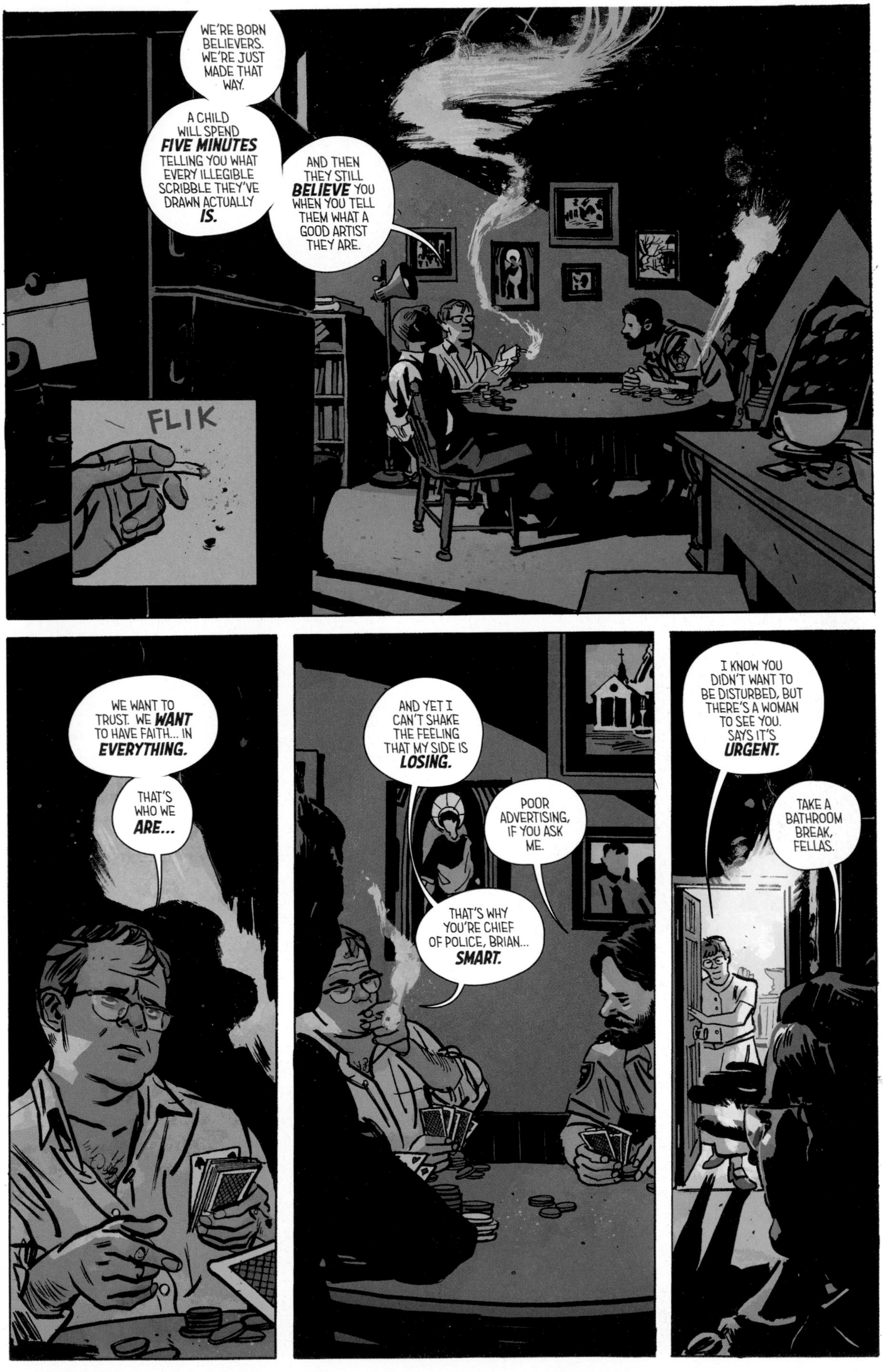
WE'RE BORN BELIEVERS. WE'RE JUST MADE THAT WAY.
A CHILD WILL SPEND **FIVE MINUTES** TELLING YOU WHAT EVERY ILLEGIBLE SCRIBBLE THEY'VE DRAWN ACTUALLY **IS.**
AND THEN THEY STILL **BELIEVE** YOU WHEN YOU TELL THEM WHAT A GOOD ARTIST THEY ARE.
FLIK
WE WANT TO TRUST. WE **WANT** TO HAVE FAITH... IN **EVERYTHING.**
THAT'S WHO WE **ARE...**
AND YET I CAN'T SHAKE THE FEELING THAT MY SIDE IS **LOSING.**
POOR ADVERTISING, IF YOU ASK ME.
THAT'S WHY YOU'RE CHIEF OF POLICE, BRIAN... **SMART.**
I KNOW YOU DIDN'T WANT TO BE DISTURBED, BUT THERE'S A WOMAN TO SEE YOU. SAYS IT'S **URGENT.**
TAKE A BATHROOM BREAK, FELLAS.

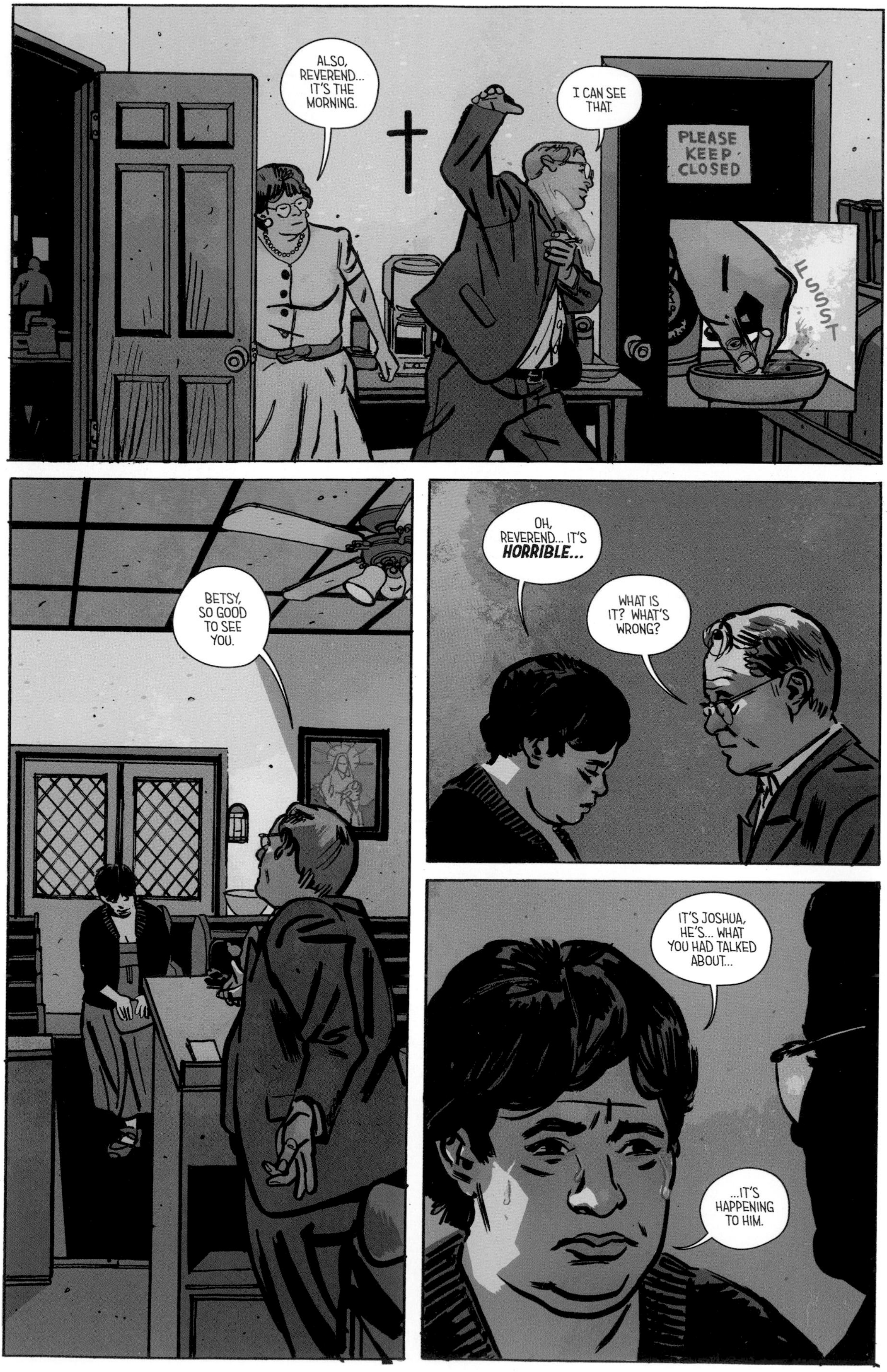
ALSO, REVEREND... IT'S THE MORNING.
I CAN SEE THAT.
PLEASE KEEP CLOSED
TSSSST
BETSY, SO GOOD TO SEE YOU.
OH, REVEREND... IT'S HORRIBLE...
WHAT IS IT? WHAT'S WRONG?
IT'S JOSHUA, HE'S... WHAT YOU HAD TALKED ABOUT...
...IT'S HAPPENING TO HIM.

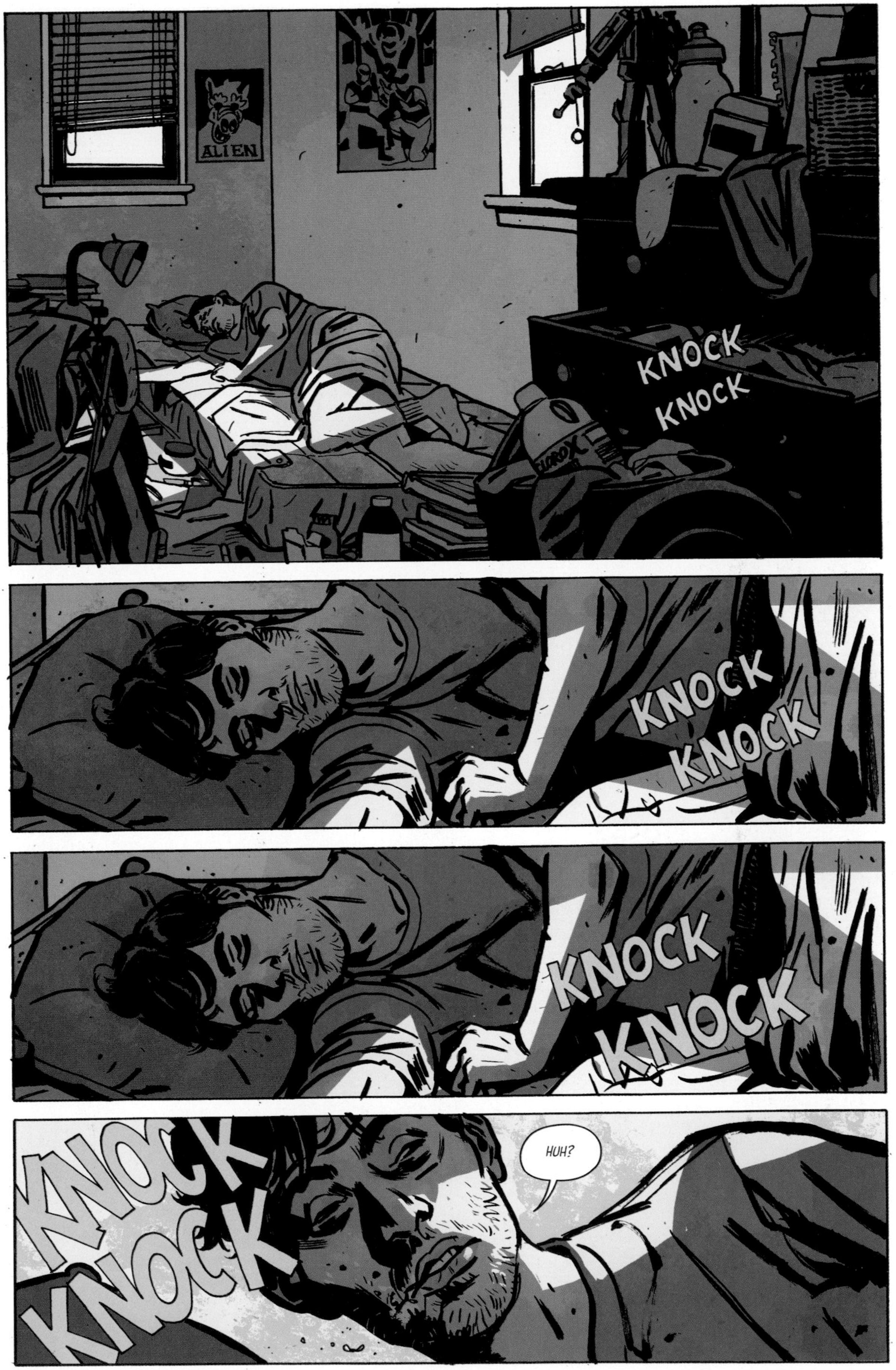
ALIEN
KNOCK KNOCK
KNOCK KNOCK
KNOCK KNOCK
KNOCK KNOCK
HUH?

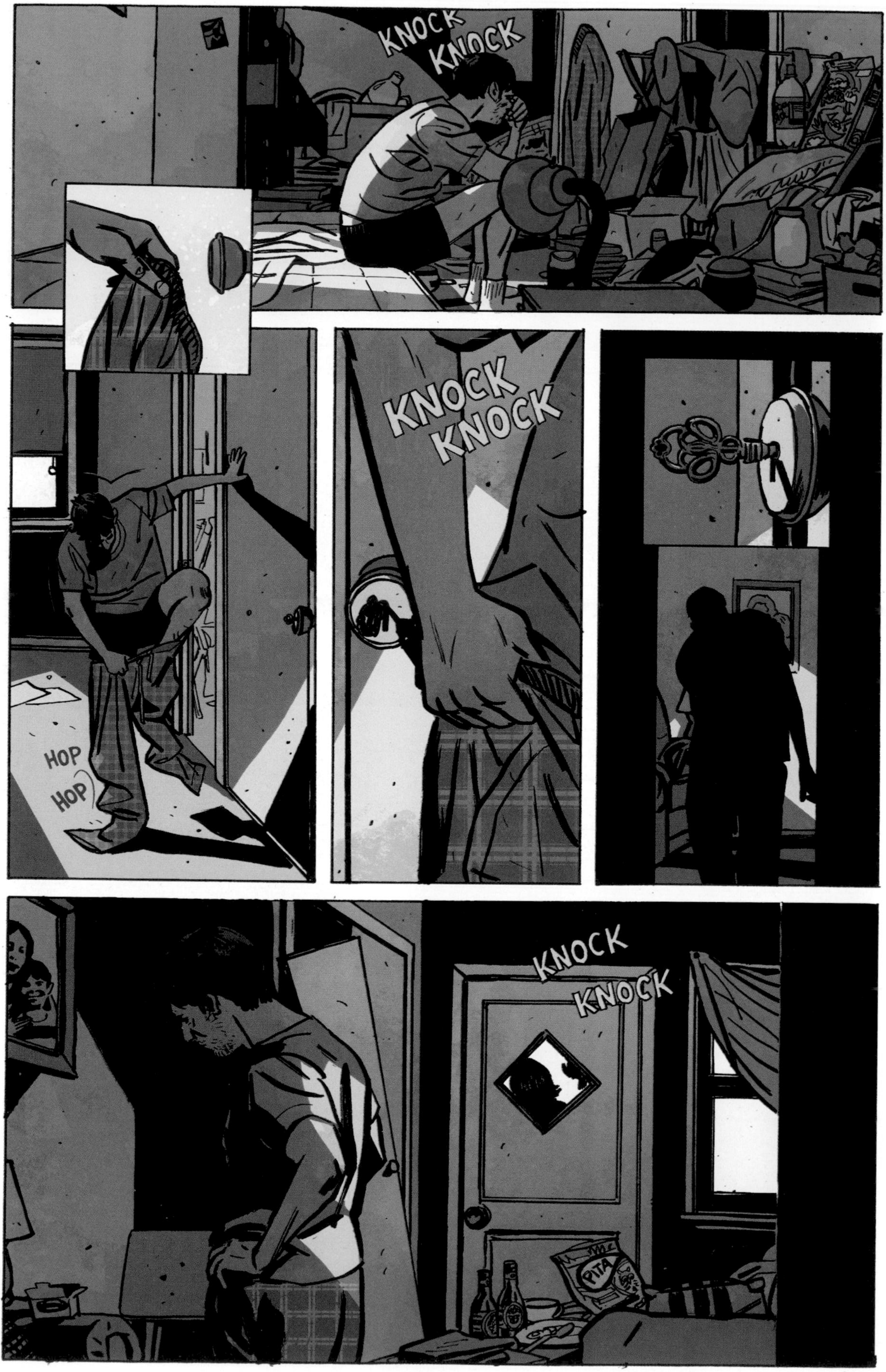
KNOCK
KNOCK
HOP
HOP
KNOCK
KNOCK
KNOCK
KNOCK
PITA

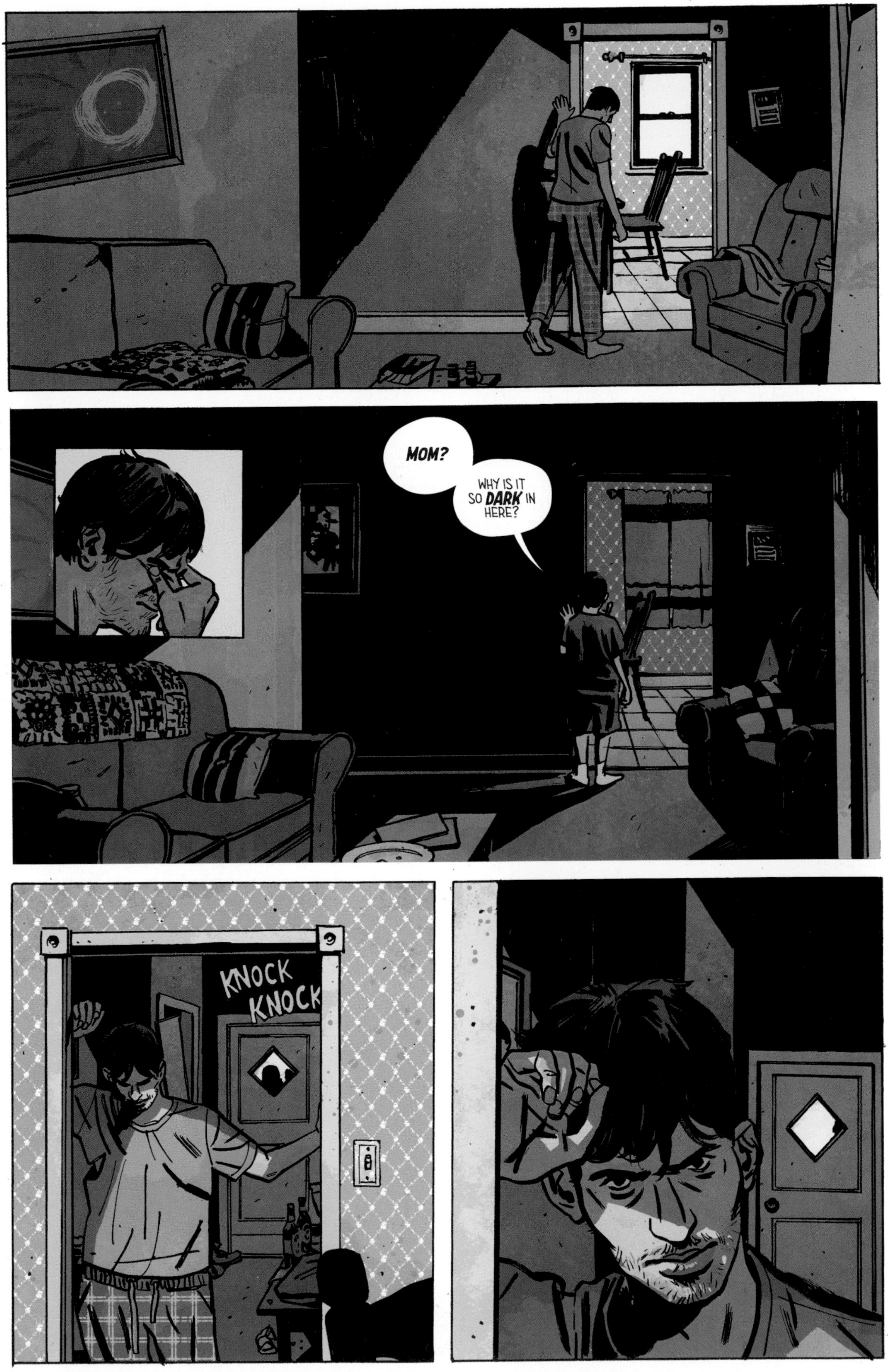
MOM?
WHY IS IT SO DARK IN HERE?
KNOCK KNOCK

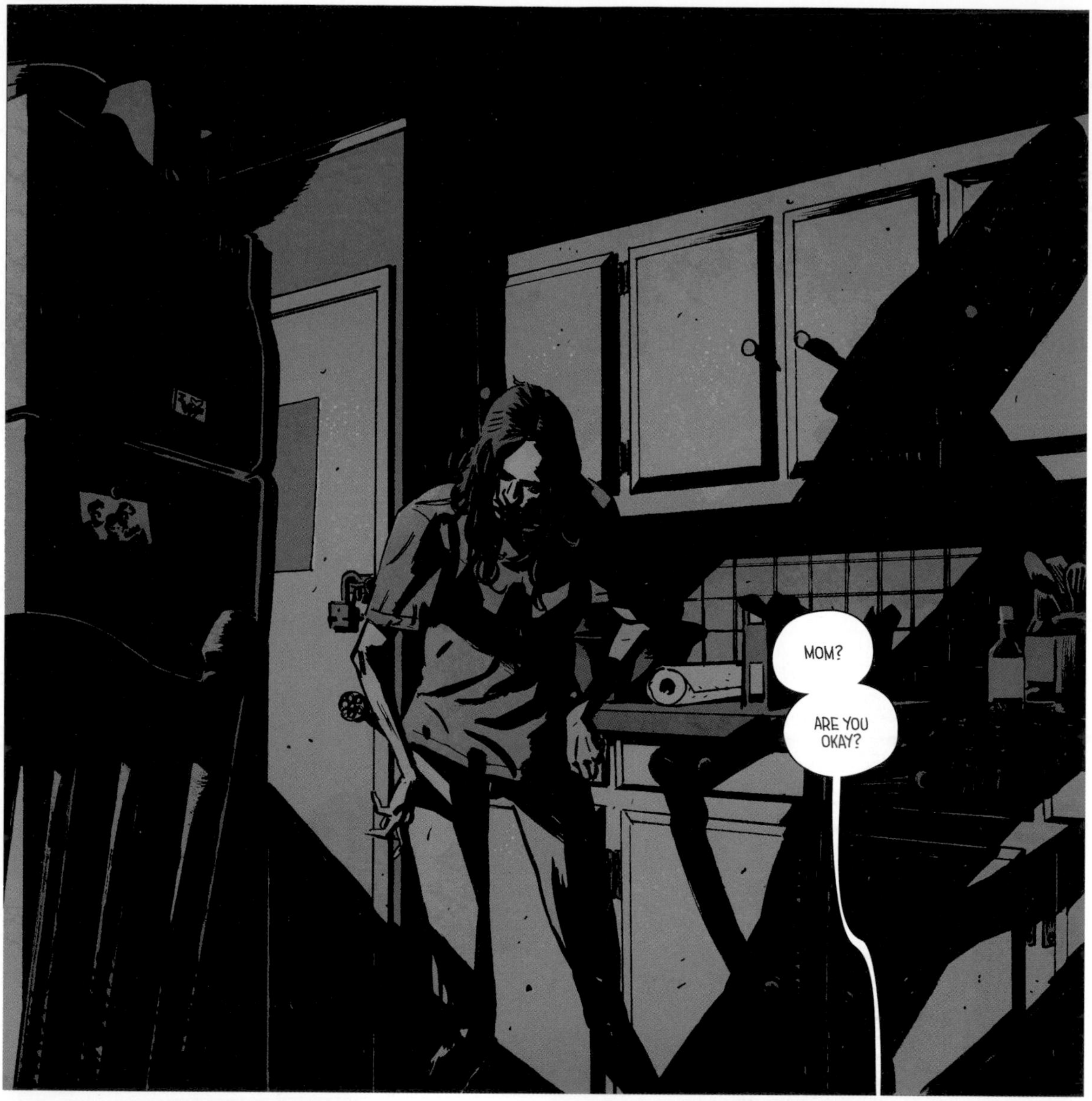
MOM?
ARE YOU OKAY?

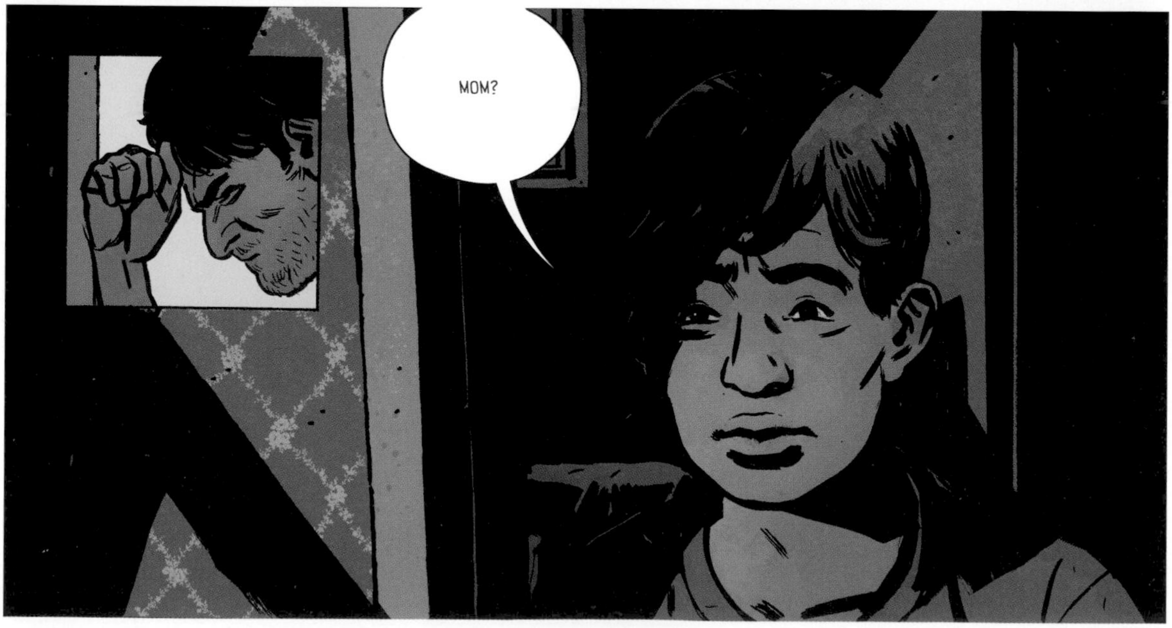
MOM?

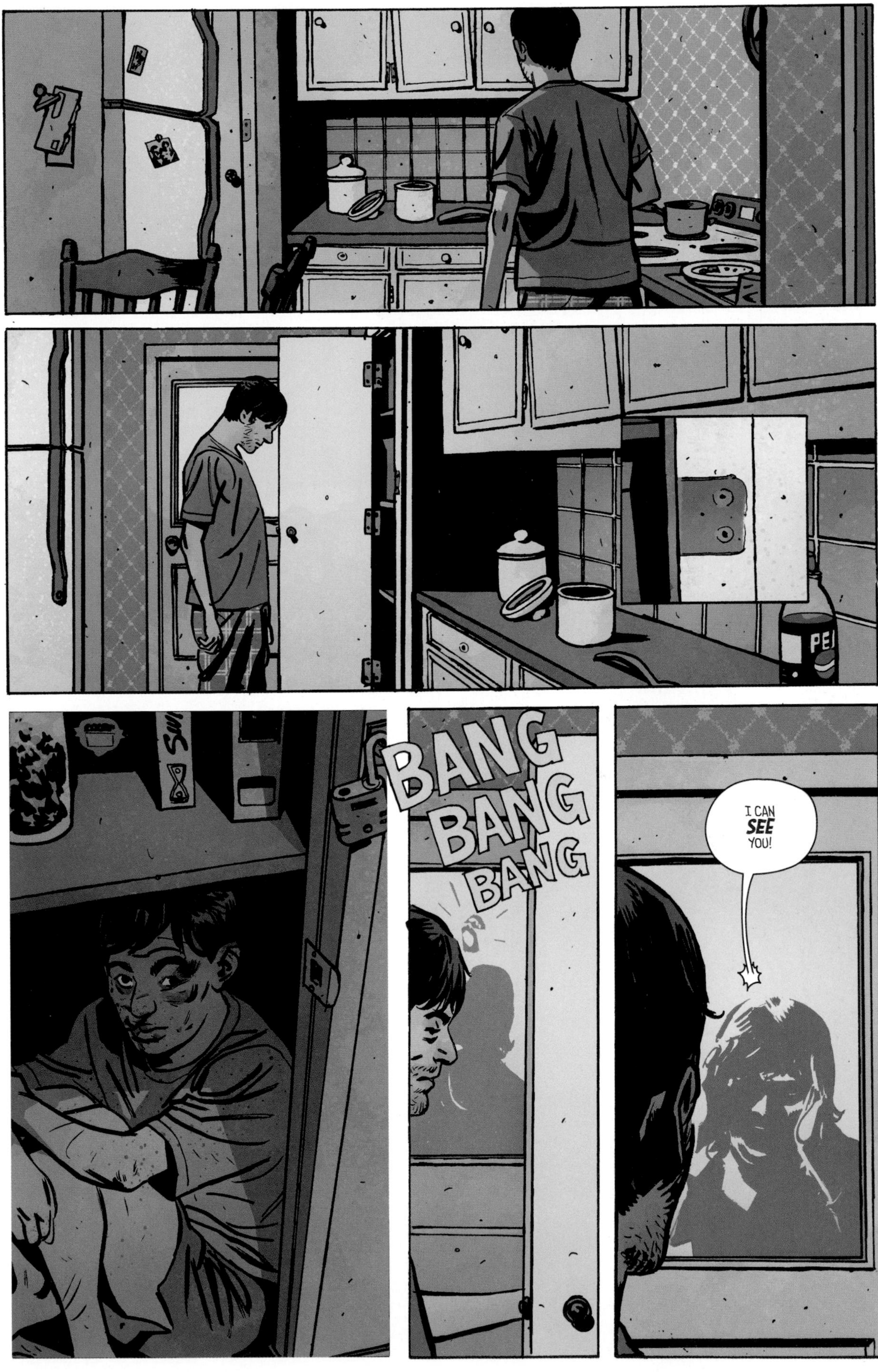

BANG
BANG
BANG
I CAN SEE YOU!

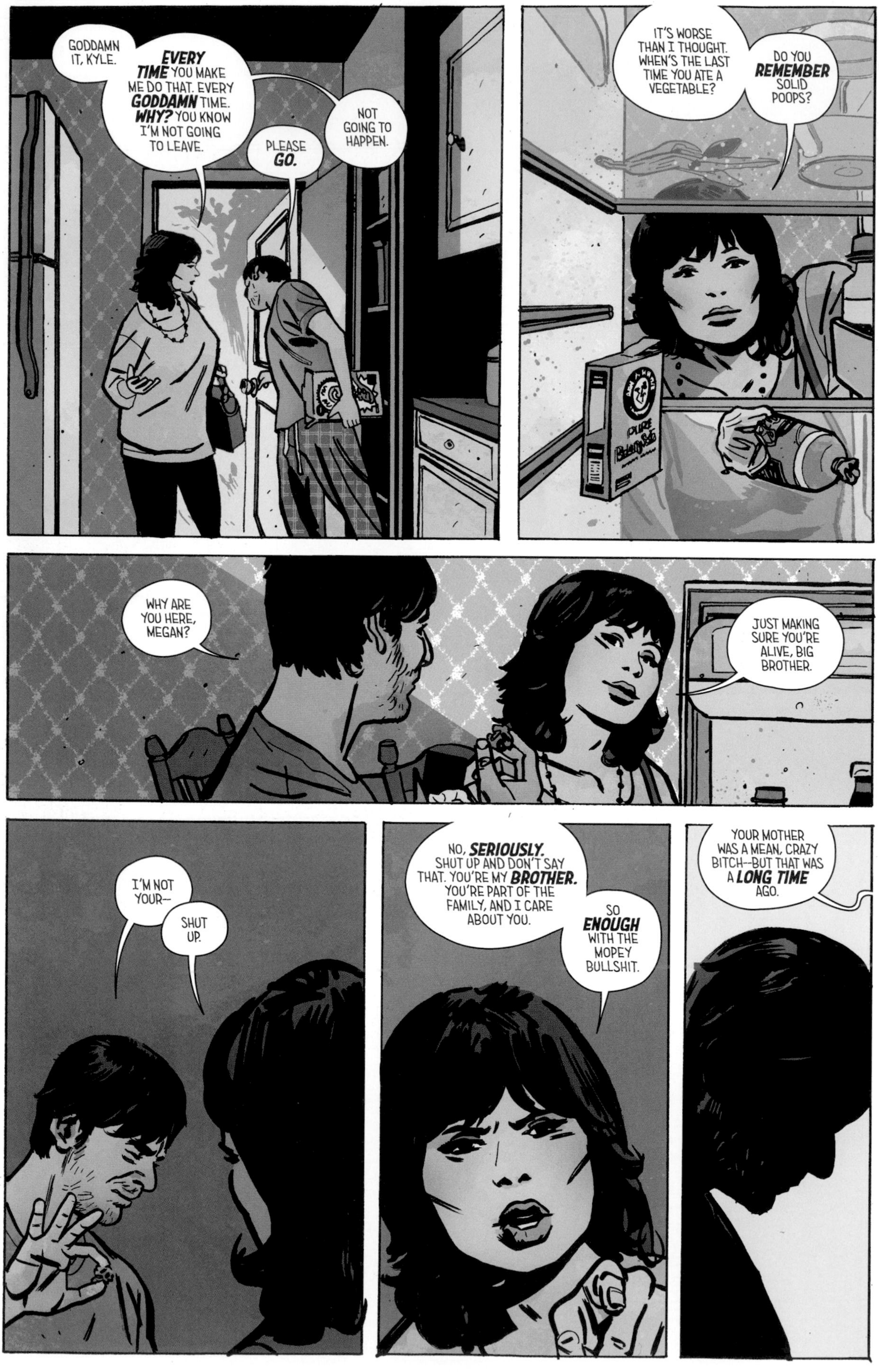
GODDAMN IT, KYLE.
EVERY TIME YOU MAKE ME DO THAT. EVERY GODDAMN TIME. WHY? YOU KNOW I'M NOT GOING TO LEAVE.
PLEASE GO.
NOT GOING TO HAPPEN.
IT'S WORSE THAN I THOUGHT. WHEN'S THE LAST TIME YOU ATE A VEGETABLE?
DO YOU REMEMBER SOLID POOPS?
PURE
WHY ARE YOU HERE, MEGAN?
JUST MAKING SURE YOU'RE ALIVE, BIG BROTHER.
I'M NOT YOUR--
SHUT UP.
NO, SERIOUSLY. SHUT UP AND DON'T SAY THAT. YOU'RE MY BROTHER. YOU'RE PART OF THE FAMILY, AND I CARE ABOUT YOU.
SO ENOUGH WITH THE MOPEY BULLSHIT.
YOUR MOTHER WAS A MEAN, CRAZY BITCH--BUT THAT WAS A LONG TIME AGO.

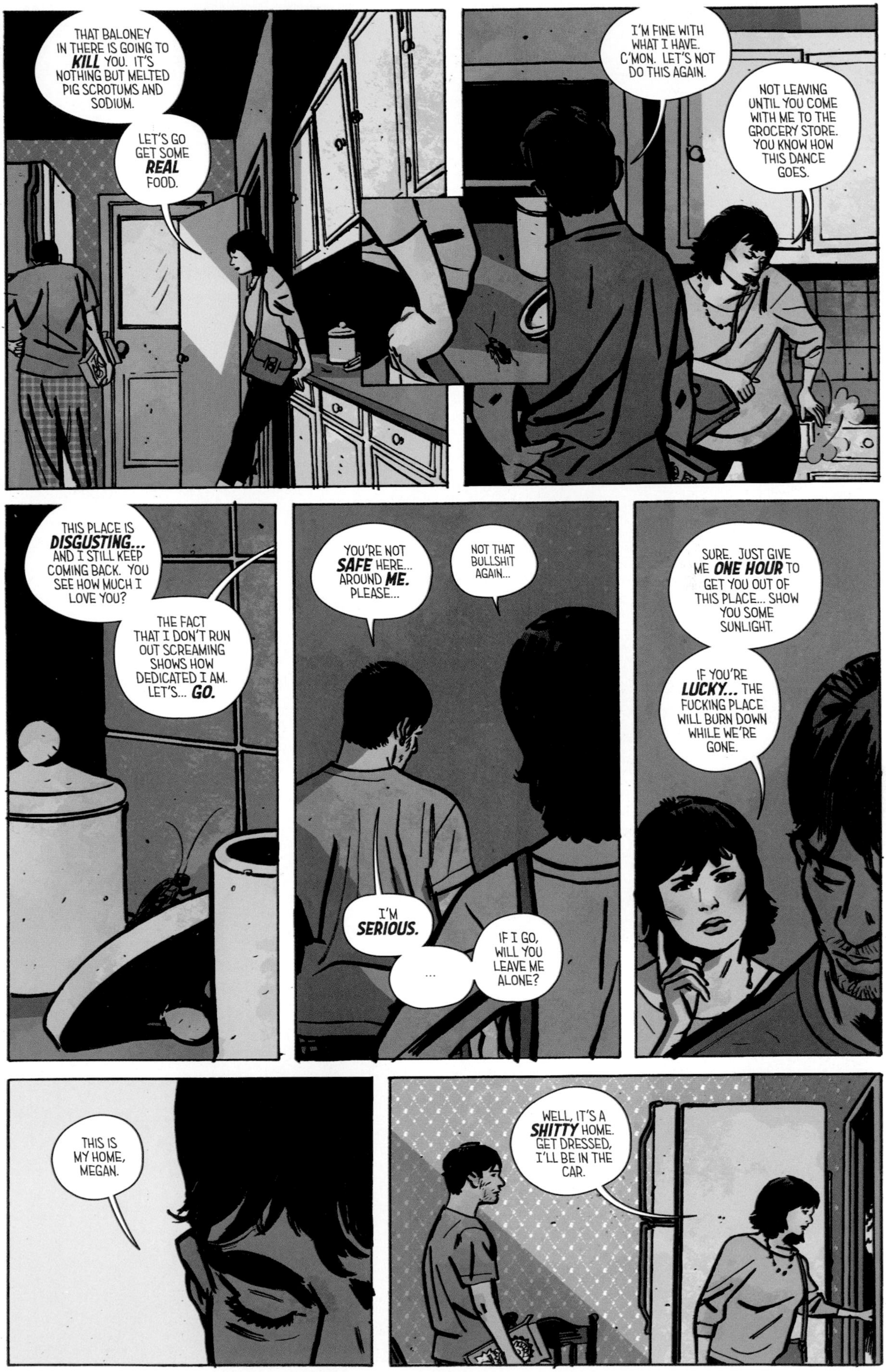
THAT BALONEY IN THERE IS GOING TO KILL YOU. IT'S NOTHING BUT MELTED PIG SCROTUMS AND SODIUM.
LET'S GO GET SOME REAL FOOD.
I'M FINE WITH WHAT I HAVE. C'MON. LET'S NOT DO THIS AGAIN.
NOT LEAVING UNTIL YOU COME WITH ME TO THE GROCERY STORE. YOU KNOW HOW THIS DANCE GOES.
THIS PLACE IS DISGUSTING... AND I STILL KEEP COMING BACK. YOU SEE HOW MUCH I LOVE YOU?
THE FACT THAT I DON'T RUN OUT SCREAMING SHOWS HOW DEDICATED I AM. LET'S... GO.
YOU'RE NOT SAFE HERE... AROUND ME. PLEASE...
NOT THAT BULLSHIT AGAIN...
I'M SERIOUS.
...
IF I GO, WILL YOU LEAVE ME ALONE?
SURE. JUST GIVE ME ONE HOUR TO GET YOU OUT OF THIS PLACE... SHOW YOU SOME SUNLIGHT.
IF YOU'RE LUCKY... THE FUCKING PLACE WILL BURN DOWN WHILE WE'RE GONE.
THIS IS MY HOME, MEGAN.
WELL, IT'S A SHITTY HOME. GET DRESSED, I'LL BE IN THE CAR.

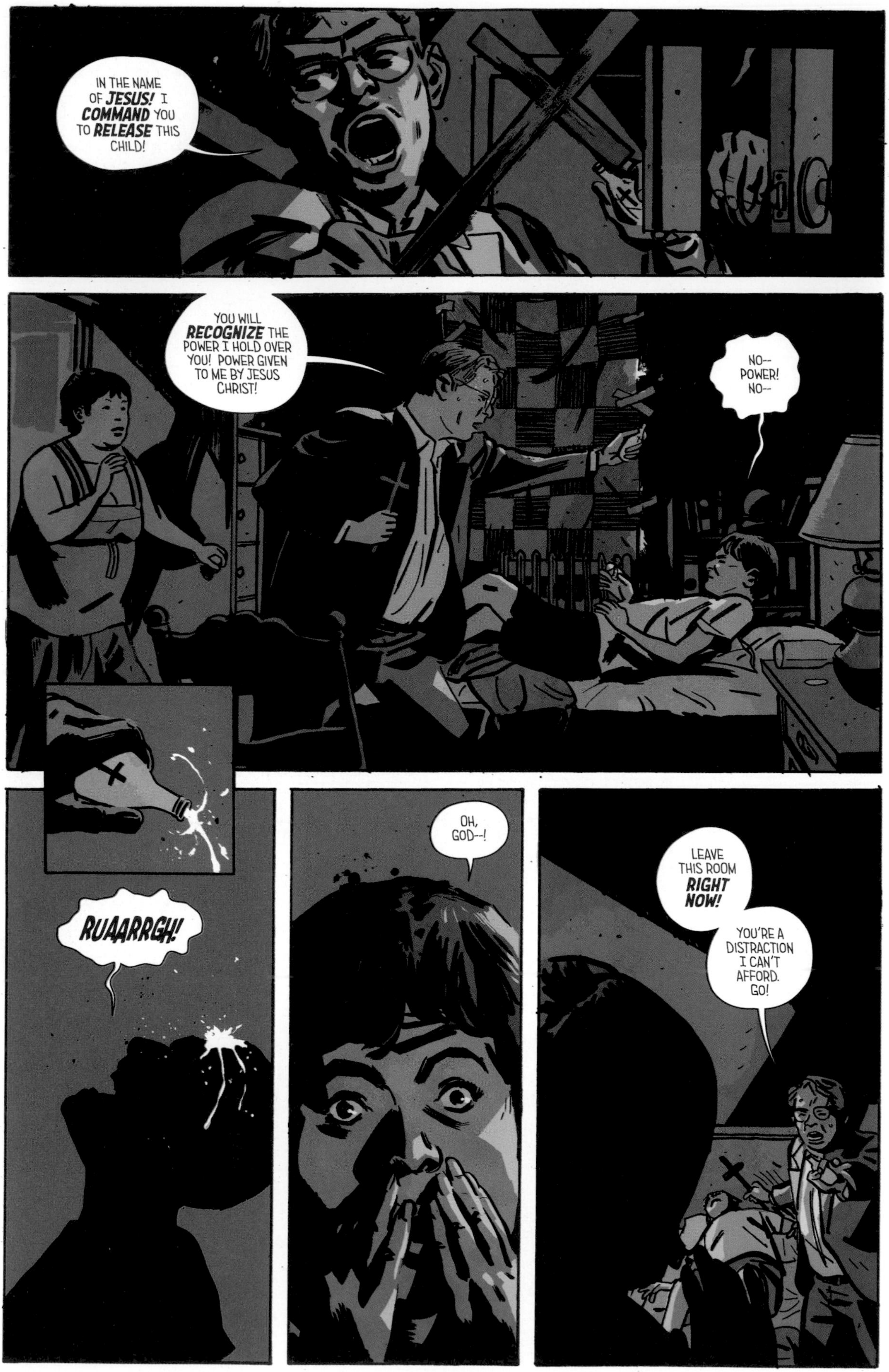
IN THE NAME OF **JESUS!** I **COMMAND** YOU TO **RELEASE** THIS CHILD!
YOU WILL **RECOGNIZE** THE POWER I HOLD OVER YOU! POWER GIVEN TO ME BY JESUS CHRIST!
NO-- POWER! NO--
RUAARRGH!
OH, GOD--!
LEAVE THIS ROOM **RIGHT NOW!**
YOU'RE A DISTRACTION I CAN'T AFFORD. GO!

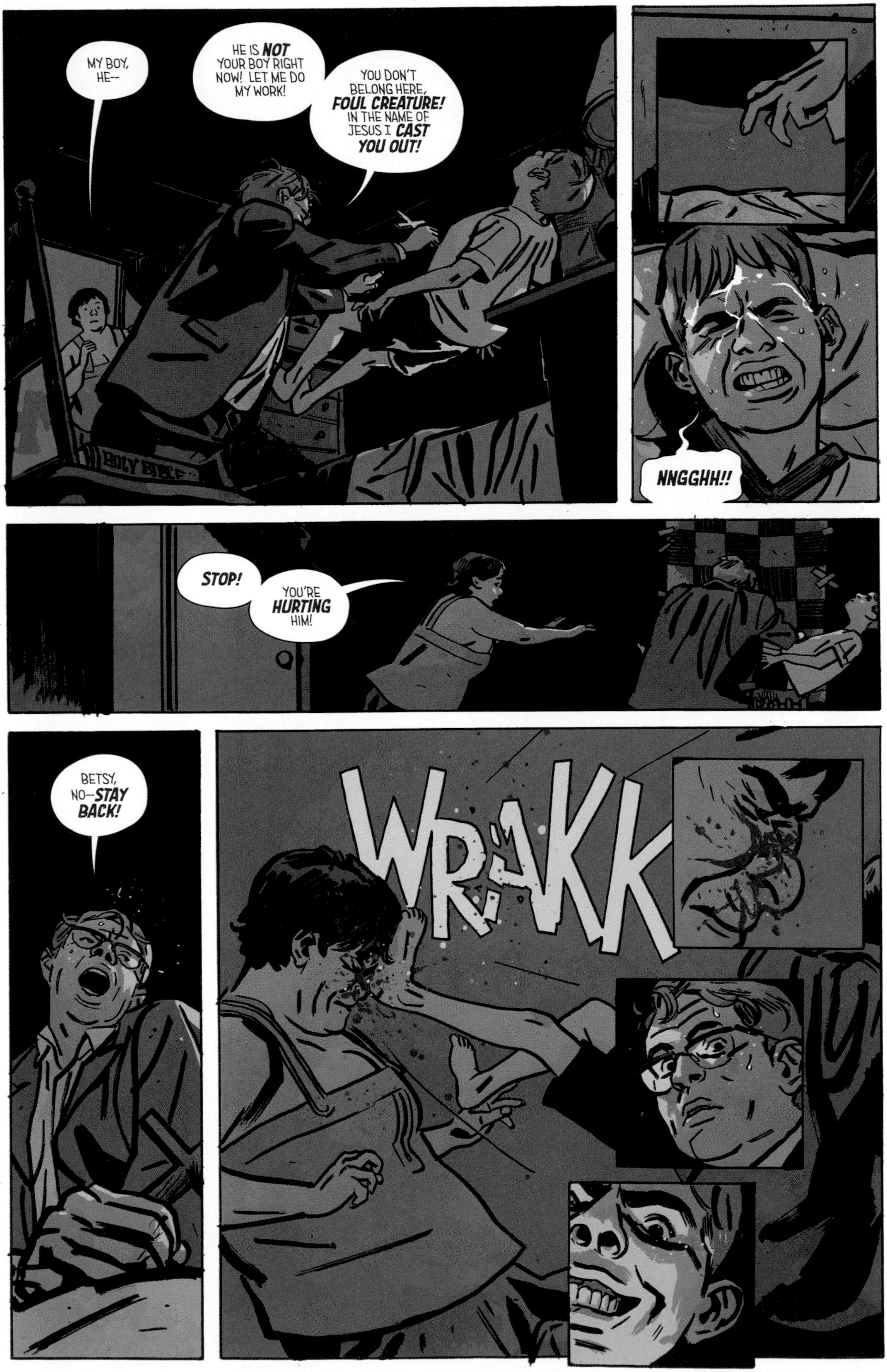

MY BOY, HE--
HE IS NOT YOUR BOY RIGHT NOW! LET ME DO MY WORK!
YOU DON'T BELONG HERE, FOUL CREATURE! IN THE NAME OF JESUS I CAST YOU OUT!
HOLY BIBLE
NNGGHH!!
STOP!
YOU'RE HURTING HIM!
BETSY, NO--STAY BACK!
WRAKK

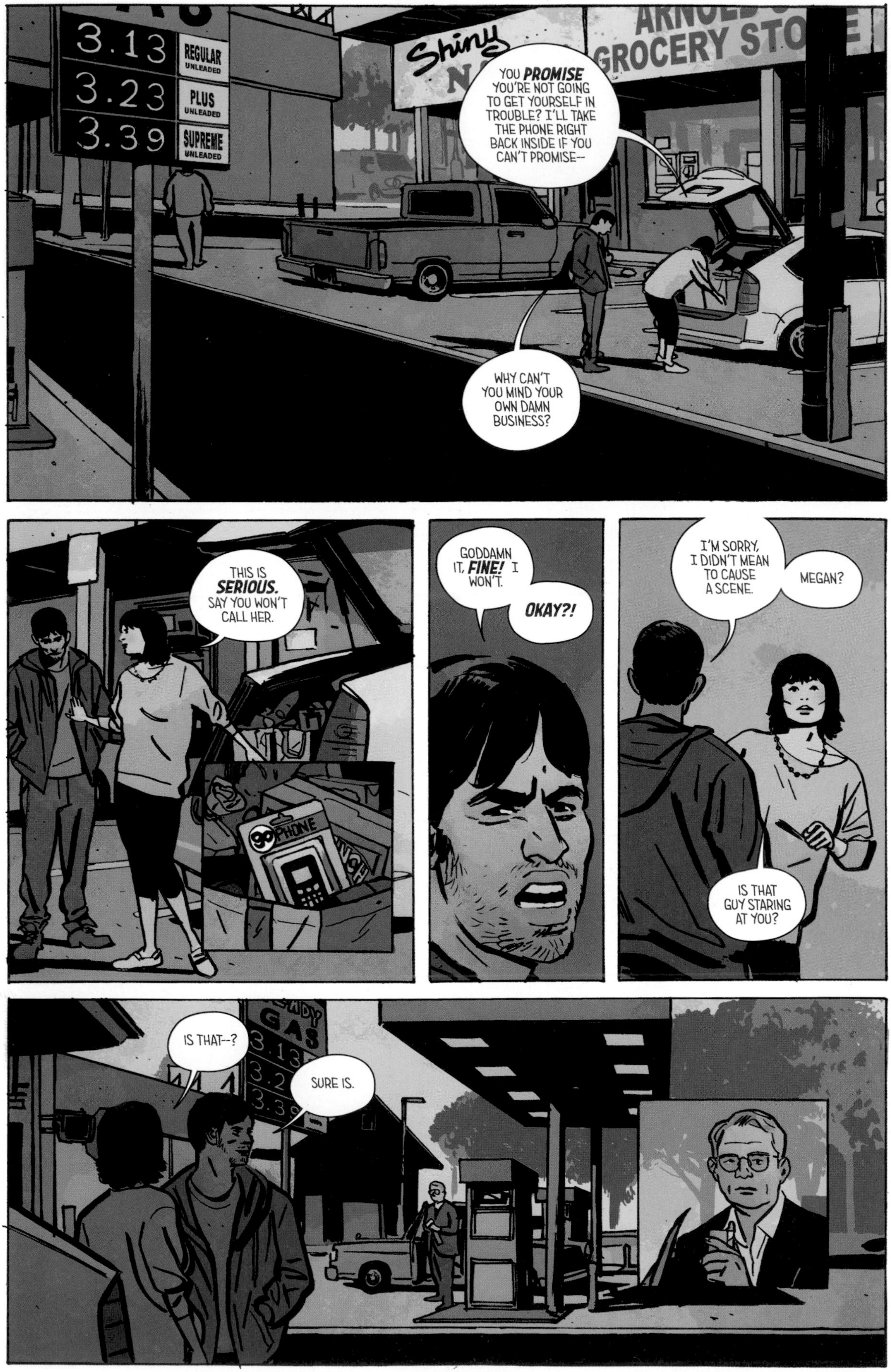
3.13 REGULAR UNLEADED
3.23 PLUS UNLEADED
3.39 SUPREME UNLEADED
GROCERY STO
Shiny
YOU **PROMISE** YOU'RE NOT GOING TO GET YOURSELF IN TROUBLE? I'LL TAKE THE PHONE RIGHT BACK INSIDE IF YOU CAN'T PROMISE--
WHY CAN'T YOU MIND YOUR OWN DAMN BUSINESS?
THIS IS **SERIOUS.** SAY YOU WON'T CALL HER.
PHONE
GODDAMN IT, **FINE!** I WON'T.
OKAY?!
I'M SORRY, I DIDN'T MEAN TO CAUSE A SCENE.
MEGAN?
IS THAT GUY STARING AT YOU?
IS THAT--?
SURE IS.
GAS

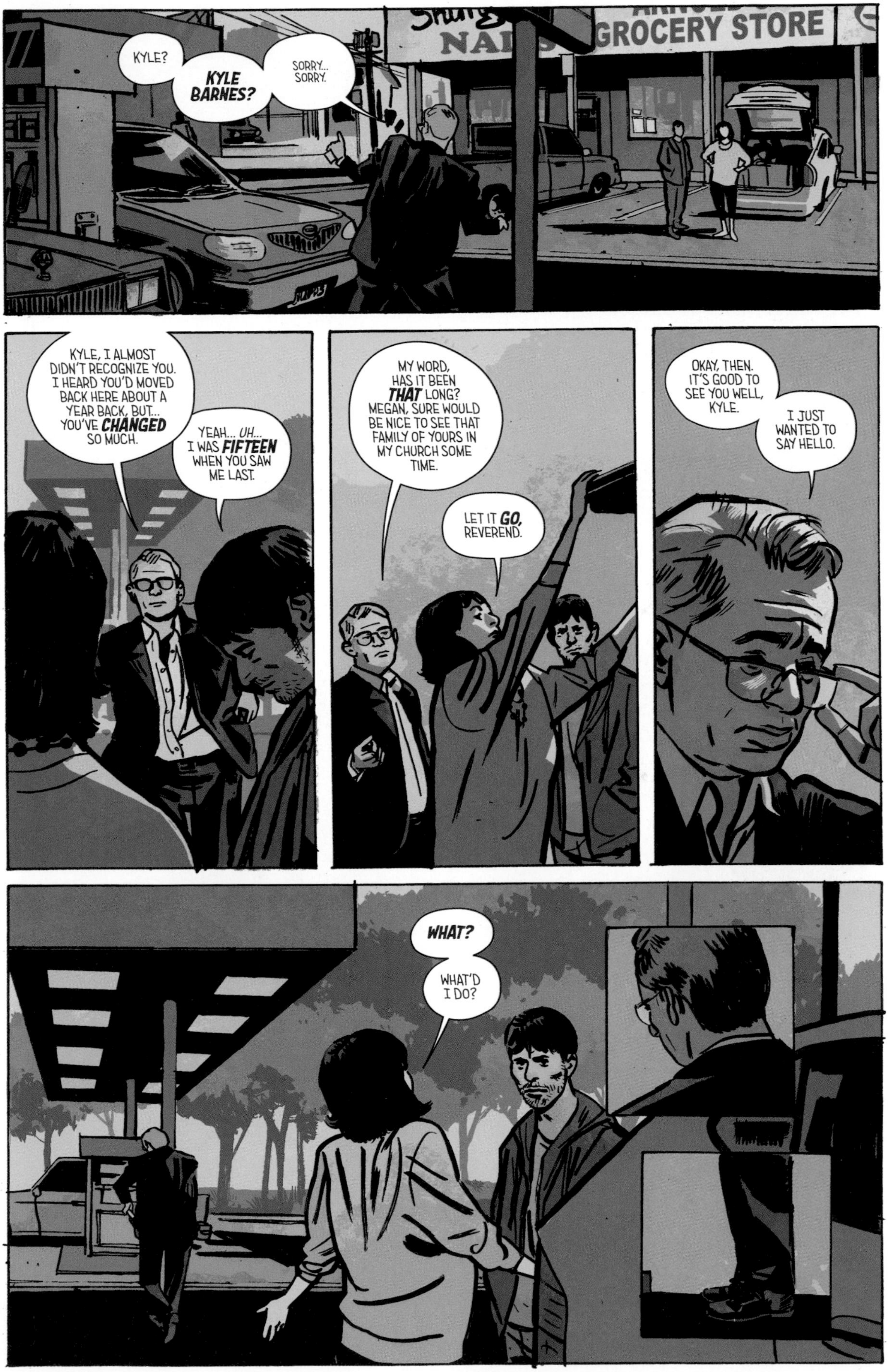

GROCERY STORE
KYLE?
KYLE BARNES?
SORRY... SORRY.
KYLE, I ALMOST DIDN'T RECOGNIZE YOU. I HEARD YOU'D MOVED BACK HERE ABOUT A YEAR BACK, BUT... YOU'VE CHANGED SO MUCH.
YEAH... UH... I WAS FIFTEEN WHEN YOU SAW ME LAST.
MY WORD, HAS IT BEEN THAT LONG? MEGAN, SURE WOULD BE NICE TO SEE THAT FAMILY OF YOURS IN MY CHURCH SOME TIME.
LET IT GO, REVEREND.
OKAY, THEN. IT'S GOOD TO SEE YOU WELL, KYLE.
I JUST WANTED TO SAY HELLO.
WHAT?
WHAT'D I DO?

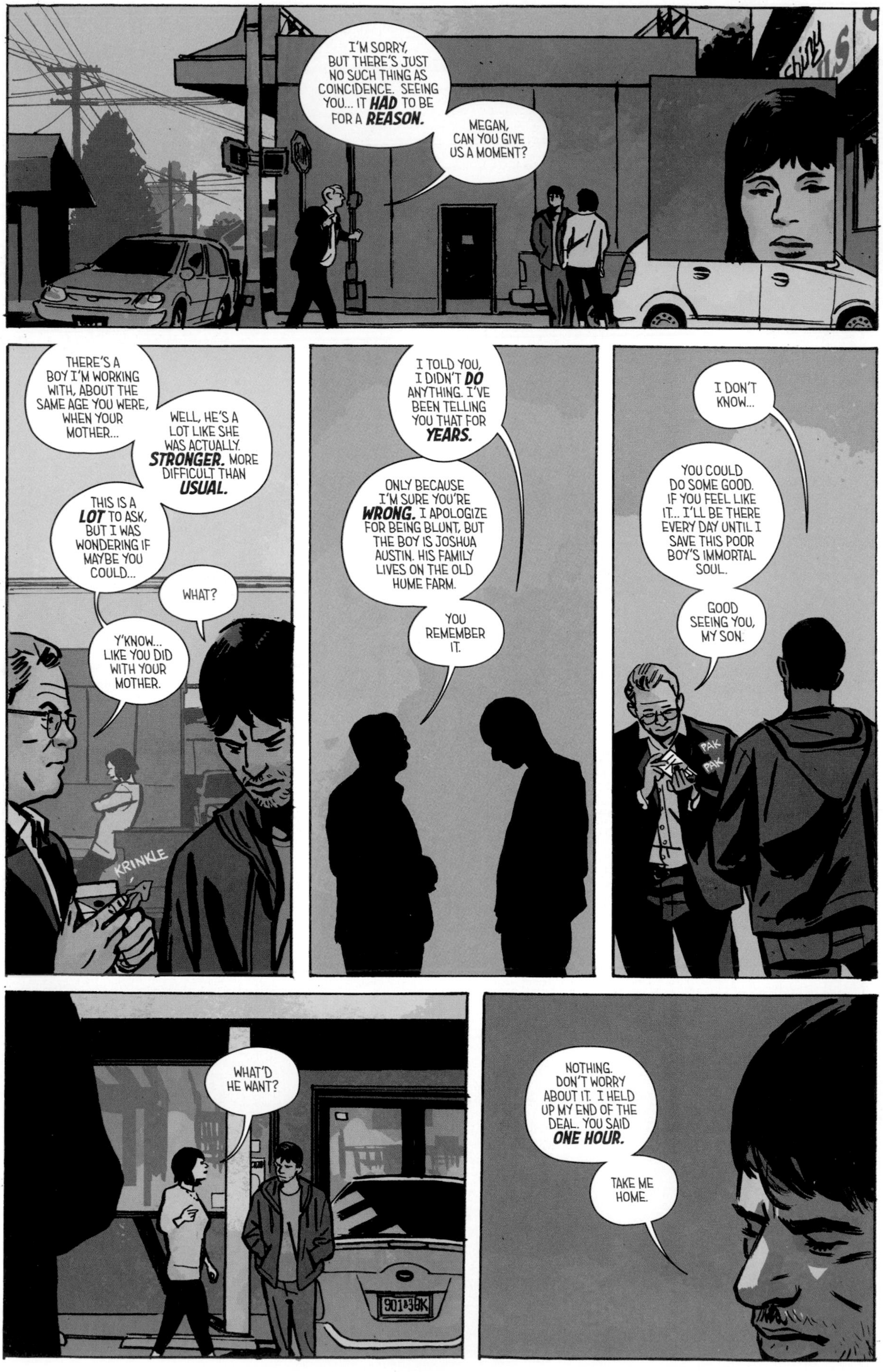
I'M SORRY, BUT THERE'S JUST NO SUCH THING AS COINCIDENCE. SEEING YOU... IT HAD TO BE FOR A REASON.
MEGAN, CAN YOU GIVE US A MOMENT?
THERE'S A BOY I'M WORKING WITH, ABOUT THE SAME AGE YOU WERE, WHEN YOUR MOTHER...
WELL, HE'S A LOT LIKE SHE WAS ACTUALLY. STRONGER. MORE DIFFICULT THAN USUAL.
THIS IS A LOT TO ASK, BUT I WAS WONDERING IF MAYBE YOU COULD...
WHAT?
Y'KNOW... LIKE YOU DID WITH YOUR MOTHER.
KRINKLE
I TOLD YOU, I DIDN'T DO ANYTHING. I'VE BEEN TELLING YOU THAT FOR YEARS.
ONLY BECAUSE I'M SURE YOU'RE WRONG. I APOLOGIZE FOR BEING BLUNT, BUT THE BOY IS JOSHUA AUSTIN. HIS FAMILY LIVES ON THE OLD HUME FARM.
YOU REMEMBER IT.
I DON'T KNOW...
YOU COULD DO SOME GOOD. IF YOU FEEL LIKE IT... I'LL BE THERE EVERY DAY UNTIL I SAVE THIS POOR BOY'S IMMORTAL SOUL.
GOOD SEEING YOU, MY SON.
PAK
PAK
WHAT'D HE WANT?
NOTHING. DON'T WORRY ABOUT IT. I HELD UP MY END OF THE DEAL. YOU SAID ONE HOUR.
TAKE ME HOME.

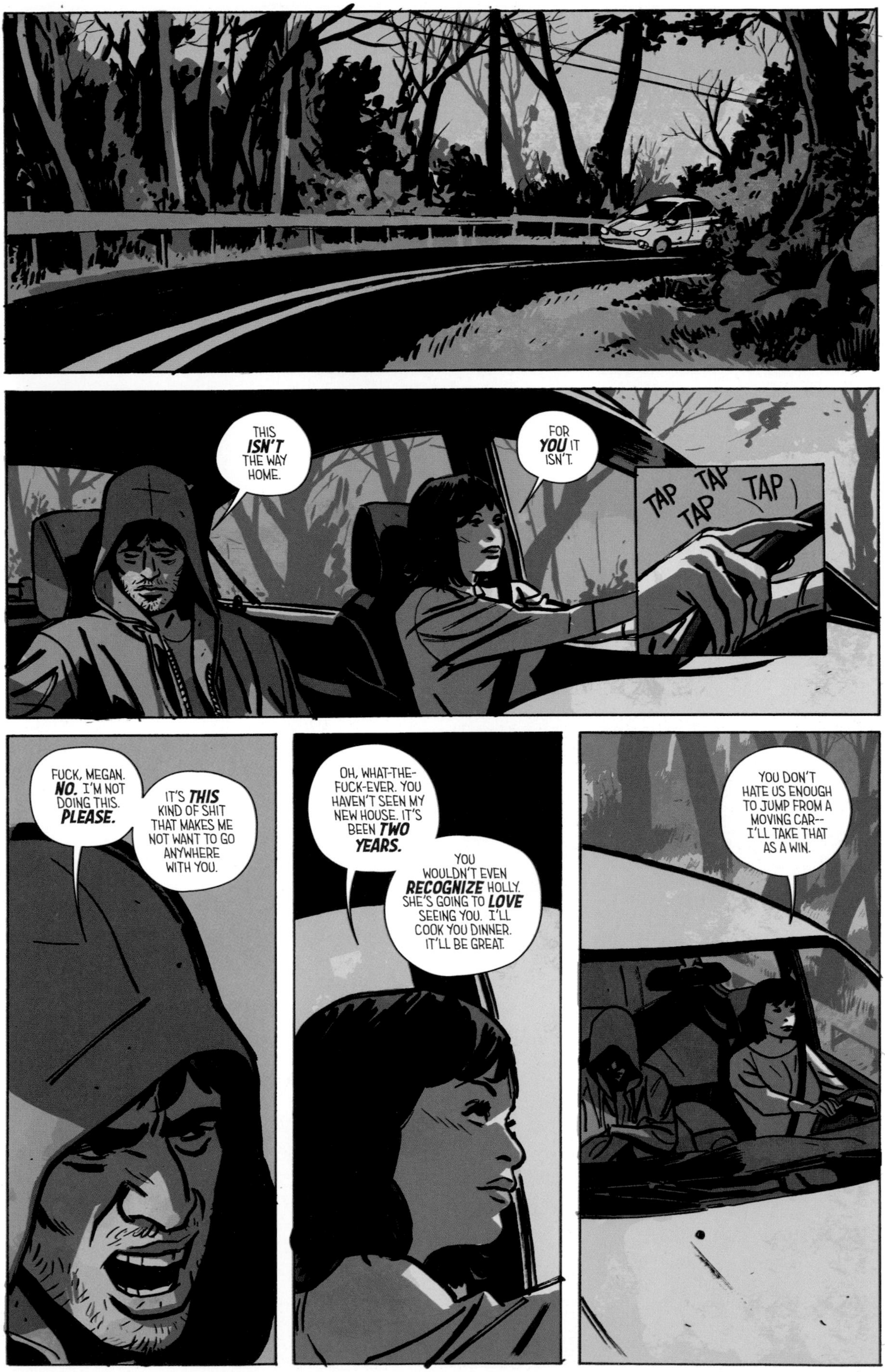
THIS ISN'T THE WAY HOME.
FOR YOU IT ISN'T.
TAP TAP TAP TAP
FUCK, MEGAN. NO. I'M NOT DOING THIS. PLEASE.
IT'S THIS KIND OF SHIT THAT MAKES ME NOT WANT TO GO ANYWHERE WITH YOU.
OH, WHAT-THE-FUCK-EVER. YOU HAVEN'T SEEN MY NEW HOUSE. IT'S BEEN TWO YEARS.
YOU WOULDN'T EVEN RECOGNIZE HOLLY. SHE'S GOING TO LOVE SEEING YOU. I'LL COOK YOU DINNER. IT'LL BE GREAT.
YOU DON'T HATE US ENOUGH TO JUMP FROM A MOVING CAR-- I'LL TAKE THAT AS A WIN.

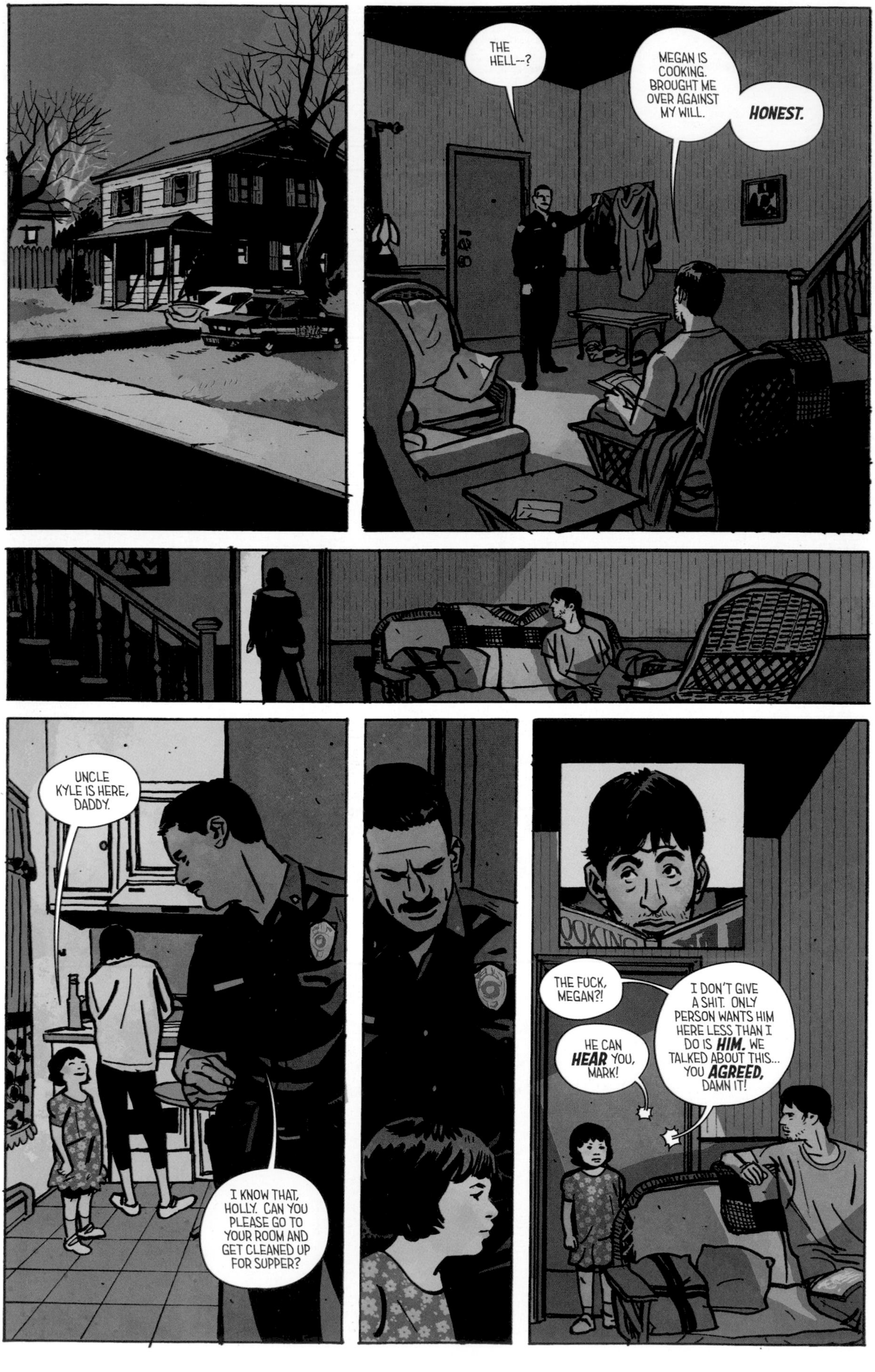
THE HELL--?
MEGAN IS COOKING. BROUGHT ME OVER AGAINST MY WILL.
HONEST.
UNCLE KYLE IS HERE, DADDY.
I KNOW THAT, HOLLY. CAN YOU PLEASE GO TO YOUR ROOM AND GET CLEANED UP FOR SUPPER?
THE FUCK, MEGAN?!
I DON'T GIVE A SHIT. ONLY PERSON WANTS HIM HERE LESS THAN I DO IS HIM. WE TALKED ABOUT THIS... YOU AGREED, DAMN IT!
HE CAN HEAR YOU, MARK!

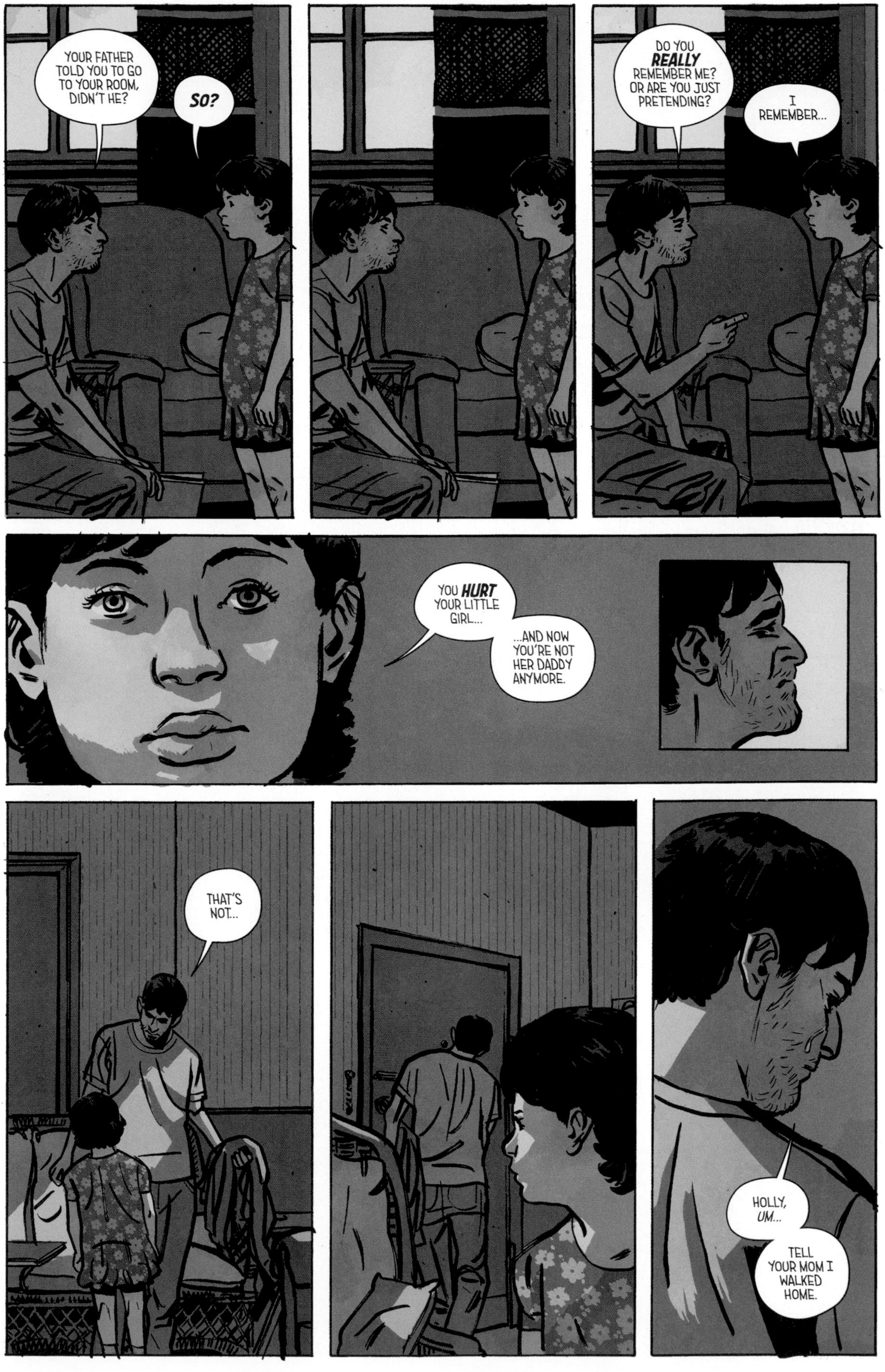
YOUR FATHER TOLD YOU TO GO TO YOUR ROOM, DIDN'T HE?
SO?
DO YOU *REALLY* REMEMBER ME? OR ARE YOU JUST PRETENDING?
I REMEMBER...
YOU *HURT* YOUR LITTLE GIRL...
...AND NOW YOU'RE NOT HER DADDY ANYMORE.
THAT'S NOT...
HOLLY, *UM*...
TELL YOUR MOM I WALKED HOME.

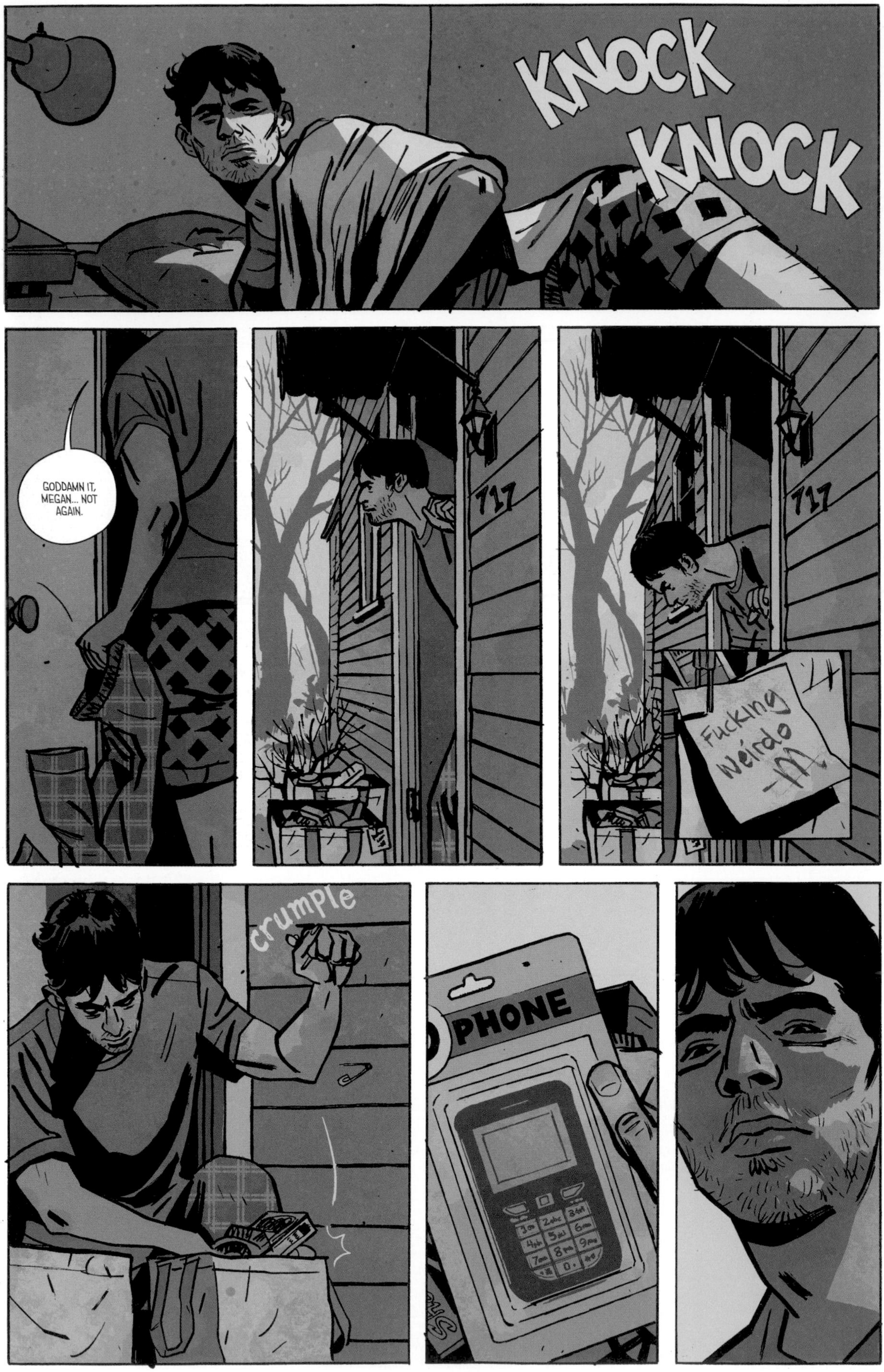
KNOCK
KNOCK
GODDAMN IT, MEGAN... NOT AGAIN.
717
717
Fucking Weirdo -M
crumple
PHONE

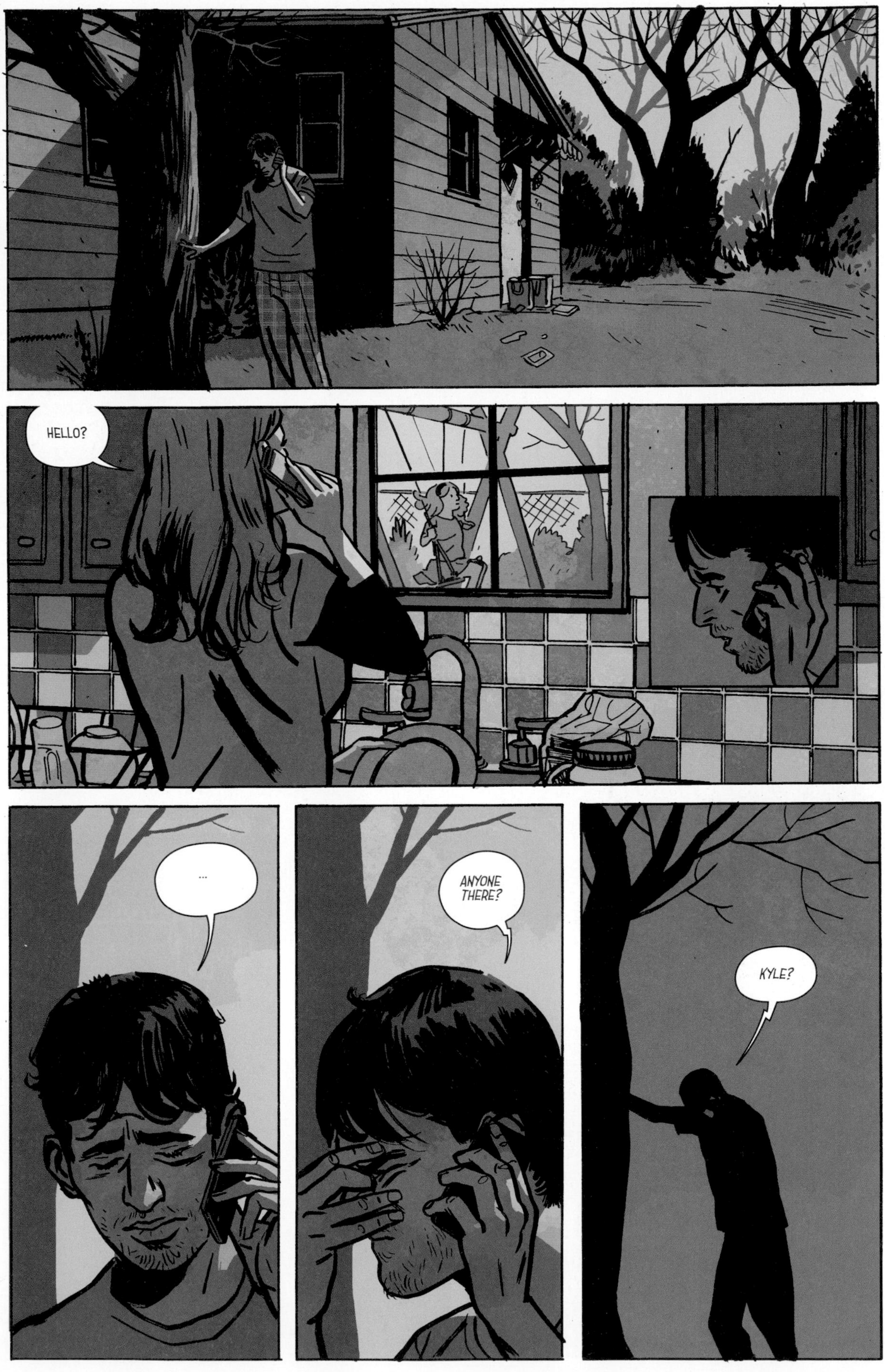
HELLO?
...
ANYONE THERE?
KYLE?

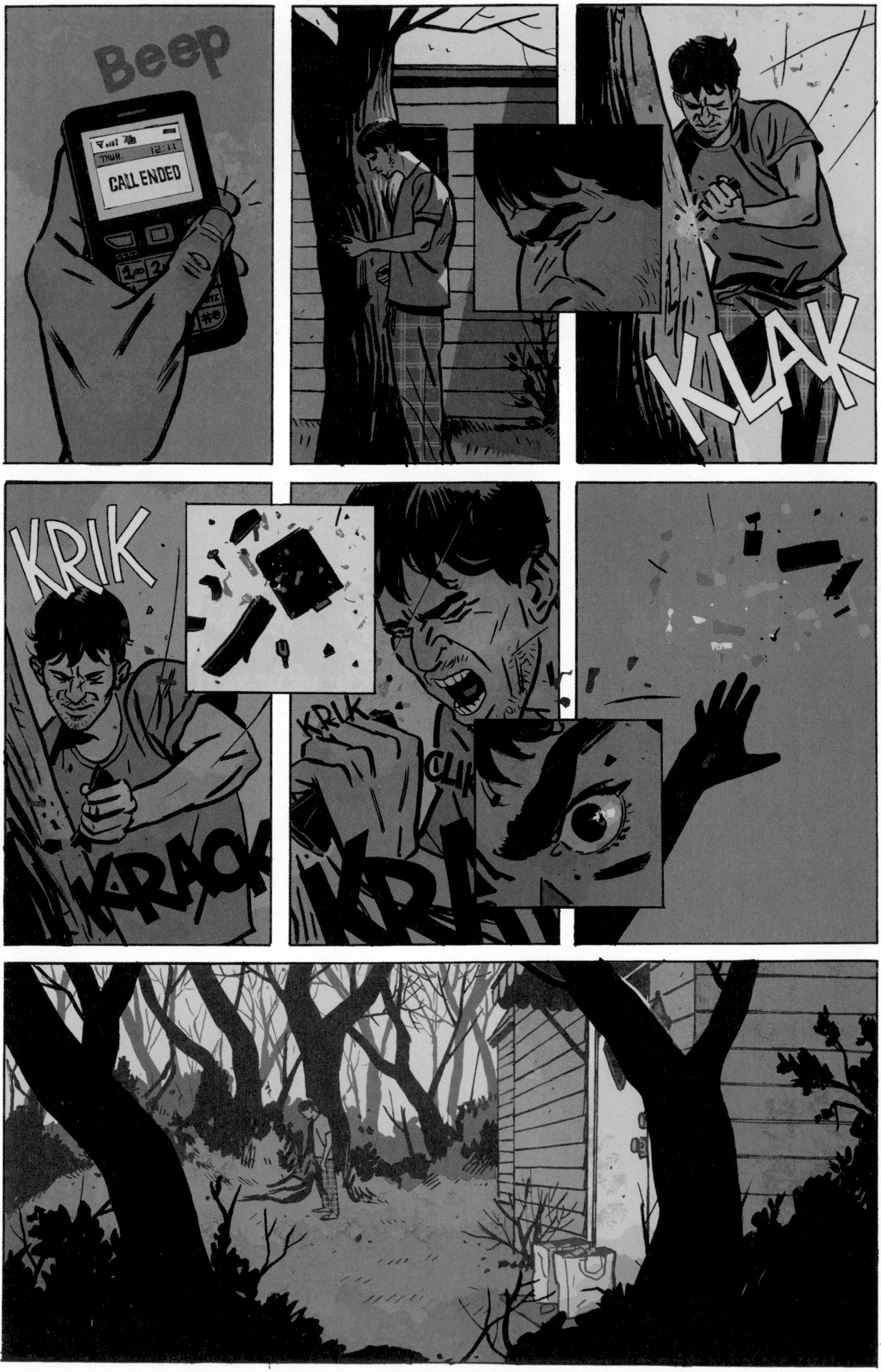
Beep
THUR. 12:11
CALL ENDED
KLAK
KRIK
KRACK
KRIK
CLIK

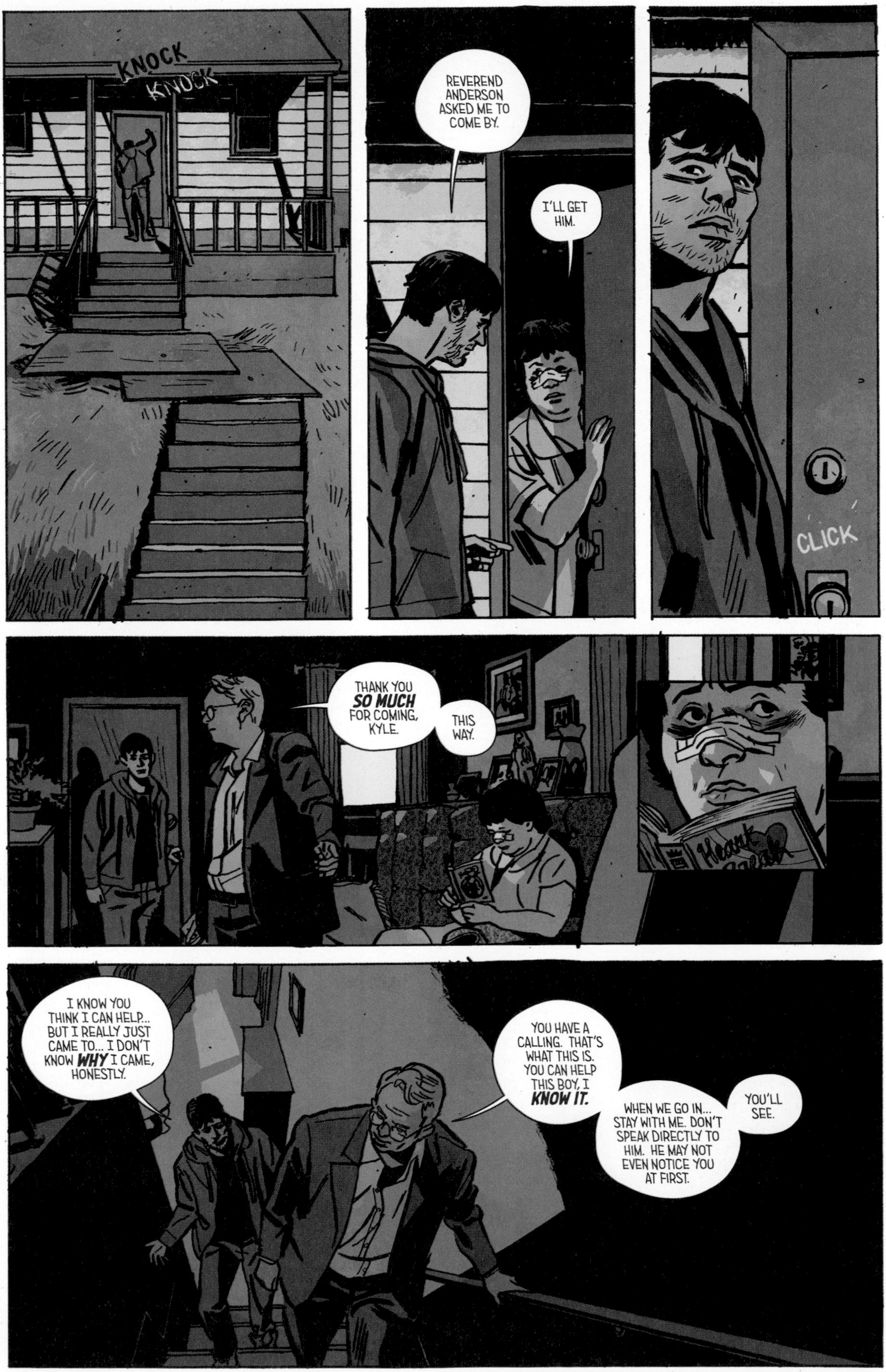
KNOCK
KNOCK
REVEREND ANDERSON ASKED ME TO COME BY.
I'LL GET HIM.
CLICK
THANK YOU **SO MUCH** FOR COMING, KYLE.
THIS WAY.
I KNOW YOU THINK I CAN HELP... BUT I REALLY JUST CAME TO... I DON'T KNOW **WHY** I CAME, HONESTLY.
YOU HAVE A CALLING. THAT'S WHAT THIS IS. YOU CAN HELP THIS BOY, I **KNOW IT.**
WHEN WE GO IN... STAY WITH ME. DON'T SPEAK DIRECTLY TO HIM. HE MAY NOT EVEN NOTICE YOU AT FIRST.
YOU'LL SEE.

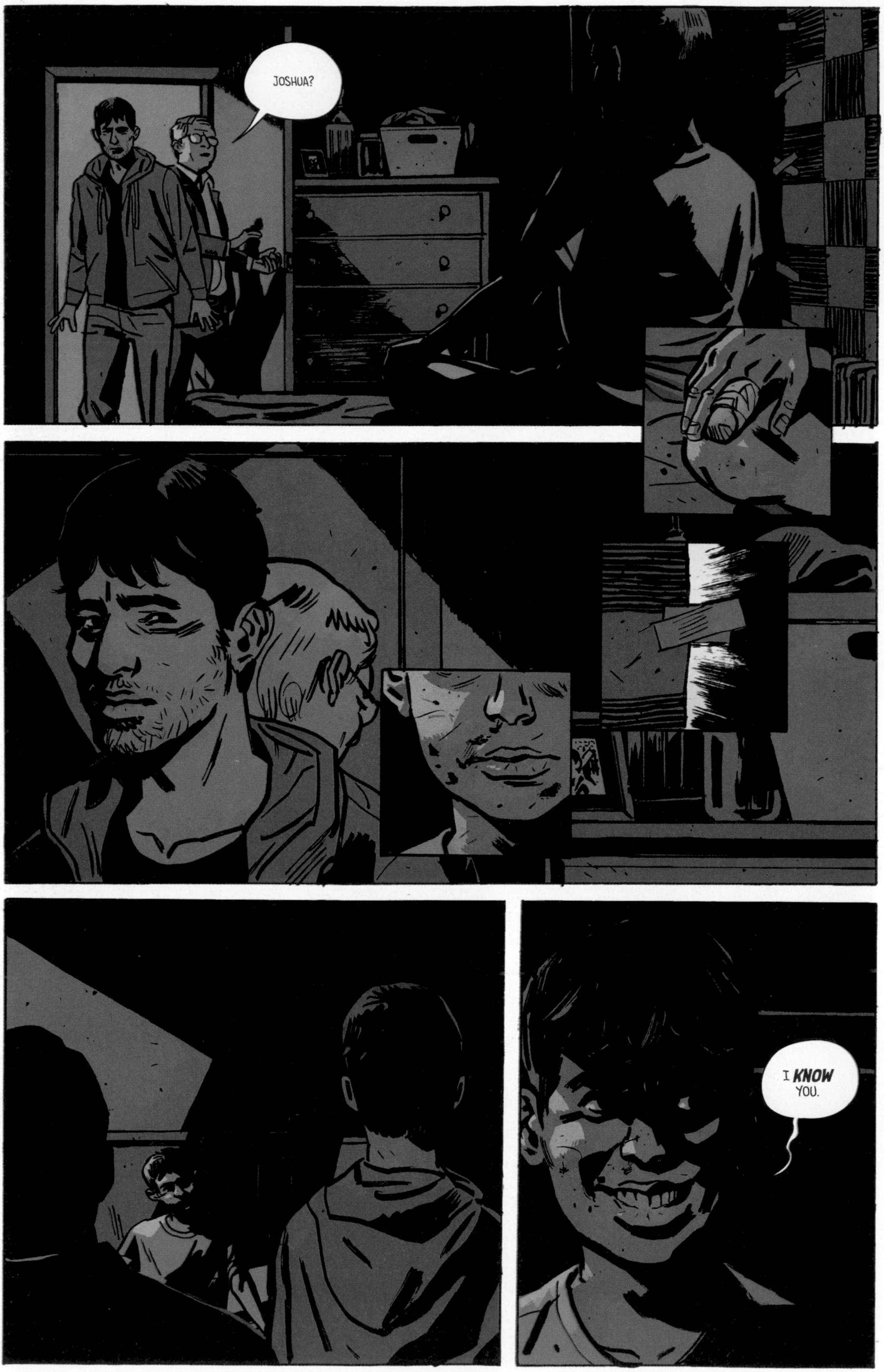
JOSHUA?
I KNOW YOU.

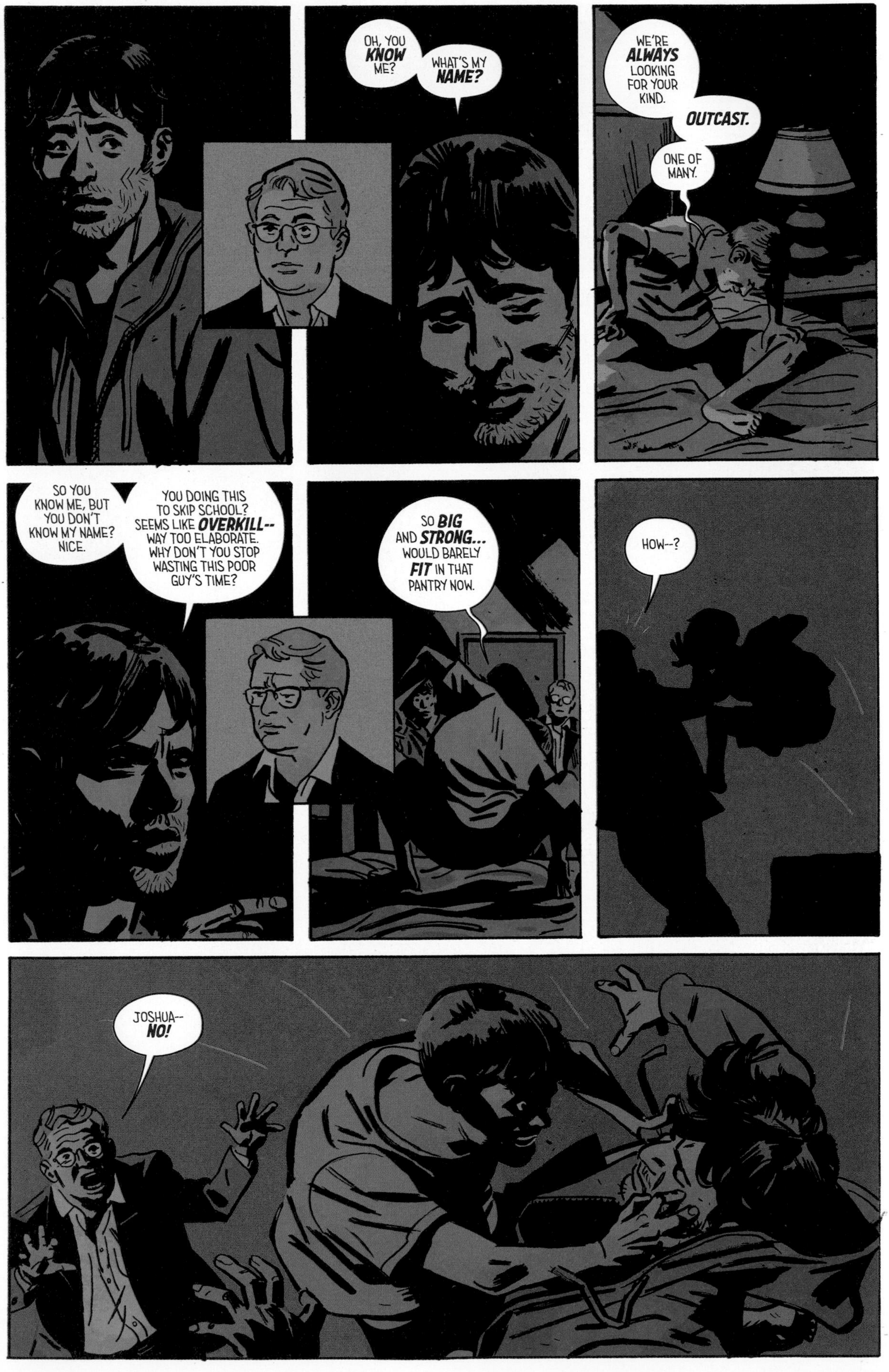
OH, YOU KNOW ME?
WHAT'S MY NAME?
WE'RE ALWAYS LOOKING FOR YOUR KIND.
OUTCAST.
ONE OF MANY.
SO YOU KNOW ME, BUT YOU DON'T KNOW MY NAME? NICE.
YOU DOING THIS TO SKIP SCHOOL? SEEMS LIKE OVERKILL-- WAY TOO ELABORATE. WHY DON'T YOU STOP WASTING THIS POOR GUY'S TIME?
SO BIG AND STRONG... WOULD BARELY FIT IN THAT PANTRY NOW.
HOW--?
JOSHUA-- NO!

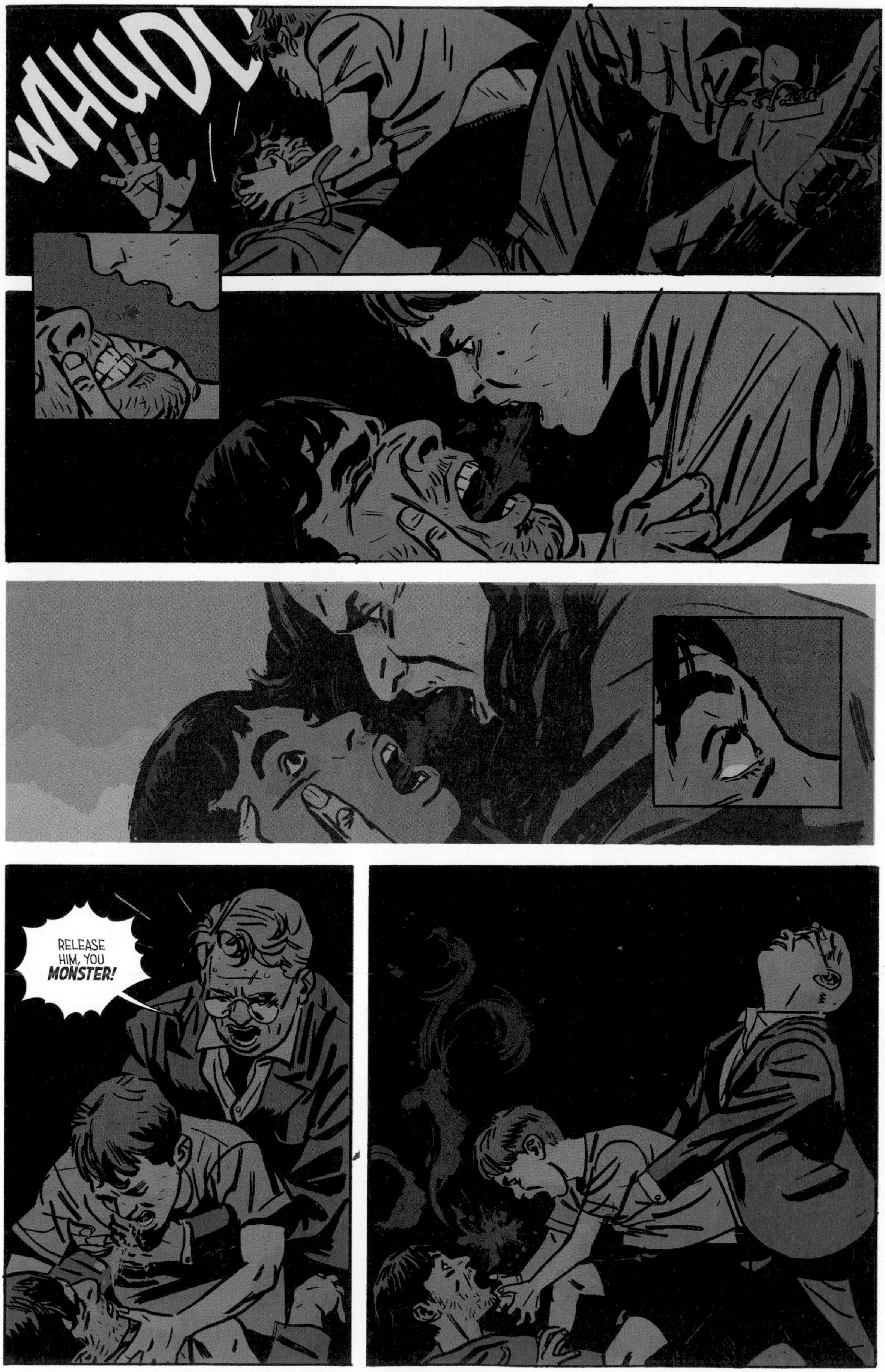
WHUD
RELEASE HIM, YOU MONSTER!

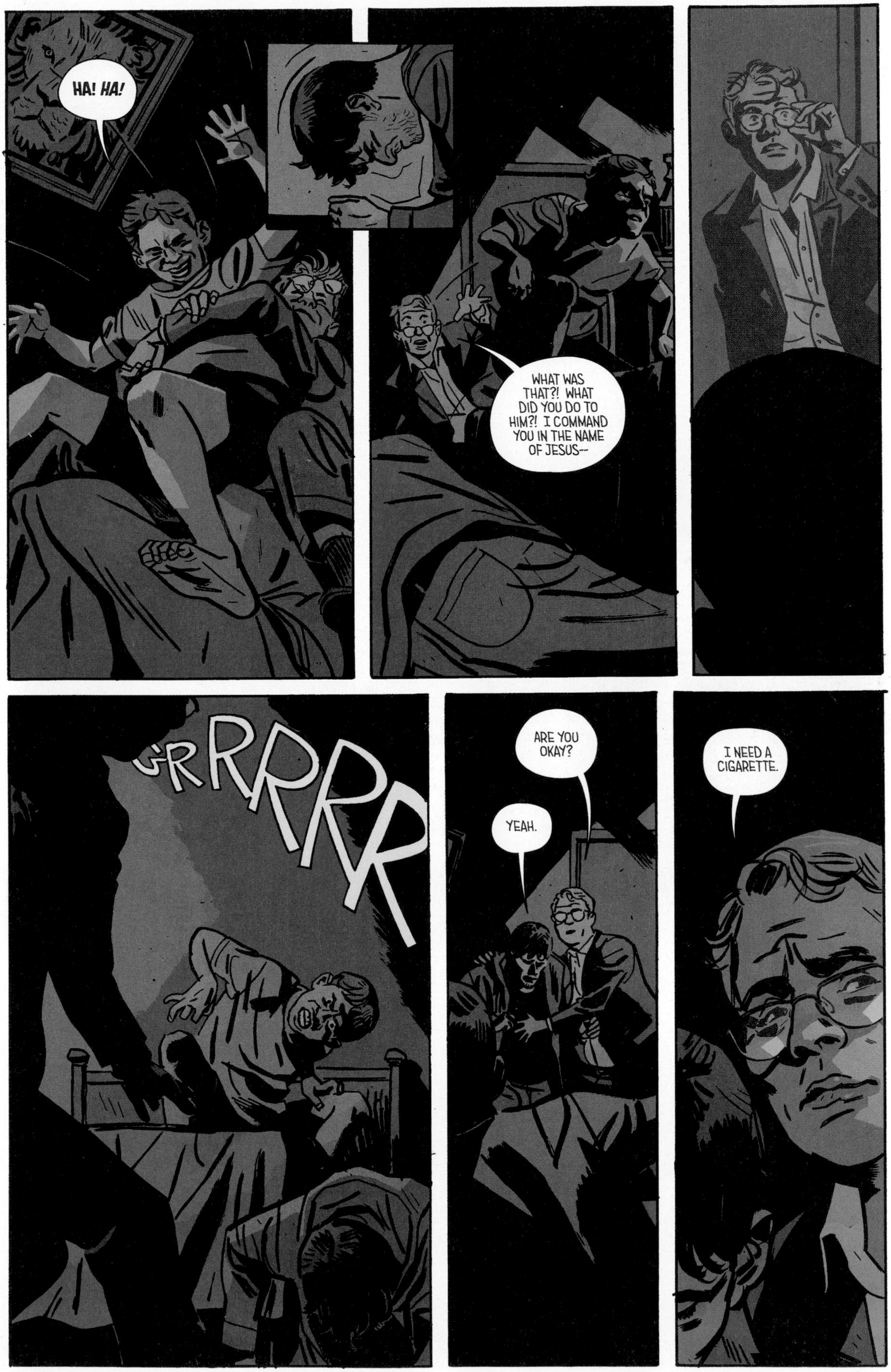
HA! HA!
WHAT WAS THAT?! WHAT DID YOU DO TO HIM?! I COMMAND YOU IN THE NAME OF JESUS--
GRRRRRR
ARE YOU OKAY?
YEAH.
I NEED A CIGARETTE.

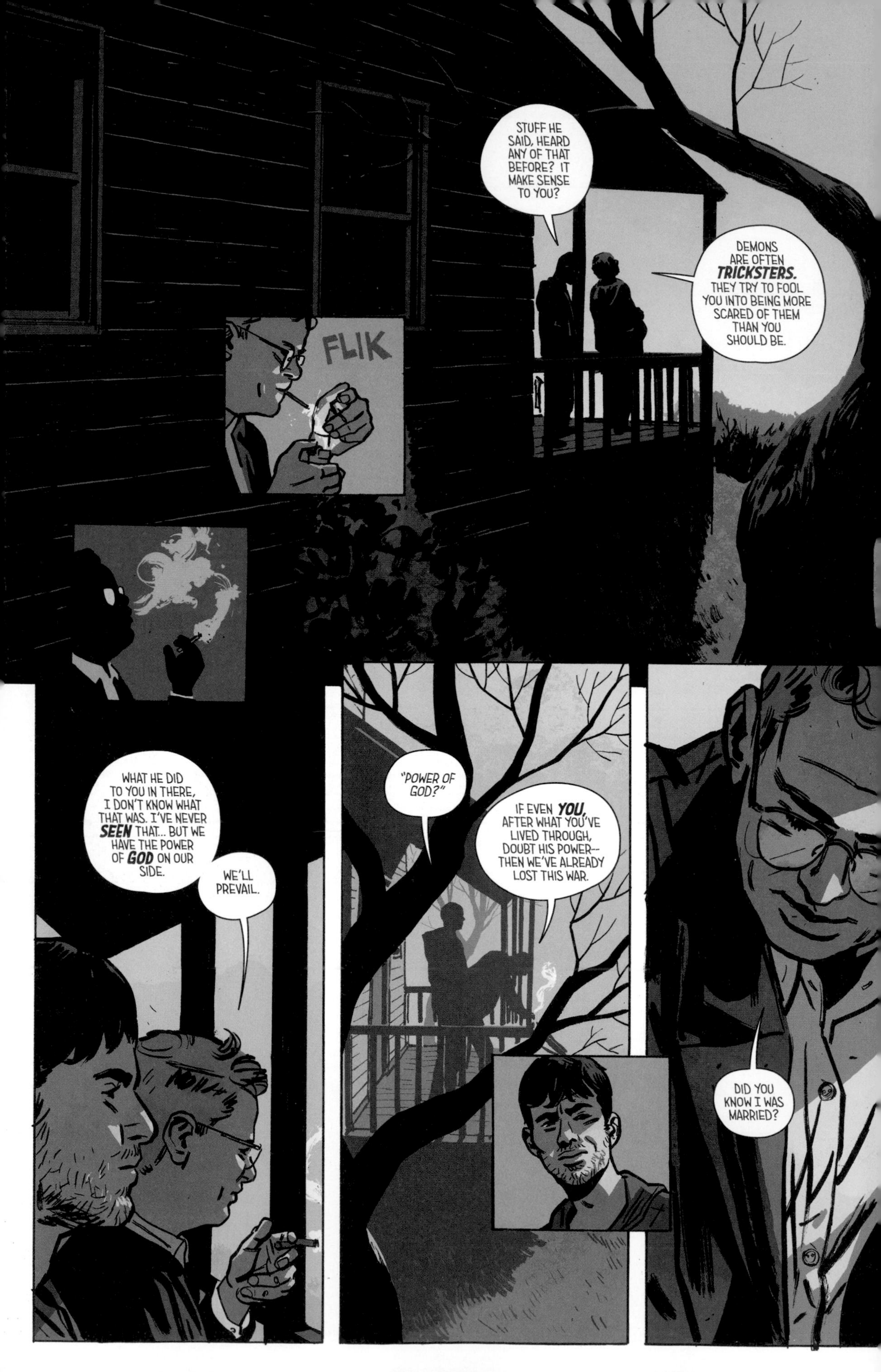
STUFF HE SAID, HEARD ANY OF THAT BEFORE? IT MAKE SENSE TO YOU?
DEMONS ARE OFTEN TRICKSTERS. THEY TRY TO FOOL YOU INTO BEING MORE SCARED OF THEM THAN YOU SHOULD BE.
FLIK
WHAT HE DID TO YOU IN THERE, I DON'T KNOW WHAT THAT WAS. I'VE NEVER SEEN THAT... BUT WE HAVE THE POWER OF GOD ON OUR SIDE.
WE'LL PREVAIL.
"POWER OF GOD?"
IF EVEN YOU, AFTER WHAT YOU'VE LIVED THROUGH, DOUBT HIS POWER-- THEN WE'VE ALREADY LOST THIS WAR.
DID YOU KNOW I WAS MARRIED?

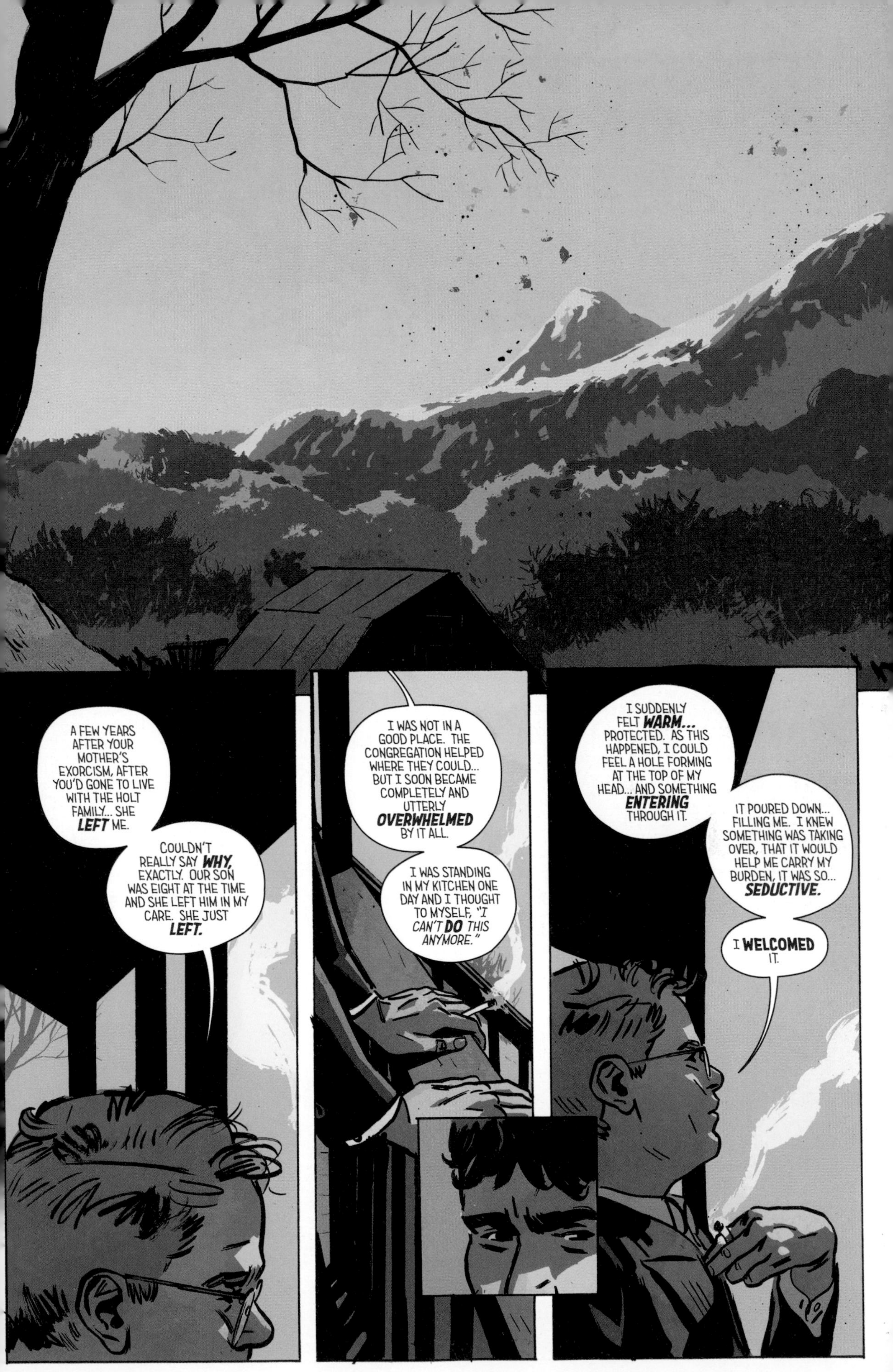
A FEW YEARS AFTER YOUR MOTHER'S EXORCISM, AFTER YOU'D GONE TO LIVE WITH THE HOLT FAMILY... SHE **LEFT** ME.
COULDN'T REALLY SAY **WHY,** EXACTLY. OUR SON WAS EIGHT AT THE TIME AND SHE LEFT HIM IN MY CARE. SHE JUST **LEFT.**
I WAS NOT IN A GOOD PLACE. THE CONGREGATION HELPED WHERE THEY COULD... BUT I SOON BECAME COMPLETELY AND UTTERLY **OVERWHELMED** BY IT ALL.
I WAS STANDING IN MY KITCHEN ONE DAY AND I THOUGHT TO MYSELF, *"I CAN'T **DO** THIS ANYMORE."*
I SUDDENLY FELT **WARM...** PROTECTED. AS THIS HAPPENED, I COULD FEEL A HOLE FORMING AT THE TOP OF MY HEAD... AND SOMETHING **ENTERING** THROUGH IT.
IT POURED DOWN... FILLING ME. I KNEW SOMETHING WAS TAKING OVER, THAT IT WOULD HELP ME CARRY MY BURDEN, IT WAS SO... **SEDUCTIVE.**
I **WELCOMED** IT.

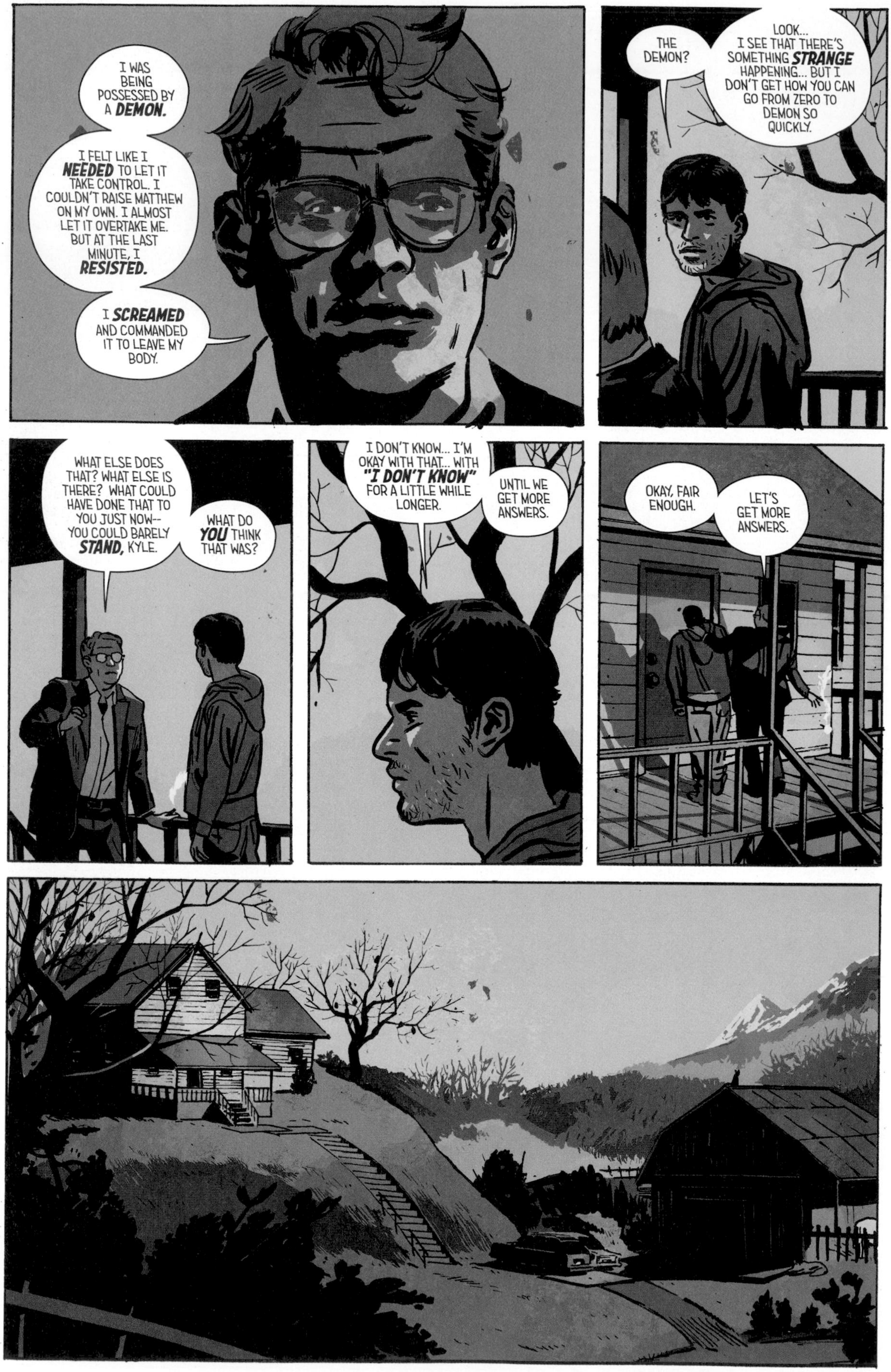
I WAS BEING POSSESSED BY A DEMON.
I FELT LIKE I NEEDED TO LET IT TAKE CONTROL. I COULDN'T RAISE MATTHEW ON MY OWN. I ALMOST LET IT OVERTAKE ME. BUT AT THE LAST MINUTE, I RESISTED.
I SCREAMED AND COMMANDED IT TO LEAVE MY BODY.
THE DEMON?
LOOK... I SEE THAT THERE'S SOMETHING STRANGE HAPPENING... BUT I DON'T GET HOW YOU CAN GO FROM ZERO TO DEMON SO QUICKLY.
WHAT ELSE DOES THAT? WHAT ELSE IS THERE? WHAT COULD HAVE DONE THAT TO YOU JUST NOW-- YOU COULD BARELY STAND, KYLE.
WHAT DO YOU THINK THAT WAS?
I DON'T KNOW... I'M OKAY WITH THAT... WITH "I DON'T KNOW" FOR A LITTLE WHILE LONGER.
UNTIL WE GET MORE ANSWERS.
OKAY, FAIR ENOUGH.
LET'S GET MORE ANSWERS.

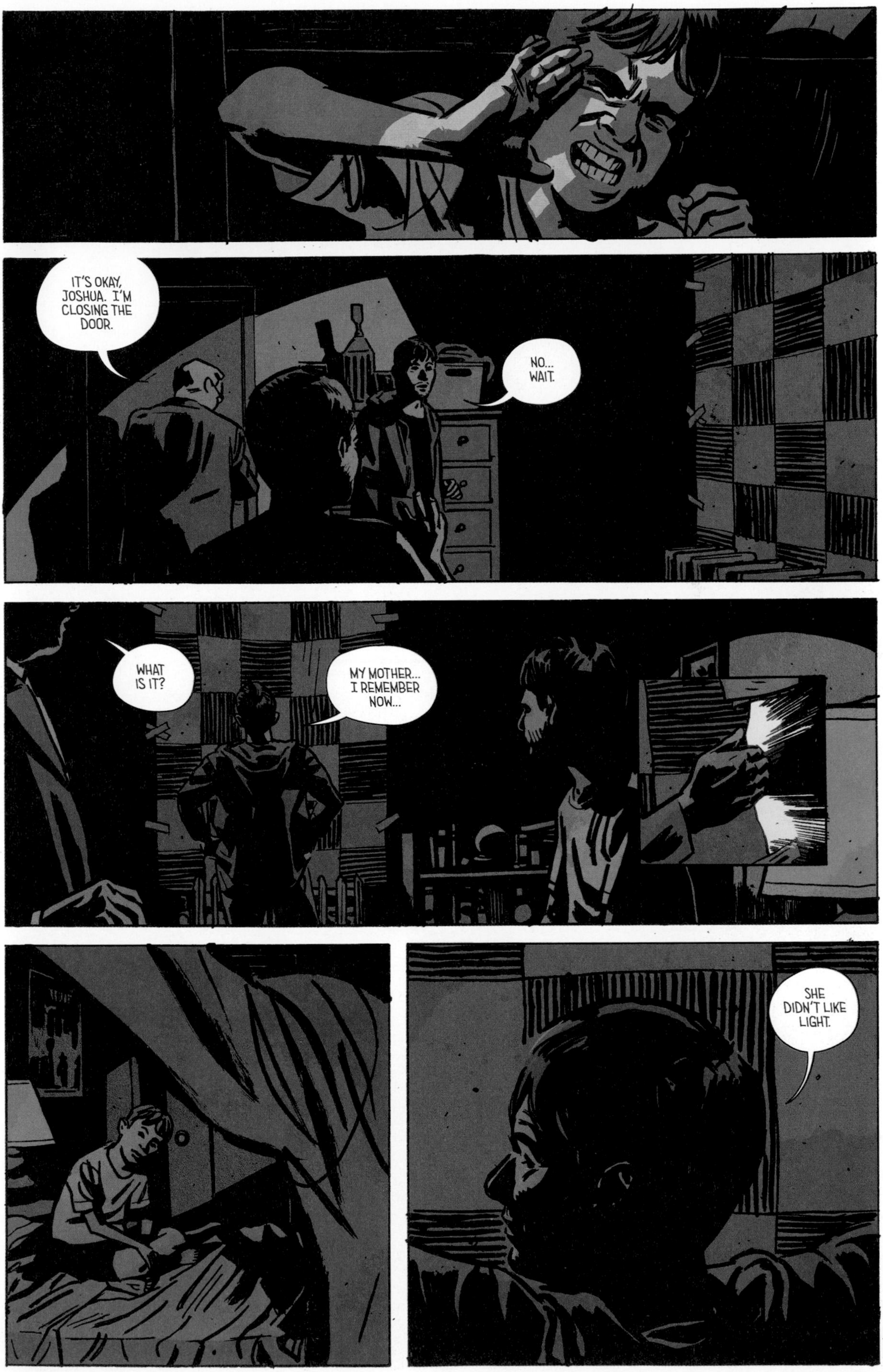
IT'S OKAY, JOSHUA. I'M CLOSING THE DOOR.
NO... WAIT.
WHAT IS IT?
MY MOTHER... I REMEMBER NOW...
SHE DIDN'T LIKE LIGHT.

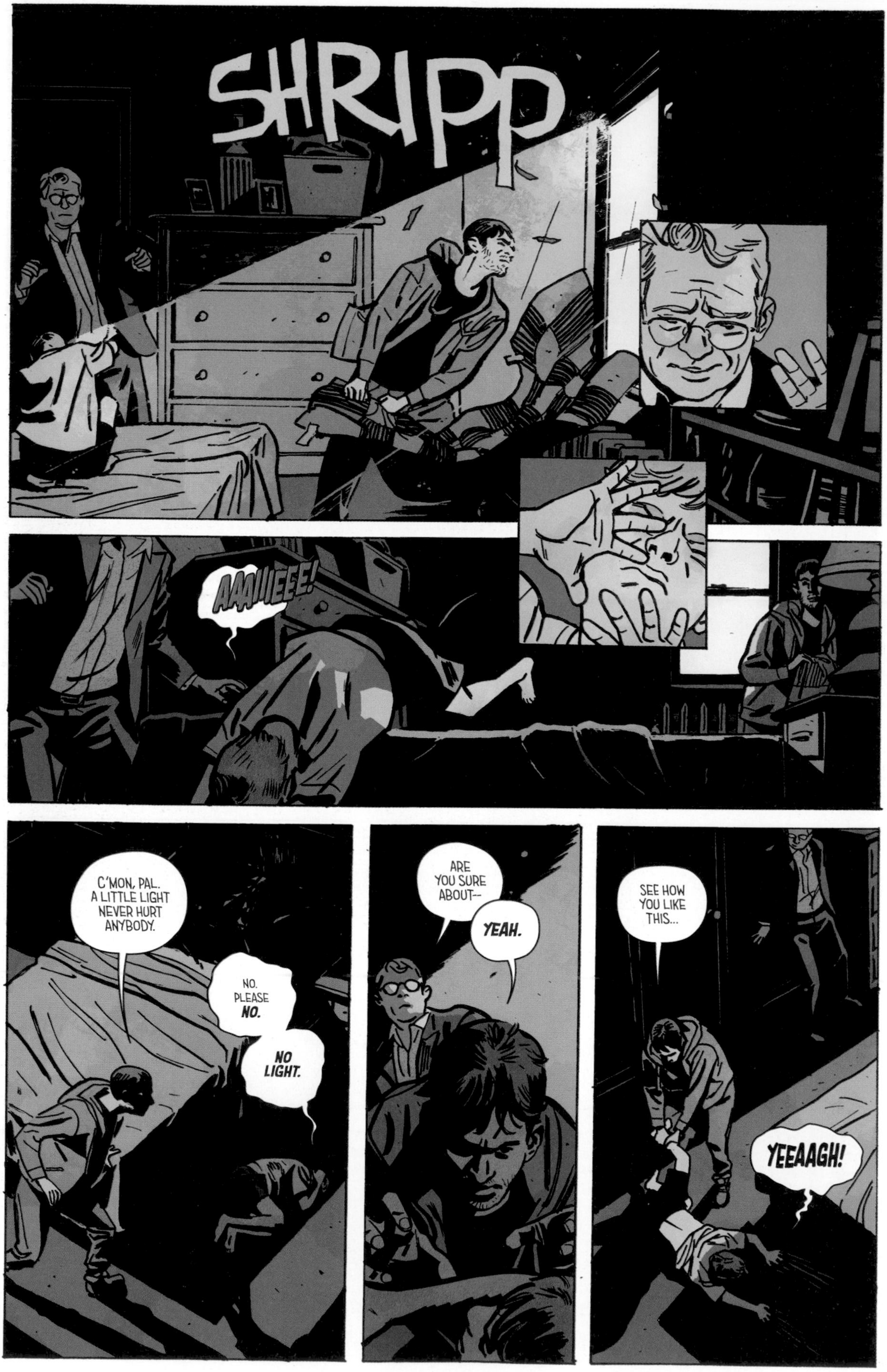
SHRIPP
AAAIIIEEE!
C'MON, PAL. A LITTLE LIGHT NEVER HURT ANYBODY.
NO. PLEASE NO.
NO LIGHT.
ARE YOU SURE ABOUT--
YEAH.
SEE HOW YOU LIKE THIS...
YEEAAGH!

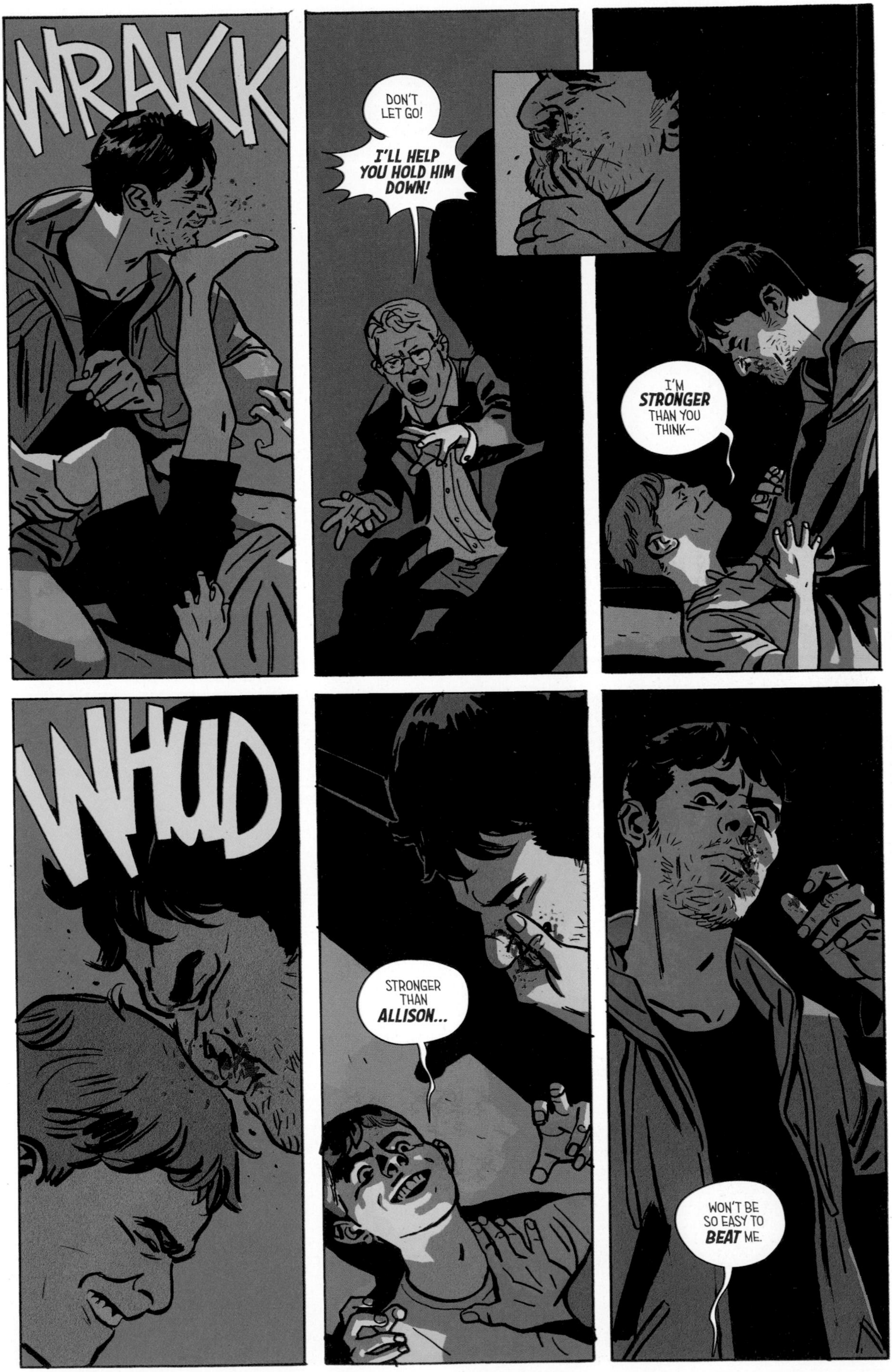
WRAKK
DON'T LET GO!
I'LL HELP YOU HOLD HIM DOWN!
I'M STRONGER THAN YOU THINK--
WHUD
STRONGER THAN ALLISON...
WON'T BE SO EASY TO BEAT ME.

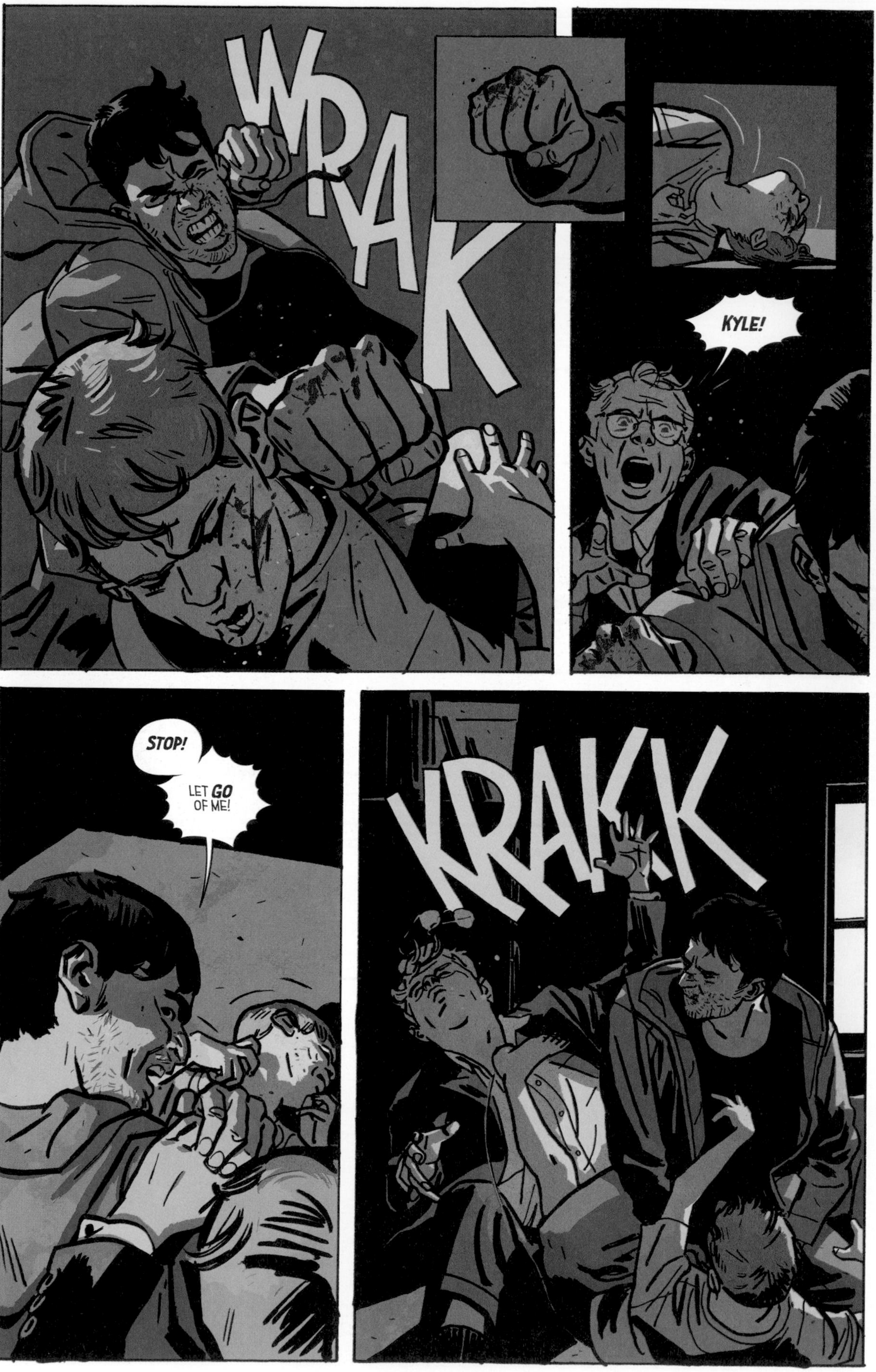
WRAK
KYLE!
STOP!
LET GO OF ME!
KRAKK

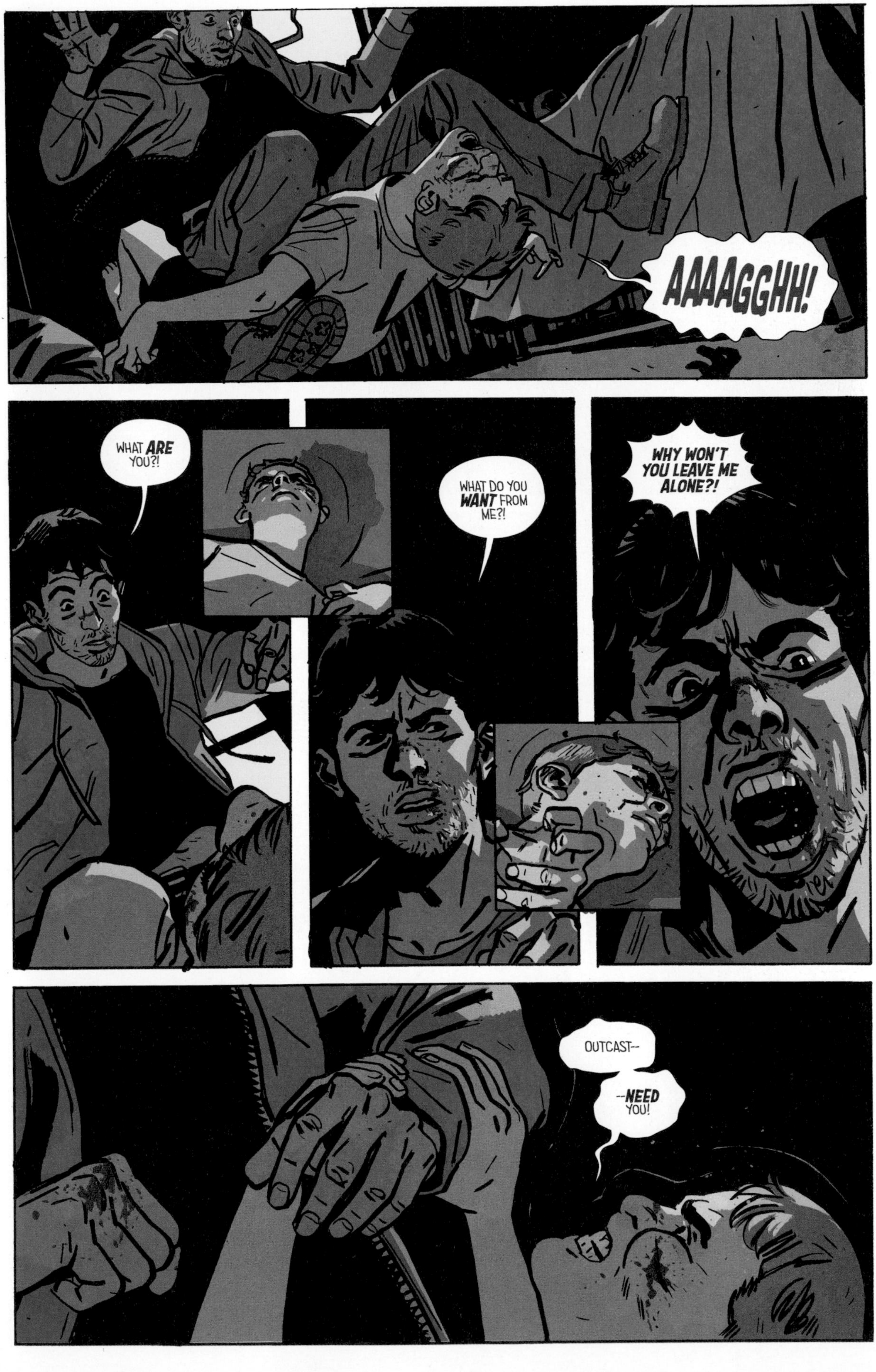
AAAAGGHH!
WHAT **ARE** YOU?!
WHAT DO YOU **WANT** FROM ME?!
WHY WON'T YOU LEAVE ME ALONE?!
OUTCAST--
--**NEED** YOU!

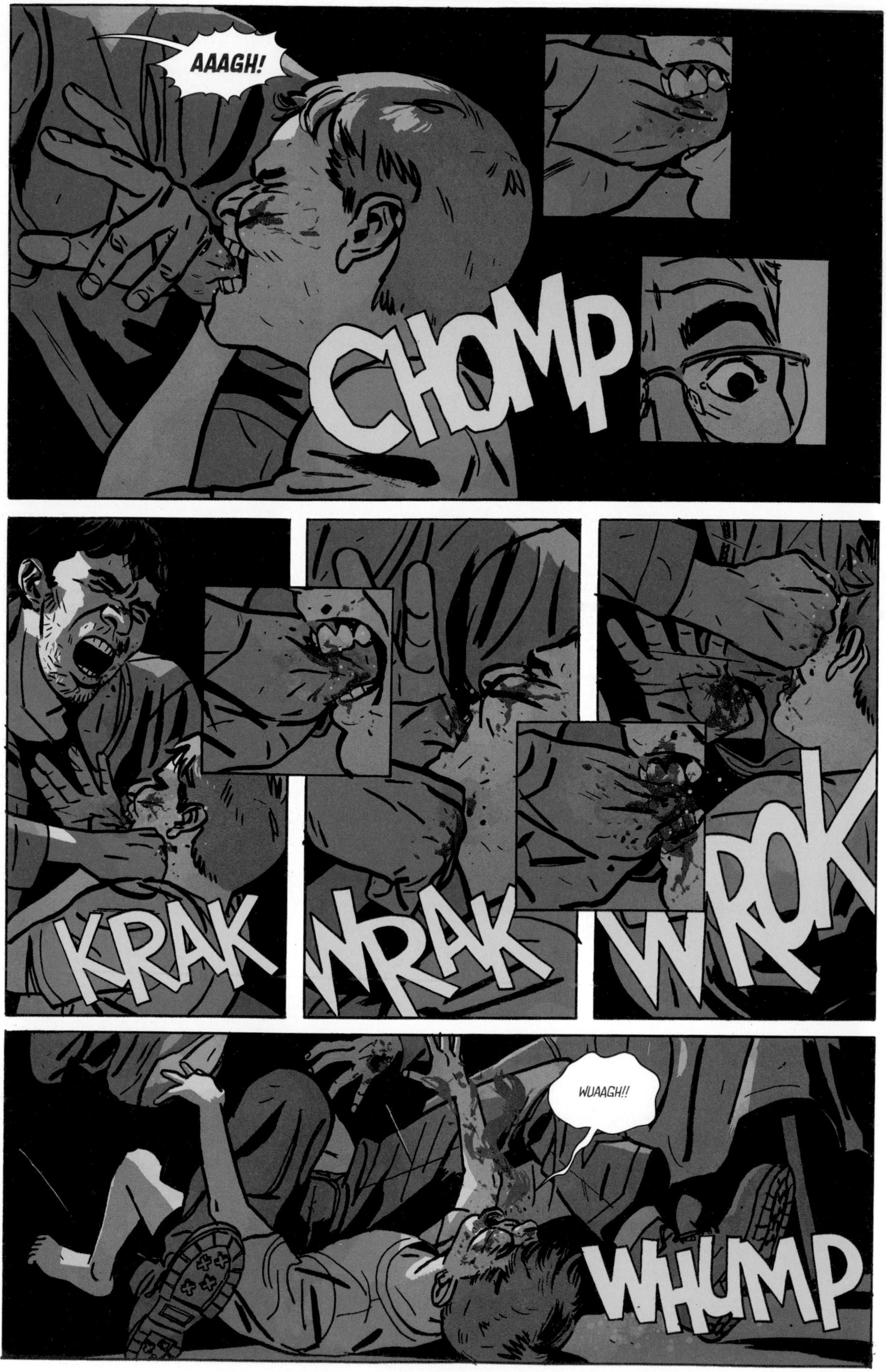
AAAGH!
CHOMP
KRAK
WRAK
WROK
WUAAGH!!
WHUMP

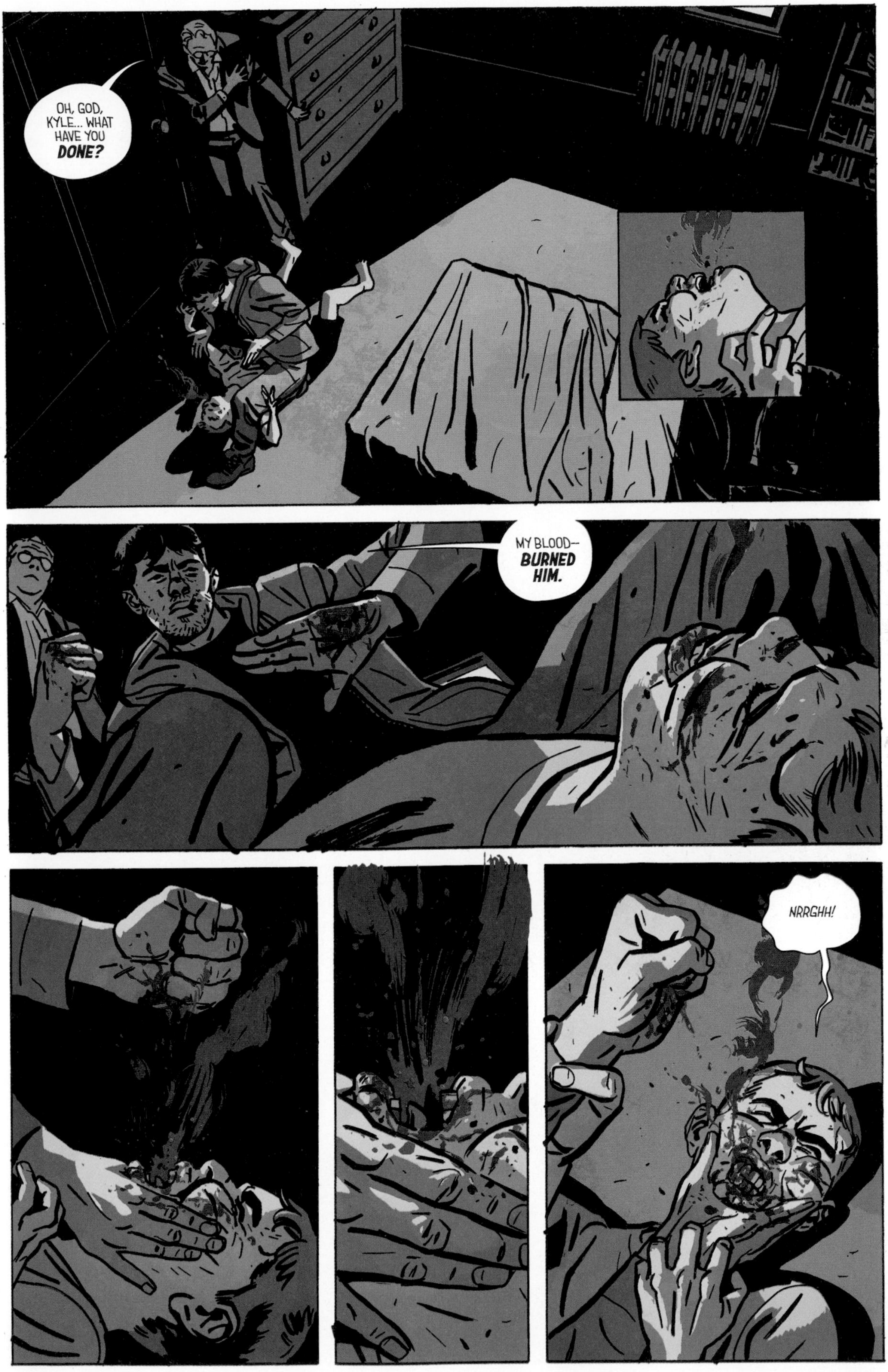

OH, GOD, KYLE... WHAT HAVE YOU DONE?
MY BLOOD-- BURNED HIM.
NRRGHH!

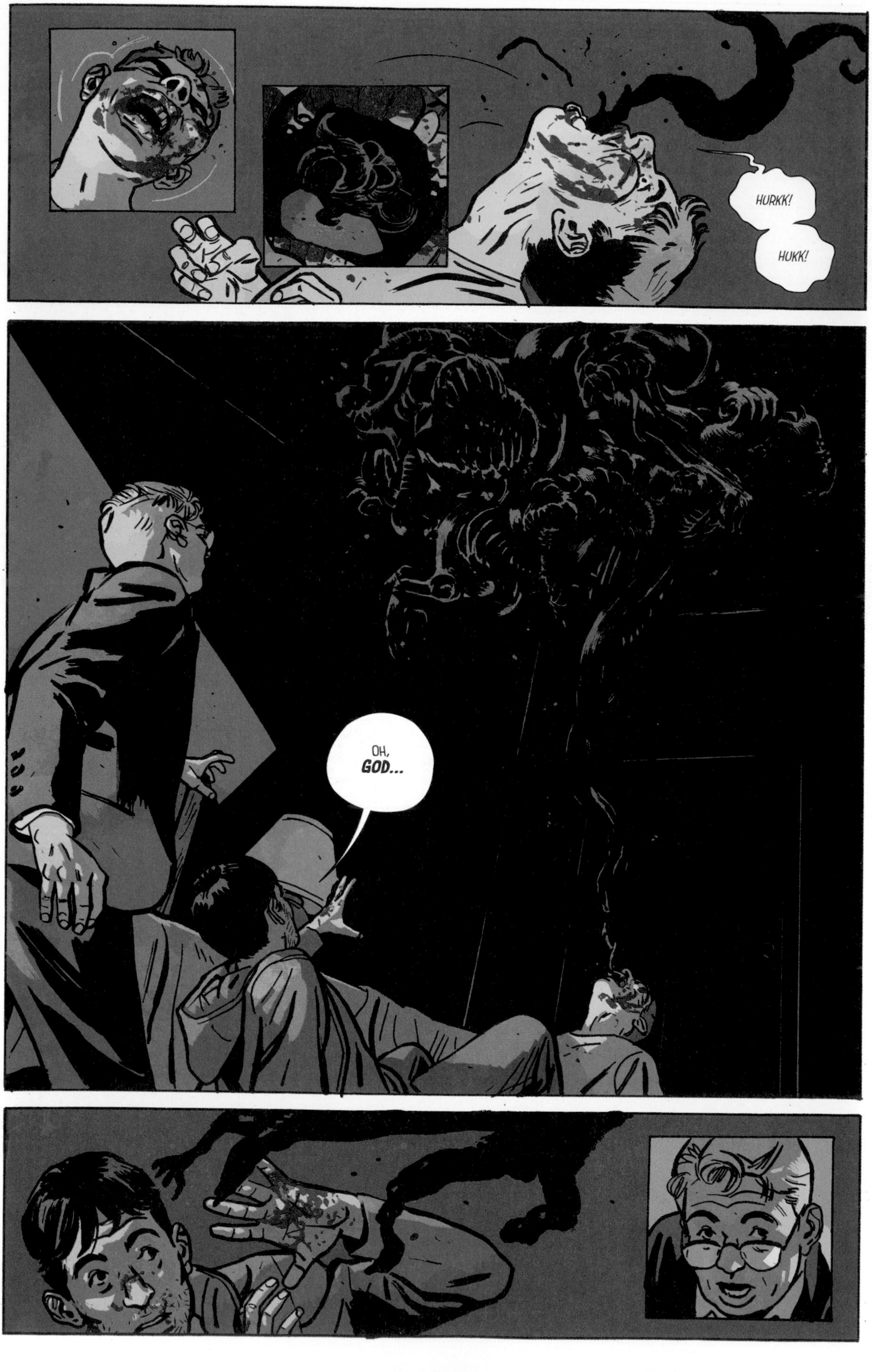
HURKK!
HUKK!
OH, GOD...

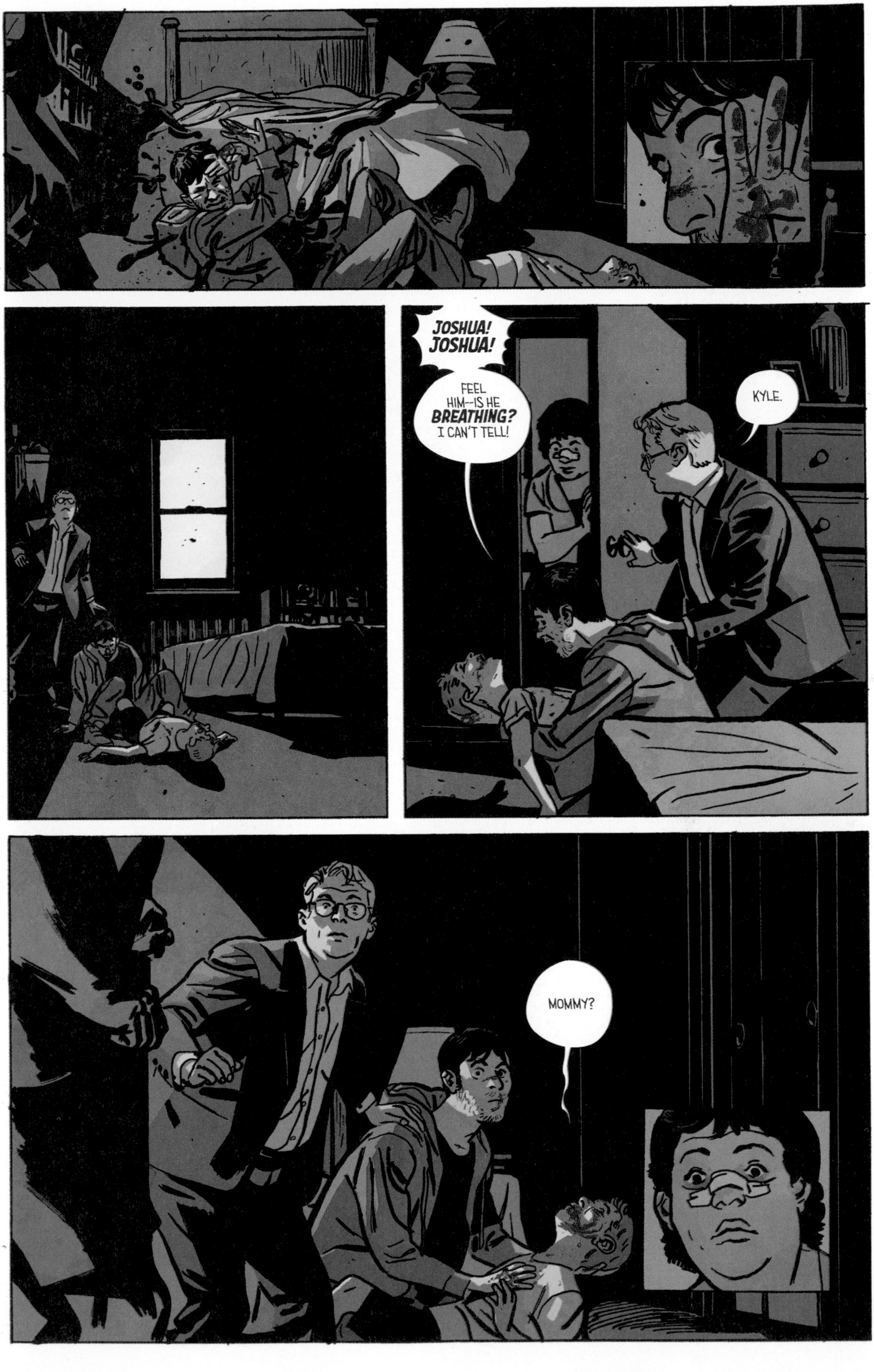
JOSHUA! JOSHUA!
FEEL HIM--IS HE BREATHING? I CAN'T TELL!
KYLE.
MOMMY?

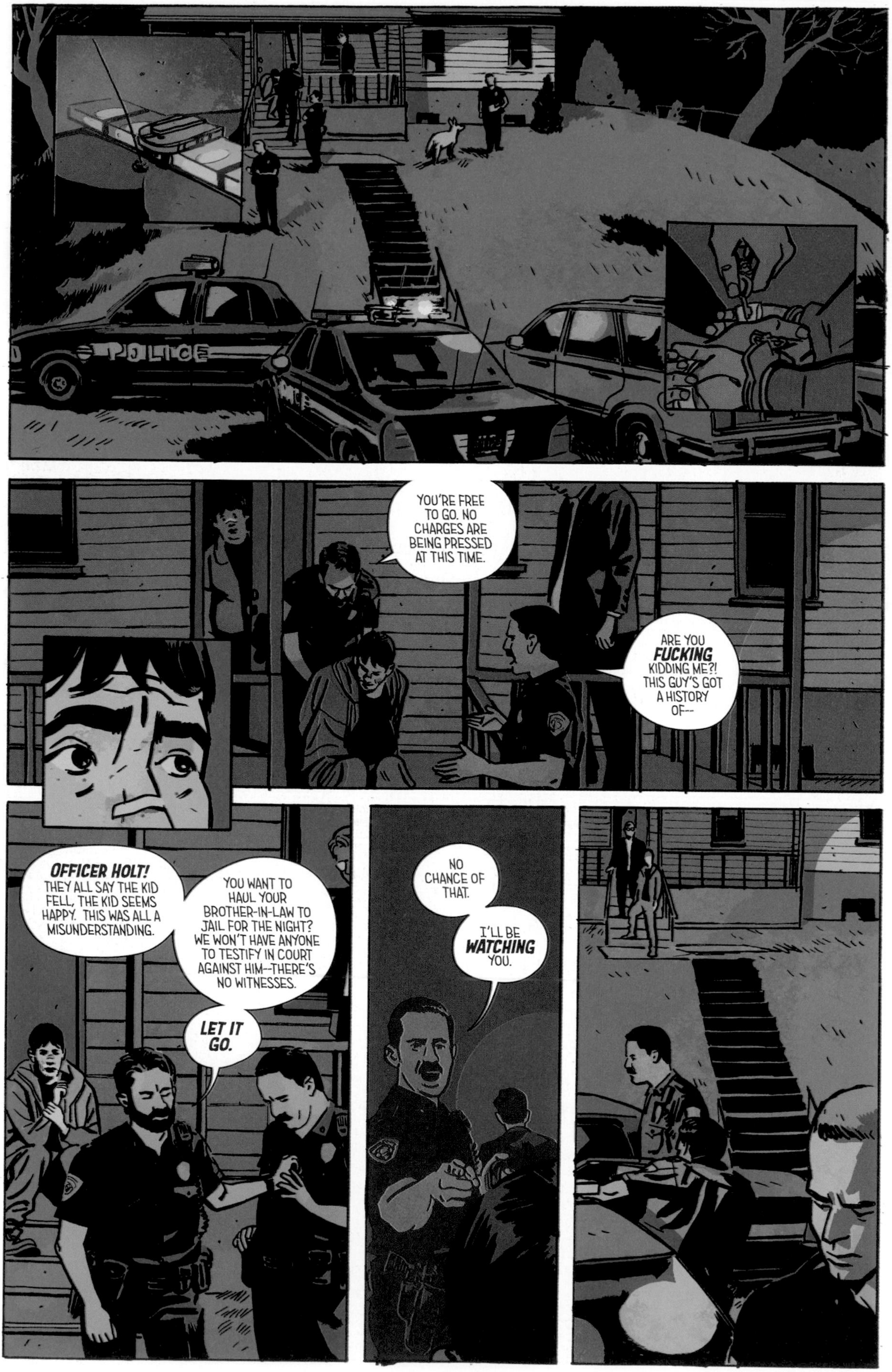
POLICE
YOU'RE FREE TO GO. NO CHARGES ARE BEING PRESSED AT THIS TIME.
ARE YOU **FUCKING** KIDDING ME?! THIS GUY'S GOT A HISTORY OF--
OFFICER HOLT! THEY ALL SAY THE KID FELL, THE KID SEEMS HAPPY. THIS WAS ALL A MISUNDERSTANDING.
YOU WANT TO HAUL YOUR BROTHER-IN-LAW TO JAIL FOR THE NIGHT? WE WON'T HAVE ANYONE TO TESTIFY IN COURT AGAINST HIM--THERE'S NO WITNESSES.
LET IT GO.
NO CHANCE OF THAT.
I'LL BE **WATCHING** YOU.

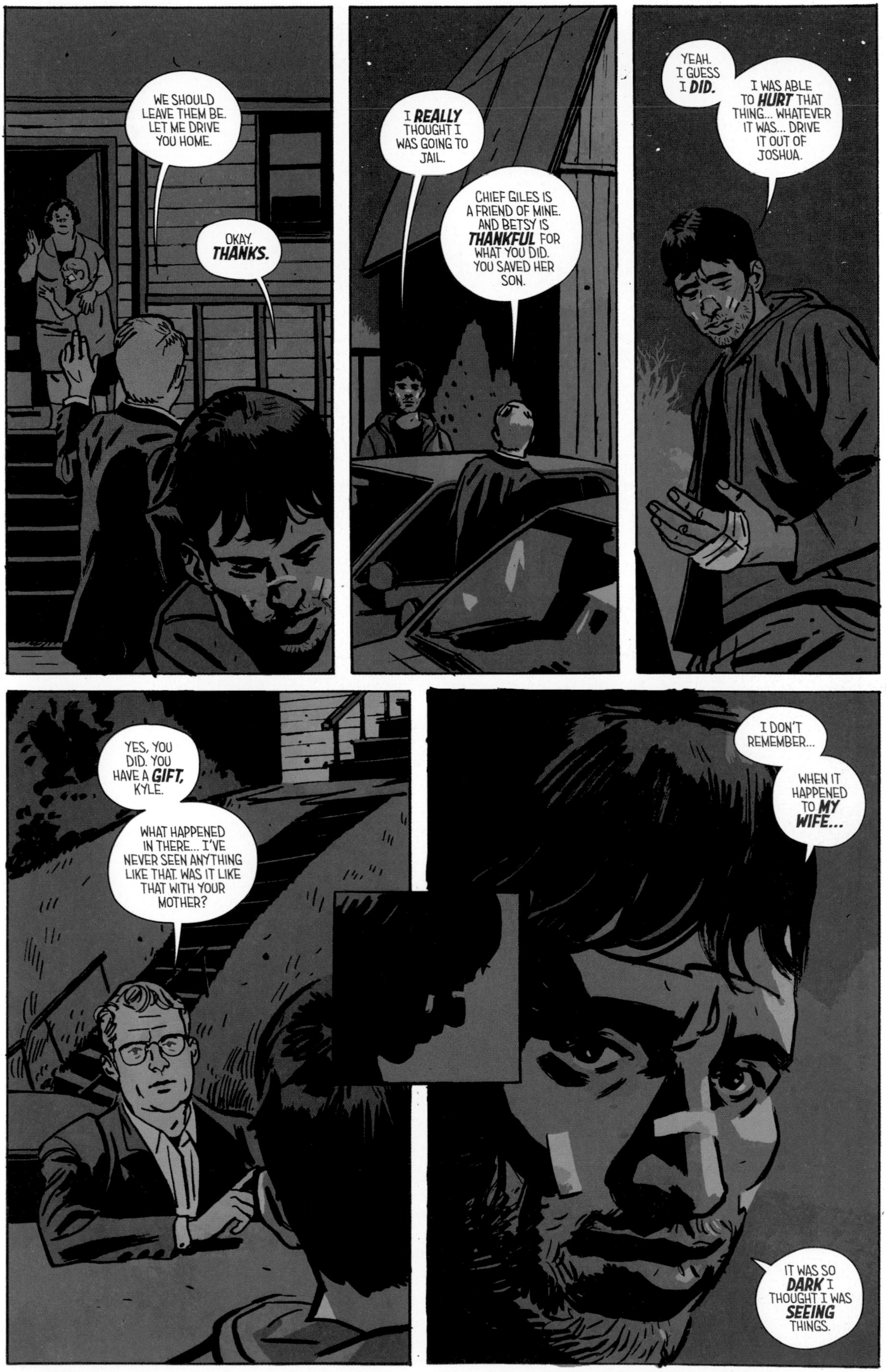
WE SHOULD LEAVE THEM BE. LET ME DRIVE YOU HOME.
OKAY. THANKS.
I REALLY THOUGHT I WAS GOING TO JAIL.
CHIEF GILES IS A FRIEND OF MINE. AND BETSY IS THANKFUL FOR WHAT YOU DID. YOU SAVED HER SON.
YEAH. I GUESS I DID.
I WAS ABLE TO HURT THAT THING... WHATEVER IT WAS... DRIVE IT OUT OF JOSHUA.
YES, YOU DID. YOU HAVE A GIFT, KYLE.
WHAT HAPPENED IN THERE... I'VE NEVER SEEN ANYTHING LIKE THAT. WAS IT LIKE THAT WITH YOUR MOTHER?
I DON'T REMEMBER...
WHEN IT HAPPENED TO MY WIFE...
IT WAS SO DARK I THOUGHT I WAS SEEING THINGS.

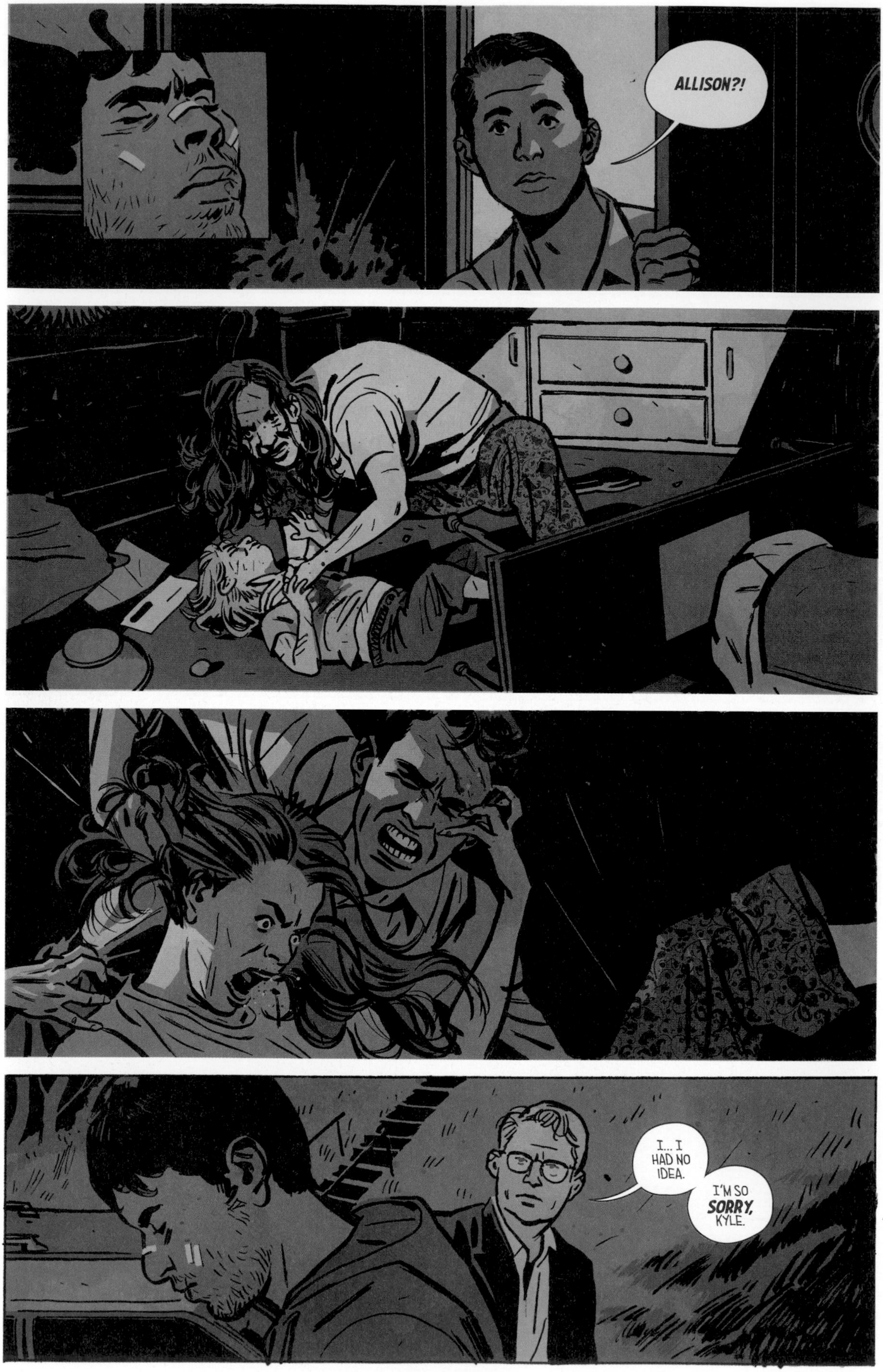
ALLISON?!
I... I HAD NO IDEA.
I'M SO SORRY, KYLE.

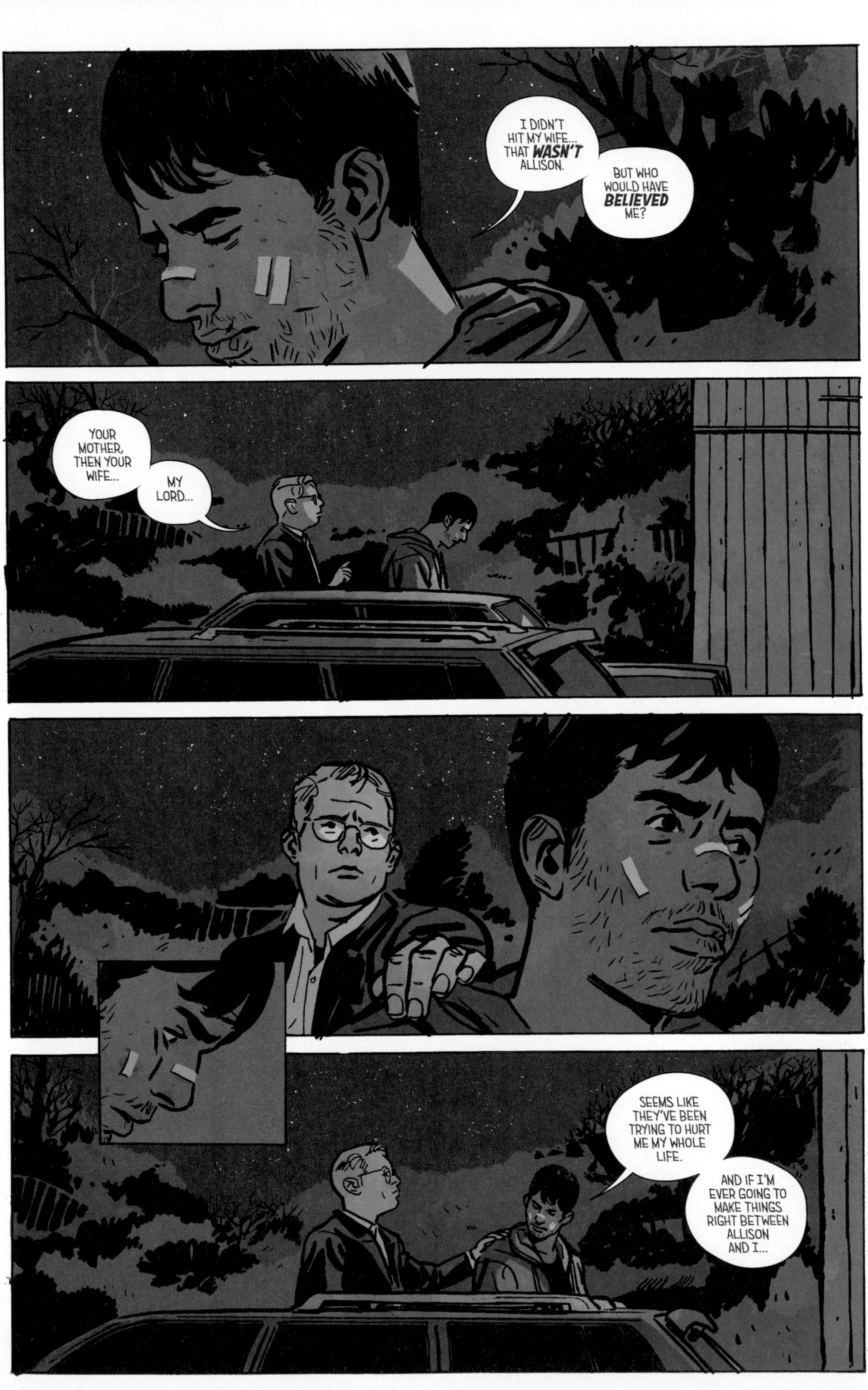
I DIDN'T HIT MY WIFE... THAT **WASN'T** ALLISON.
BUT WHO WOULD HAVE **BELIEVED** ME?
YOUR MOTHER, THEN YOUR WIFE...
MY LORD...
SEEMS LIKE THEY'VE BEEN TRYING TO HURT ME MY WHOLE LIFE.
AND IF I'M EVER GOING TO MAKE THINGS RIGHT BETWEEN ALLISON AND I...

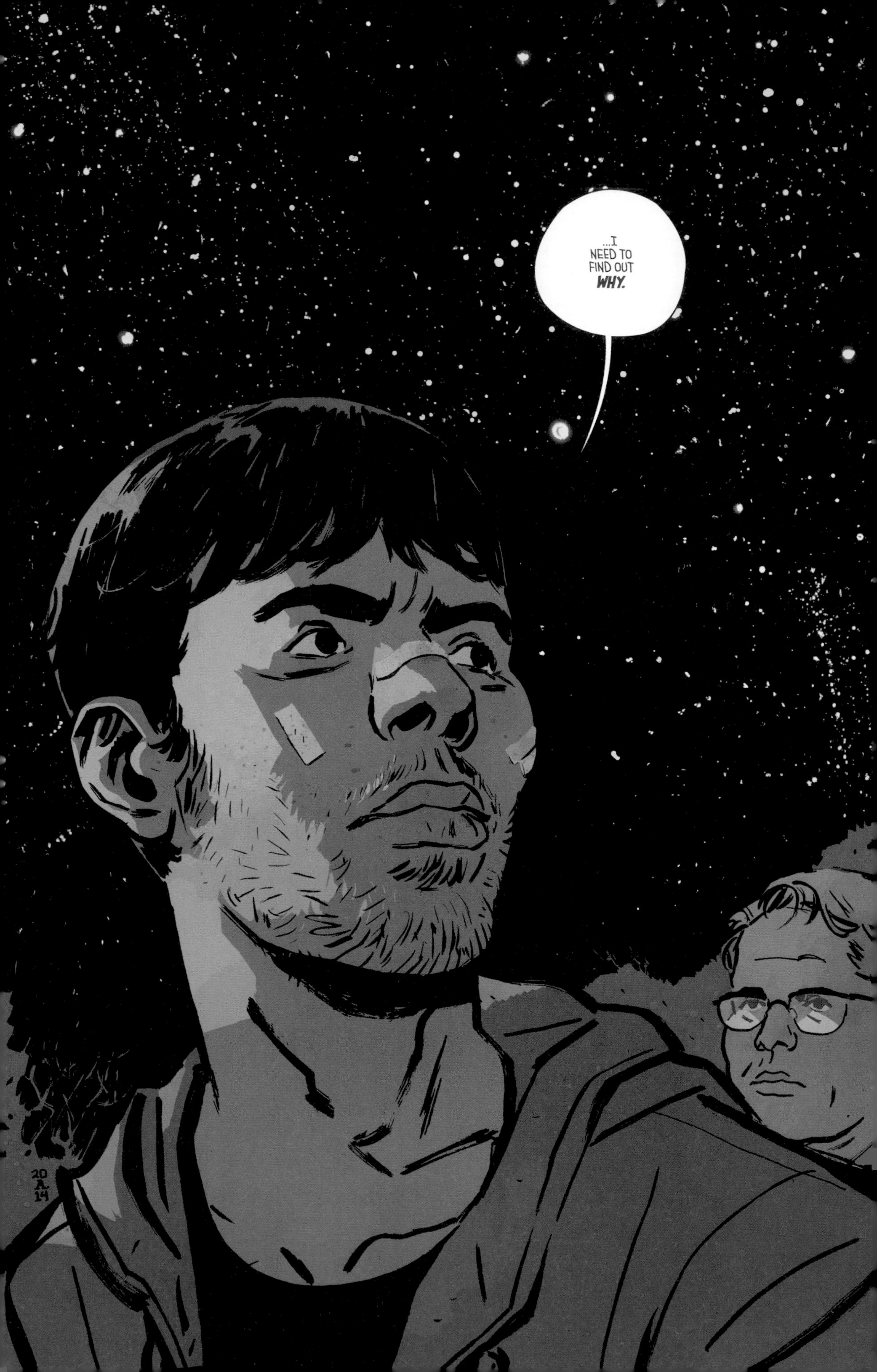
...I NEED TO FIND OUT **WHY.**

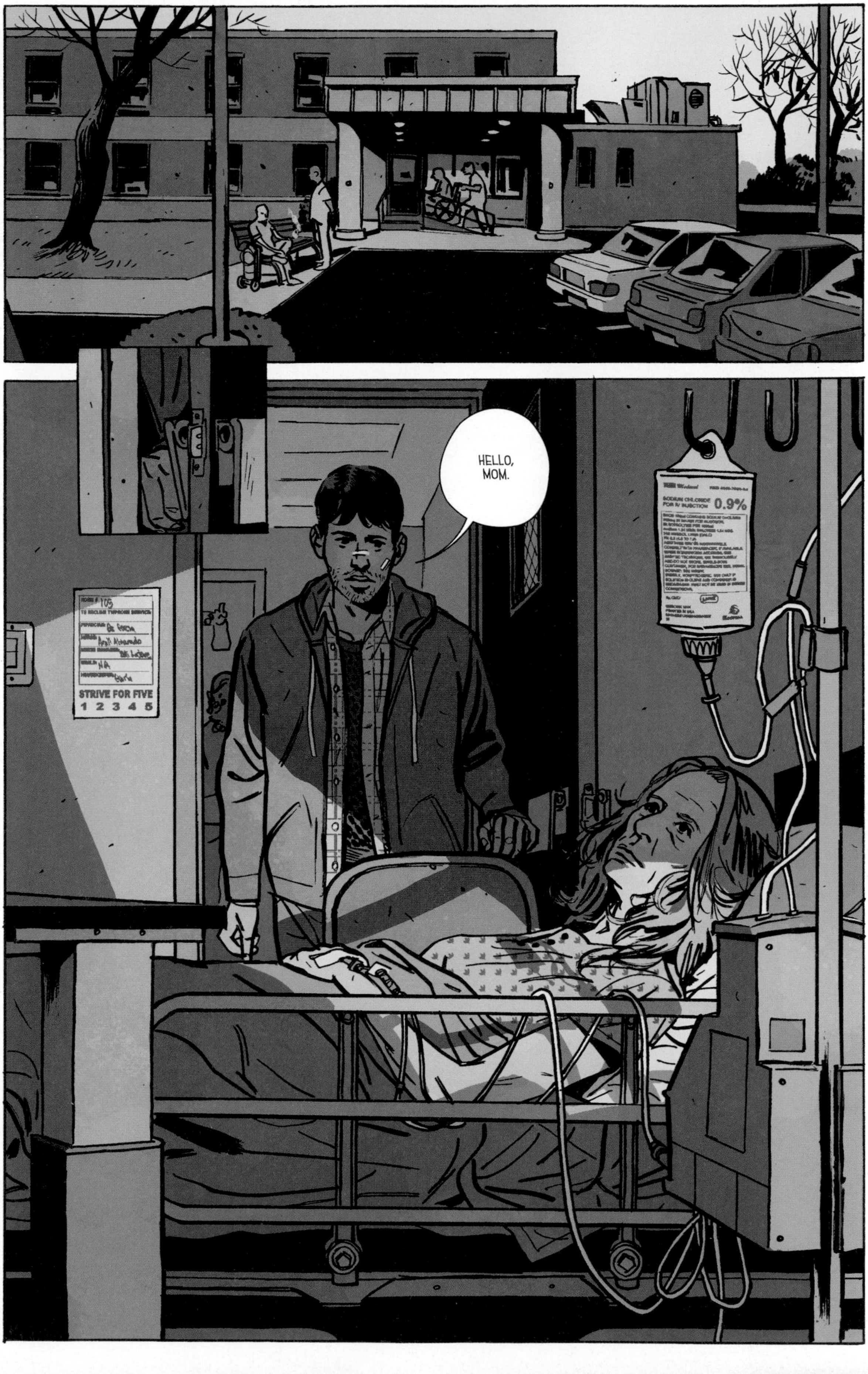
HELLO, MOM.
STRIVE FOR FIVE
1 2 3 4 5
0.9%

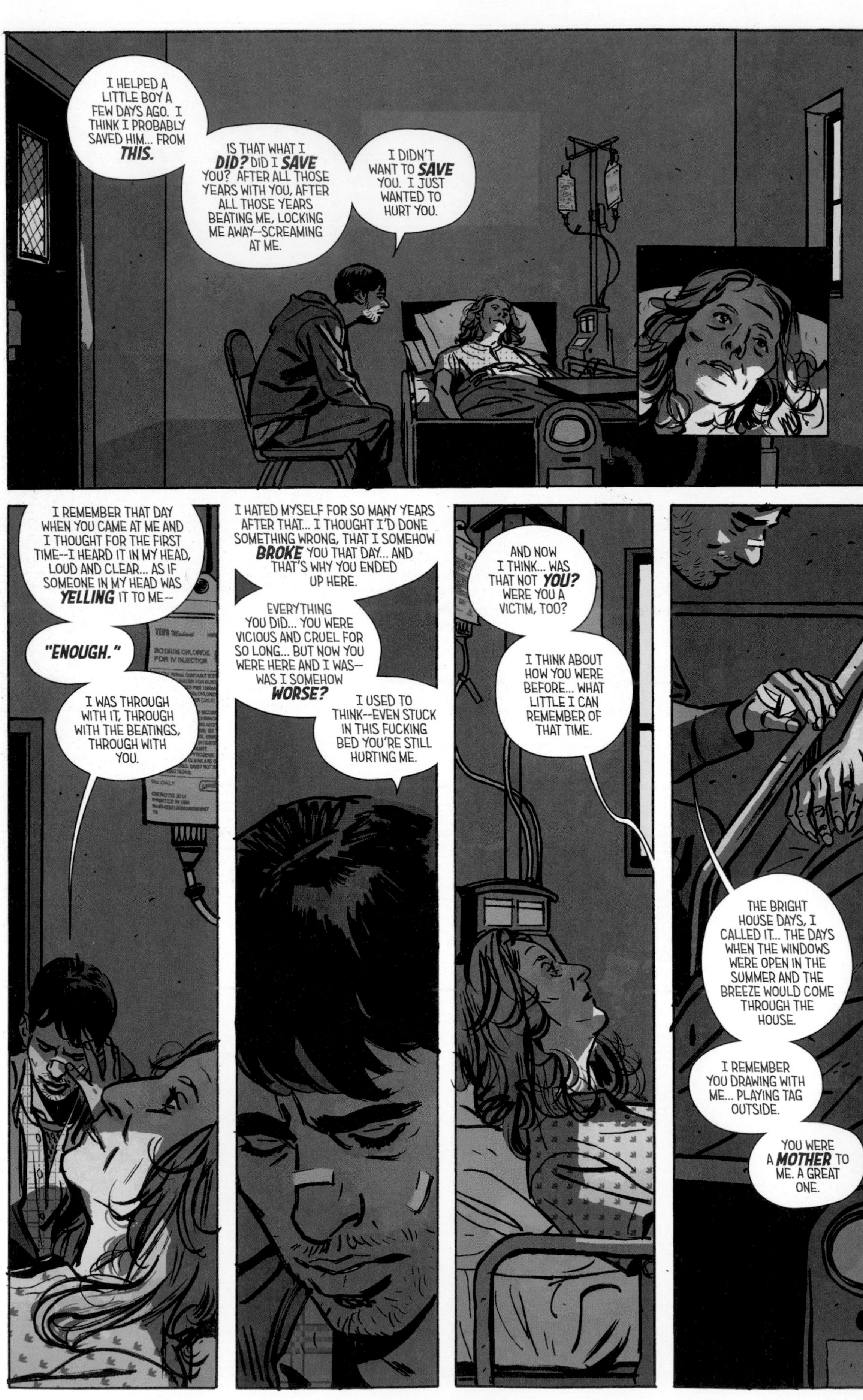
I HELPED A LITTLE BOY A FEW DAYS AGO. I THINK I PROBABLY SAVED HIM... FROM THIS.
IS THAT WHAT I DID? DID I SAVE YOU? AFTER ALL THOSE YEARS WITH YOU, AFTER ALL THOSE YEARS BEATING ME, LOCKING ME AWAY--SCREAMING AT ME.
I DIDN'T WANT TO SAVE YOU. I JUST WANTED TO HURT YOU.
I REMEMBER THAT DAY WHEN YOU CAME AT ME AND I THOUGHT FOR THE FIRST TIME--I HEARD IT IN MY HEAD, LOUD AND CLEAR... AS IF SOMEONE IN MY HEAD WAS YELLING IT TO ME--
"ENOUGH."
I WAS THROUGH WITH IT, THROUGH WITH THE BEATINGS, THROUGH WITH YOU.
I HATED MYSELF FOR SO MANY YEARS AFTER THAT... I THOUGHT I'D DONE SOMETHING WRONG, THAT I SOMEHOW BROKE YOU THAT DAY... AND THAT'S WHY YOU ENDED UP HERE.
EVERYTHING YOU DID... YOU WERE VICIOUS AND CRUEL FOR SO LONG... BUT NOW YOU WERE HERE AND I WAS--WAS I SOMEHOW WORSE?
I USED TO THINK--EVEN STUCK IN THIS FUCKING BED YOU'RE STILL HURTING ME.
AND NOW I THINK... WAS THAT NOT YOU? WERE YOU A VICTIM, TOO?
I THINK ABOUT HOW YOU WERE BEFORE... WHAT LITTLE I CAN REMEMBER OF THAT TIME.
THE BRIGHT HOUSE DAYS, I CALLED IT... THE DAYS WHEN THE WINDOWS WERE OPEN IN THE SUMMER AND THE BREEZE WOULD COME THROUGH THE HOUSE.
I REMEMBER YOU DRAWING WITH ME... PLAYING TAG OUTSIDE.
YOU WERE A MOTHER TO ME. A GREAT ONE.

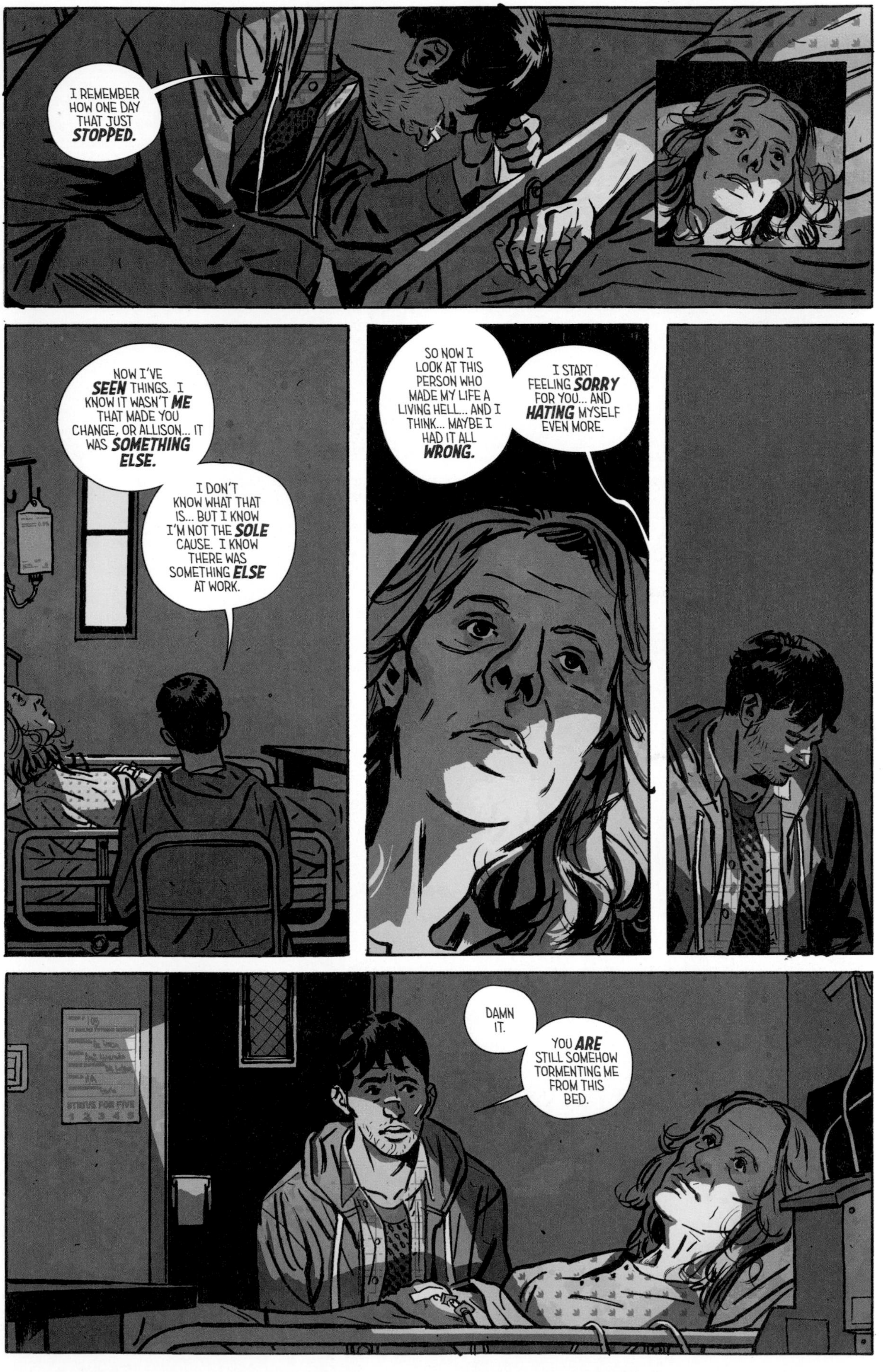
I REMEMBER HOW ONE DAY THAT JUST STOPPED.
NOW I'VE SEEN THINGS. I KNOW IT WASN'T ME THAT MADE YOU CHANGE, OR ALLISON... IT WAS SOMETHING ELSE.
I DON'T KNOW WHAT THAT IS... BUT I KNOW I'M NOT THE SOLE CAUSE. I KNOW THERE WAS SOMETHING ELSE AT WORK.
SO NOW I LOOK AT THIS PERSON WHO MADE MY LIFE A LIVING HELL... AND I THINK... MAYBE I HAD IT ALL WRONG.
I START FEELING SORRY FOR YOU... AND HATING MYSELF EVEN MORE.
STRIVE FOR FIVE
1 2 3 4 5
DAMN IT.
YOU ARE STILL SOMEHOW TORMENTING ME FROM THIS BED.

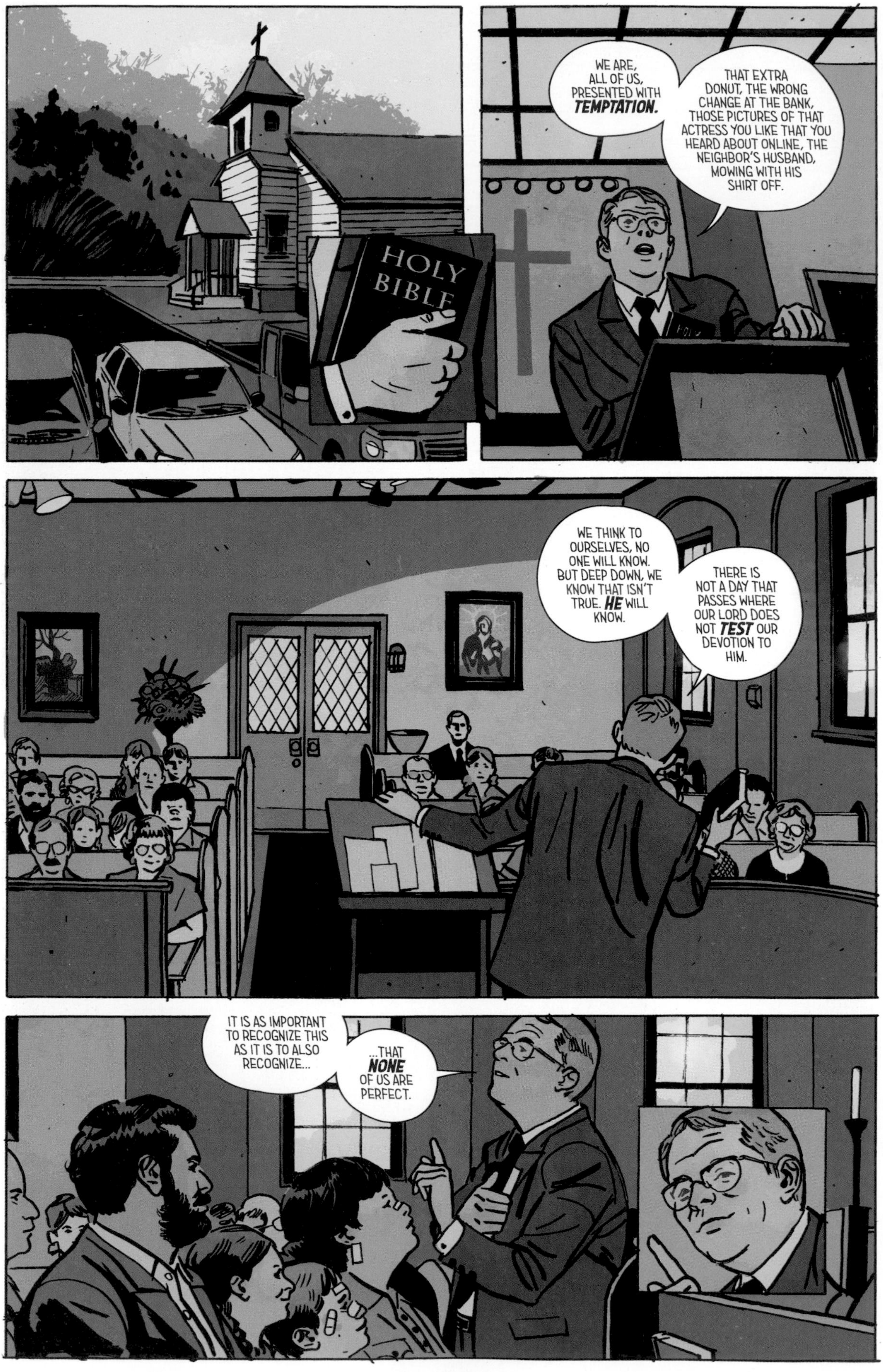
HOLY BIBLE
WE ARE, ALL OF US, PRESENTED WITH TEMPTATION.
THAT EXTRA DONUT, THE WRONG CHANGE AT THE BANK, THOSE PICTURES OF THAT ACTRESS YOU LIKE THAT YOU HEARD ABOUT ONLINE, THE NEIGHBOR'S HUSBAND, MOWING WITH HIS SHIRT OFF.
WE THINK TO OURSELVES, NO ONE WILL KNOW. BUT DEEP DOWN, WE KNOW THAT ISN'T TRUE. HE WILL KNOW.
THERE IS NOT A DAY THAT PASSES WHERE OUR LORD DOES NOT TEST OUR DEVOTION TO HIM.
IT IS AS IMPORTANT TO RECOGNIZE THIS AS IT IS TO ALSO RECOGNIZE...
...THAT NONE OF US ARE PERFECT.

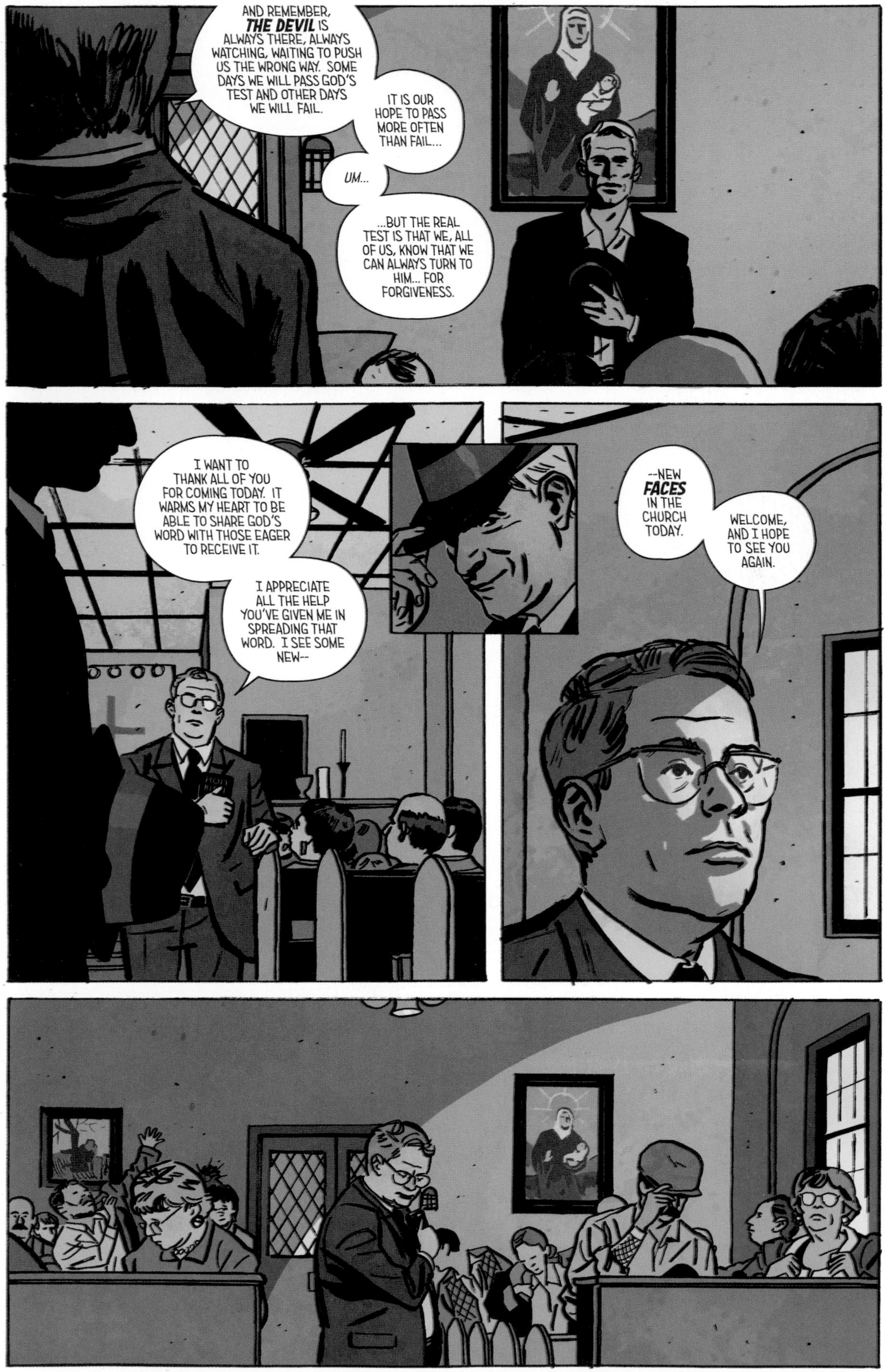

AND REMEMBER, **THE DEVIL** IS ALWAYS THERE, ALWAYS WATCHING, WAITING TO PUSH US THE WRONG WAY. SOME DAYS WE WILL PASS GOD'S TEST AND OTHER DAYS WE WILL FAIL.
IT IS OUR HOPE TO PASS MORE OFTEN THAN FAIL...
UM...
...BUT THE REAL TEST IS THAT WE, ALL OF US, KNOW THAT WE CAN ALWAYS TURN TO HIM... FOR FORGIVENESS.
I WANT TO THANK ALL OF YOU FOR COMING TODAY. IT WARMS MY HEART TO BE ABLE TO SHARE GOD'S WORD WITH THOSE EAGER TO RECEIVE IT.
I APPRECIATE ALL THE HELP YOU'VE GIVEN ME IN SPREADING THAT WORD. I SEE SOME NEW--
--NEW **FACES** IN THE CHURCH TODAY.
WELCOME, AND I HOPE TO SEE YOU AGAIN.

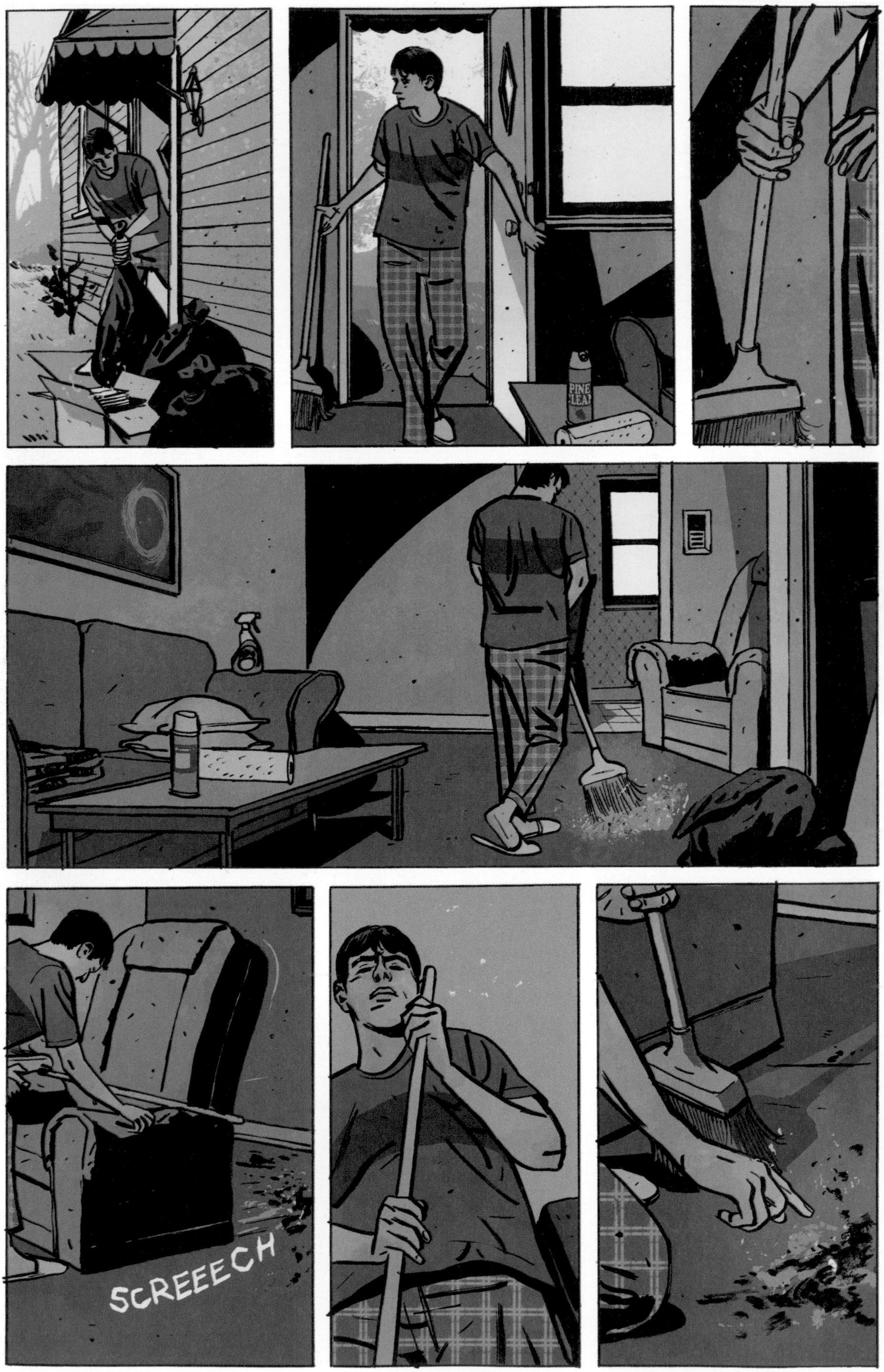
PINE CLEAN
SCREEECH

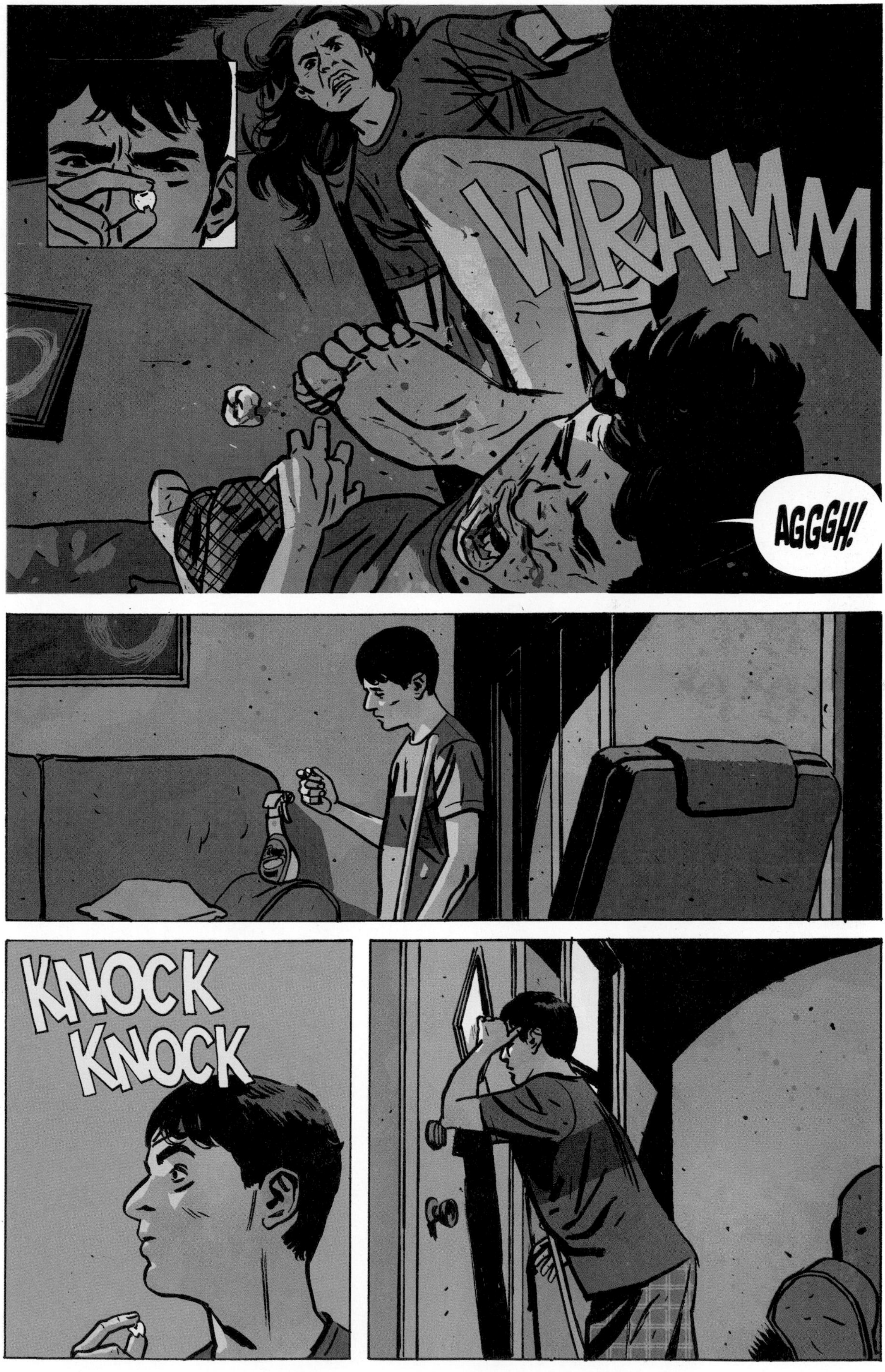
WRAMM
AGGGH!
KNOCK
KNOCK

DOING SOME CLEANING?
YEAH. *UH...*
COME ON IN.
IT LOOKED... ***WORSE*** THAN THIS?
YEAH...
...FOR A LONG TIME.
DO YOU HAVE ANOTHER...
NO, THANKFULLY IT'S NOT QUITE ***THAT*** FREQUENT. I JUST CAME HERE TO CHECK IN ON YOU... MAKE SURE YOU'RE OKAY.
I'M GOOD. BETTER, ACTUALLY.
YOU WOULDN'T HAPPEN TO BE GOING INTO TOWN AFTER THIS, WOULD YOU?
PINE CLEAN

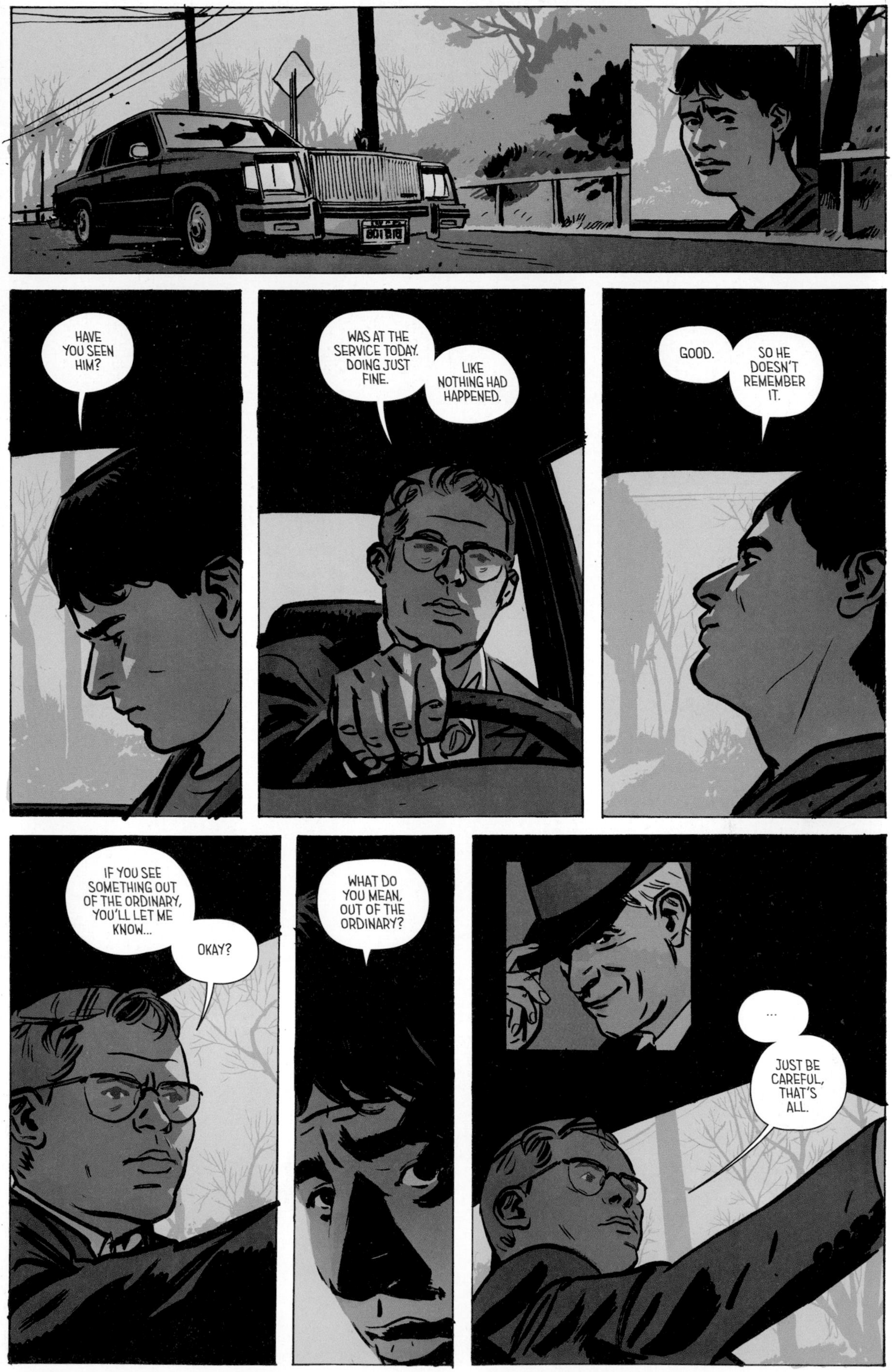
HAVE YOU SEEN HIM?
WAS AT THE SERVICE TODAY. DOING JUST FINE.
LIKE NOTHING HAD HAPPENED.
GOOD.
SO HE DOESN'T REMEMBER IT.
IF YOU SEE SOMETHING OUT OF THE ORDINARY, YOU'LL LET ME KNOW...
OKAY?
WHAT DO YOU MEAN, OUT OF THE ORDINARY?
...
JUST BE CAREFUL, THAT'S ALL.

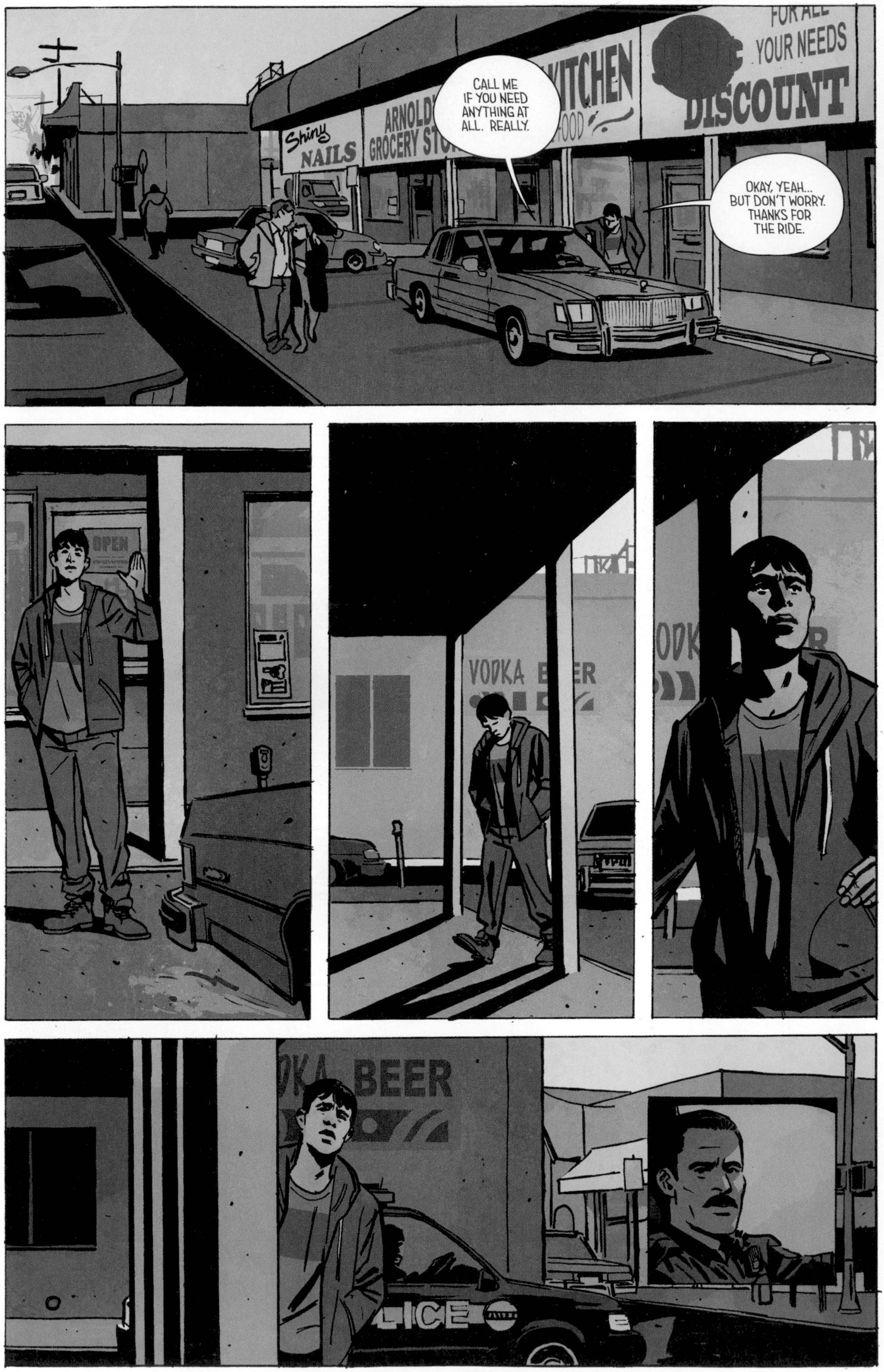
FOR ALL YOUR NEEDS
DISCOUNT
KITCHEN
Shiny NAILS
CALL ME IF YOU NEED ANYTHING AT ALL. REALLY.
OKAY, YEAH... BUT DON'T WORRY. THANKS FOR THE RIDE.
OPEN
VODKA BEER
BEER
LICE

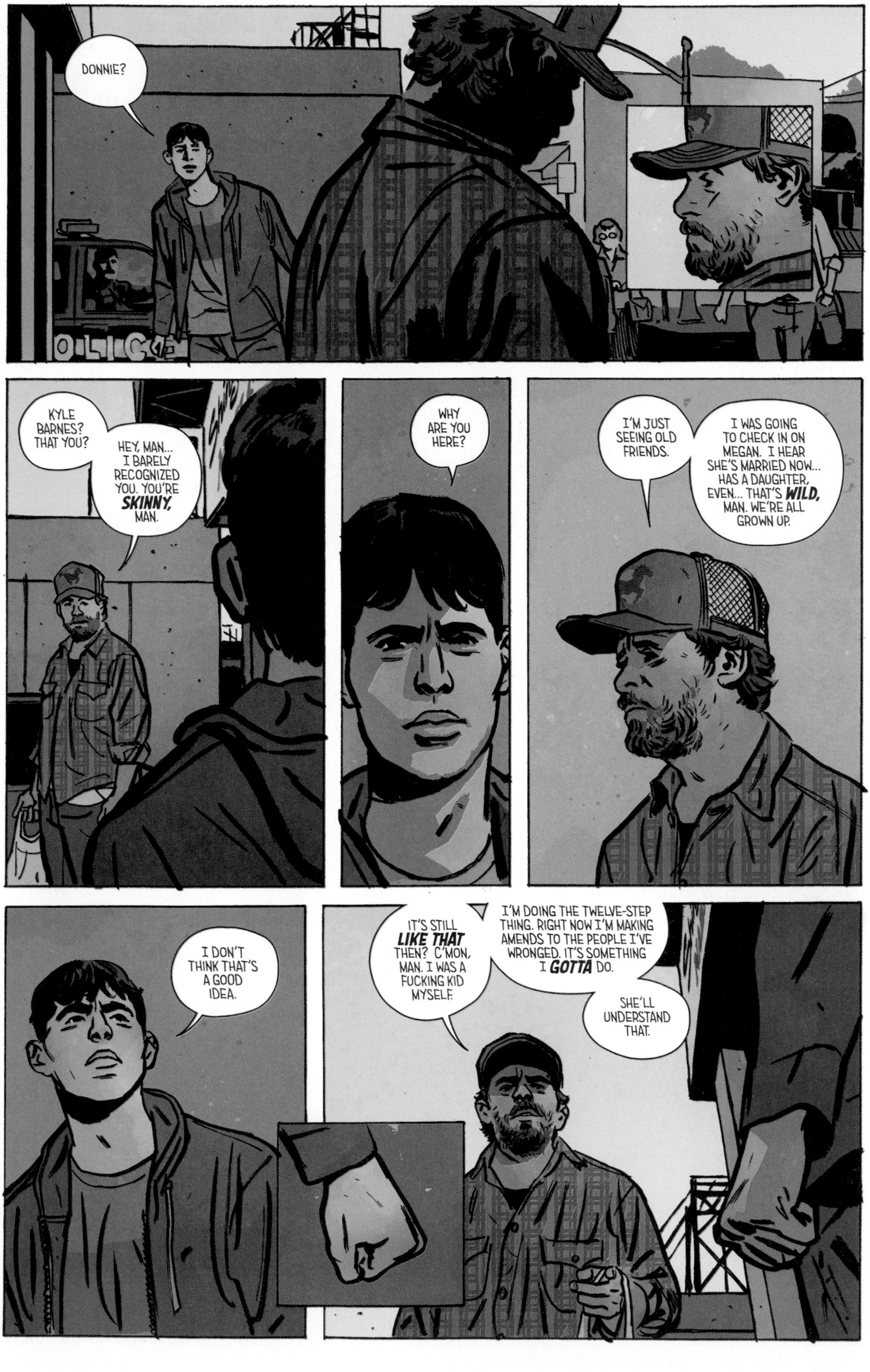
DONNIE?
KYLE BARNES? THAT YOU?
HEY, MAN... I BARELY RECOGNIZED YOU. YOU'RE **SKINNY,** MAN.
WHY ARE YOU HERE?
I'M JUST SEEING OLD FRIENDS.
I WAS GOING TO CHECK IN ON MEGAN. I HEAR SHE'S MARRIED NOW... HAS A DAUGHTER, EVEN... THAT'S **WILD,** MAN. WE'RE ALL GROWN UP.
I DON'T THINK THAT'S A GOOD IDEA.
IT'S STILL **LIKE THAT** THEN? C'MON, MAN. I WAS A FUCKING KID MYSELF.
I'M DOING THE TWELVE-STEP THING. RIGHT NOW I'M MAKING AMENDS TO THE PEOPLE I'VE WRONGED. IT'S SOMETHING I **GOTTA** DO.
SHE'LL UNDERSTAND THAT.

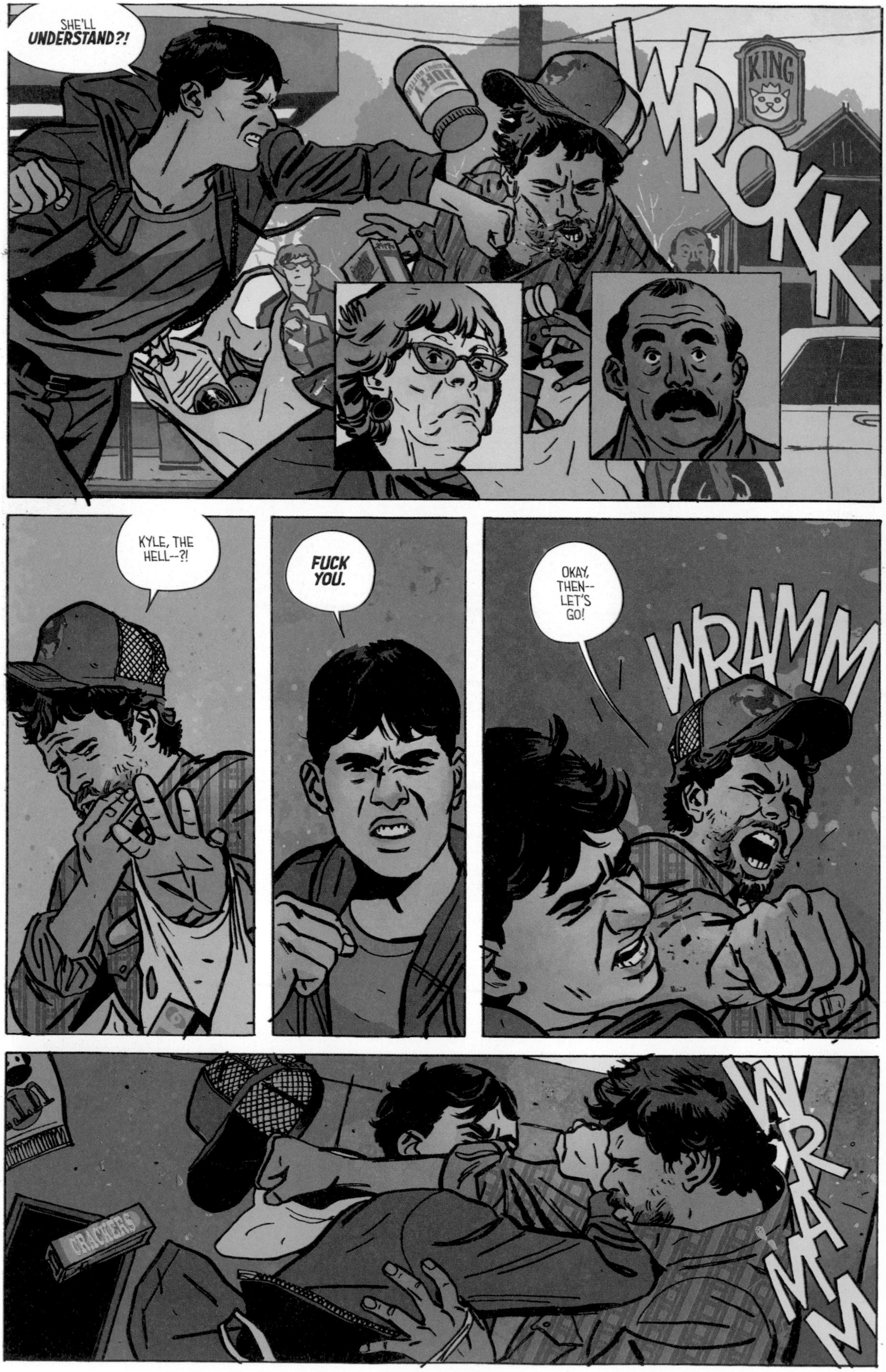
SHE'LL **UNDERSTAND?!**
WROKK
KING
KYLE, THE HELL--?!
FUCK YOU.
OKAY, THEN-- LET'S GO!
WRAMM
WRAMM
CRACKERS

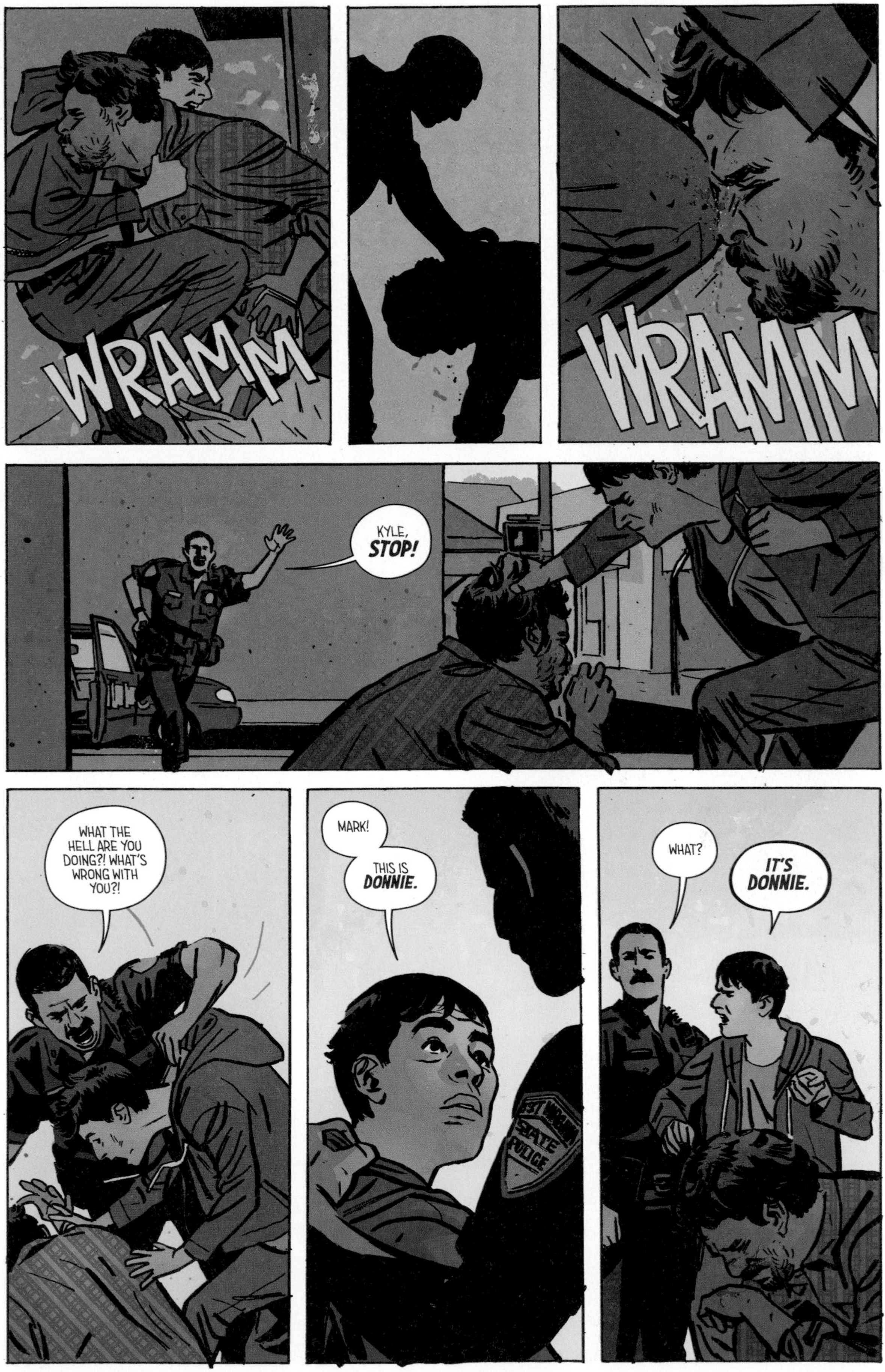
WRAMM
WRAMM
KYLE, STOP!
WHAT THE HELL ARE YOU DOING?! WHAT'S WRONG WITH YOU?!
MARK!
THIS IS DONNIE.
WHAT?
IT'S DONNIE.

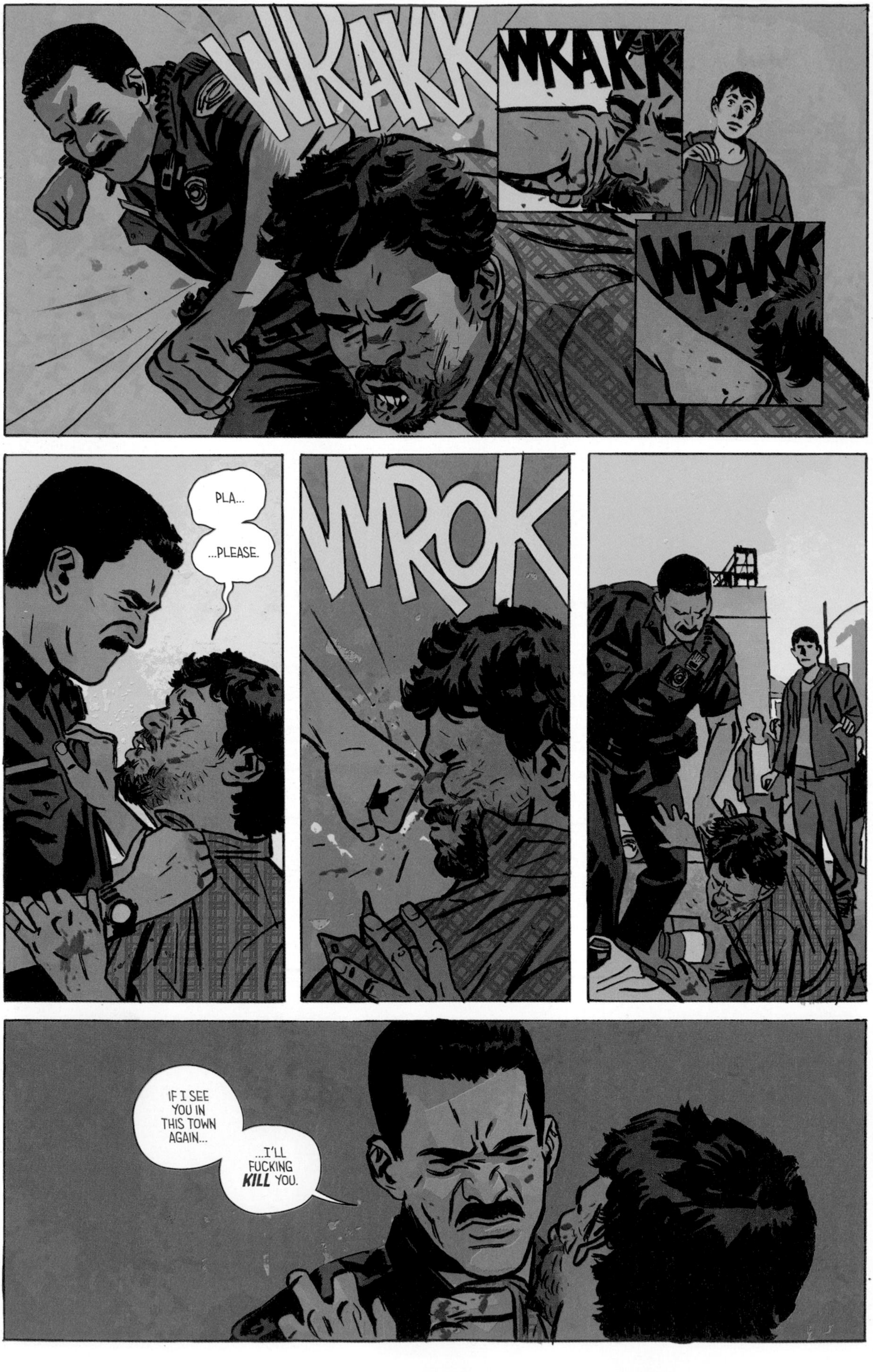
WRAKK
WRAKK
WRAKK
PLA...
...PLEASE.
WROK
IF I SEE YOU IN THIS TOWN AGAIN...
...I'LL FUCKING **KILL** YOU.

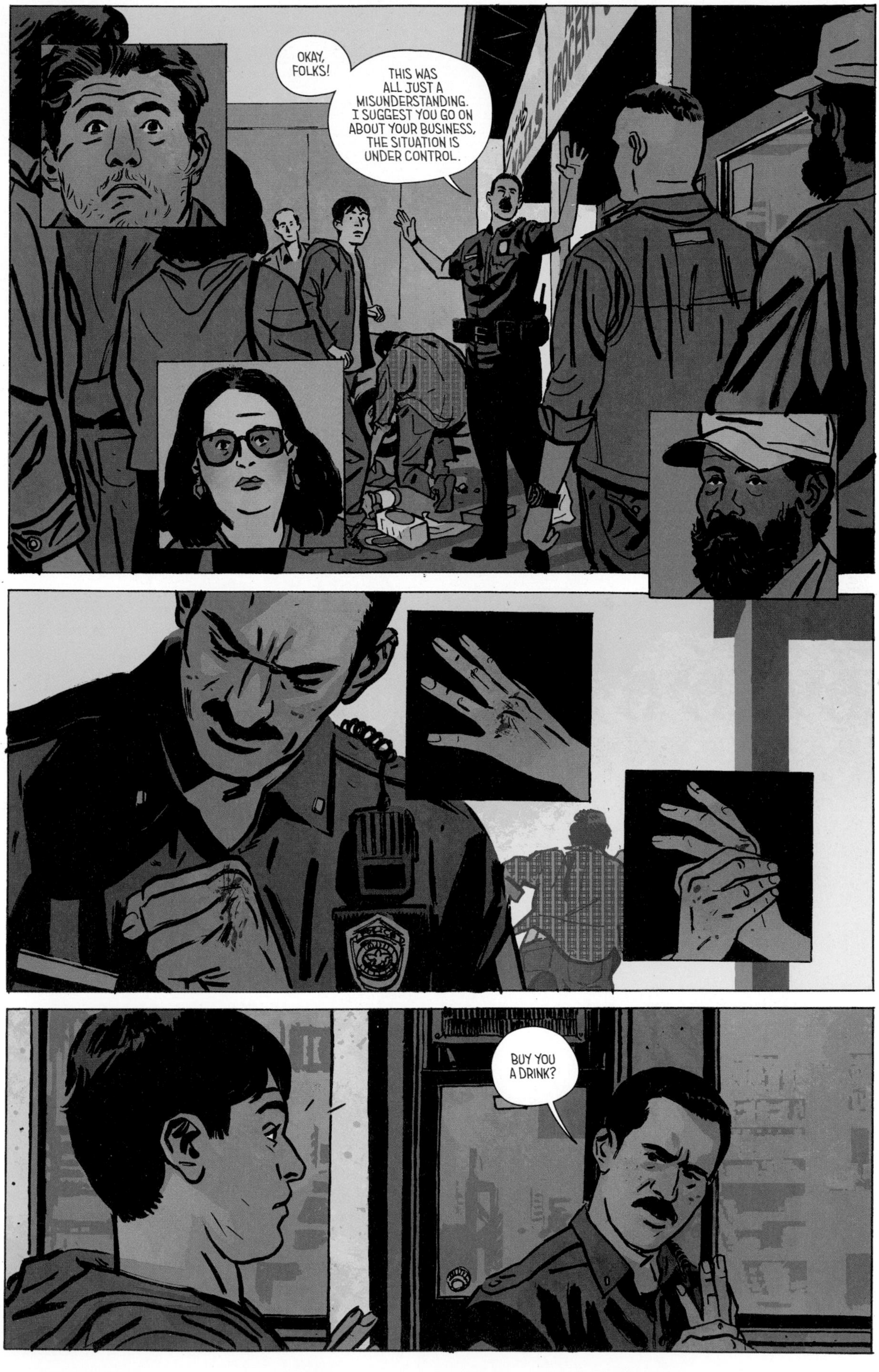
OKAY, FOLKS!
THIS WAS ALL JUST A MISUNDERSTANDING. I SUGGEST YOU GO ON ABOUT YOUR BUSINESS, THE SITUATION IS UNDER CONTROL.
BUY YOU A DRINK?

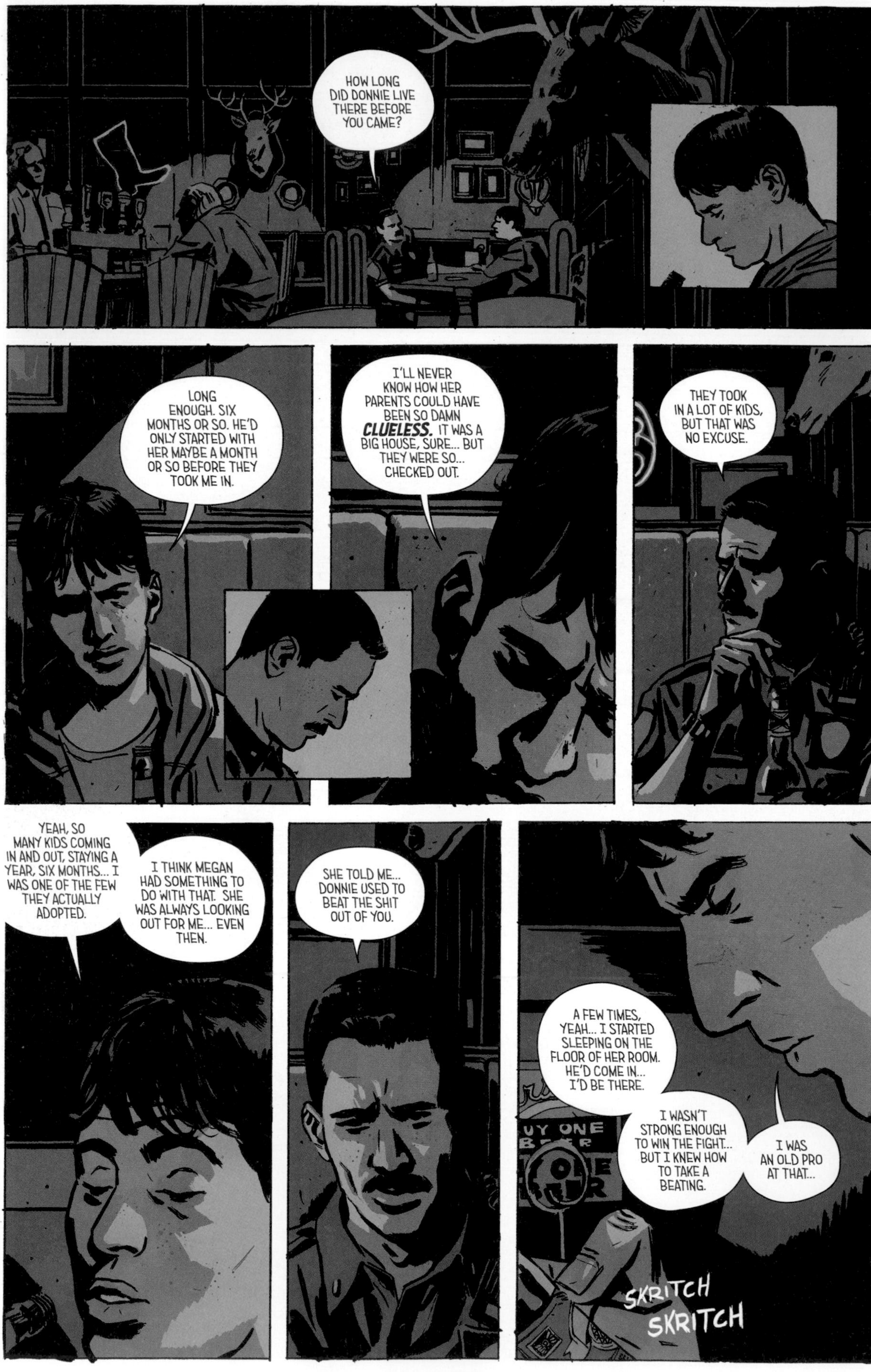
HOW LONG DID DONNIE LIVE THERE BEFORE YOU CAME?
LONG ENOUGH. SIX MONTHS OR SO. HE'D ONLY STARTED WITH HER MAYBE A MONTH OR SO BEFORE THEY TOOK ME IN.
I'LL NEVER KNOW HOW HER PARENTS COULD HAVE BEEN SO DAMN CLUELESS. IT WAS A BIG HOUSE, SURE... BUT THEY WERE SO... CHECKED OUT.
THEY TOOK IN A LOT OF KIDS, BUT THAT WAS NO EXCUSE.
YEAH, SO MANY KIDS COMING IN AND OUT, STAYING A YEAR, SIX MONTHS... I WAS ONE OF THE FEW THEY ACTUALLY ADOPTED.
I THINK MEGAN HAD SOMETHING TO DO WITH THAT. SHE WAS ALWAYS LOOKING OUT FOR ME... EVEN THEN.
SHE TOLD ME... DONNIE USED TO BEAT THE SHIT OUT OF YOU.
A FEW TIMES, YEAH... I STARTED SLEEPING ON THE FLOOR OF HER ROOM. HE'D COME IN... I'D BE THERE.
I WASN'T STRONG ENOUGH TO WIN THE FIGHT... BUT I KNEW HOW TO TAKE A BEATING.
I WAS AN OLD PRO AT THAT...
SKRITCH SKRITCH

EVENTUALLY... HE GAVE UP AND STOPPED COMING AROUND. THEN HE FINALLY MOVED ON TO ANOTHER HOME.

NEVER KNEW WHERE THAT WAS... NEVER *CARED.*

Y'KNOW... I STILL CAN'T FIGURE IT OUT.

WHAT?

MAN LIKE YOU, EVERYTHING MEGAN TOLD ME ABOUT YOU... THEN YOU GO AND BEAT *YOUR DAUGHTER* UP?

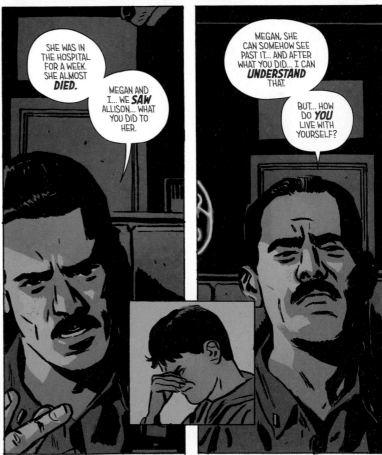

SHE WAS IN THE HOSPITAL FOR A WEEK. SHE ALMOST *DIED.*

MEGAN AND I... WE *SAW* ALLISON... WHAT YOU DID TO HER.

MEGAN, SHE CAN SOMEHOW SEE PAST IT... AND AFTER WHAT YOU DID... I CAN *UNDERSTAND* THAT.

BUT... HOW DO *YOU* LIVE WITH YOURSELF?

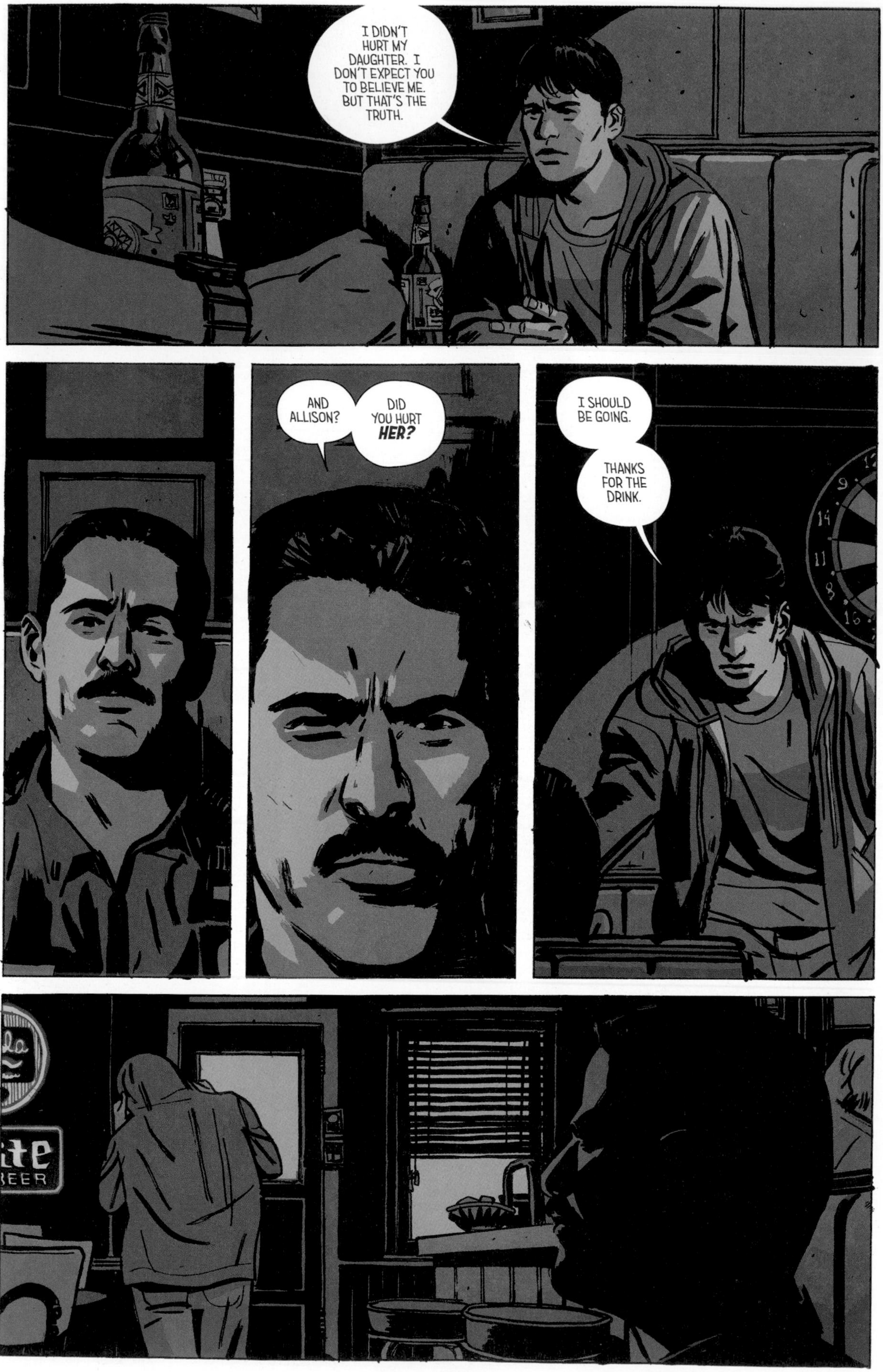
I DIDN'T HURT MY DAUGHTER. I DON'T EXPECT YOU TO BELIEVE ME. BUT THAT'S THE TRUTH.
AND ALLISON?
DID YOU HURT **HER?**
I SHOULD BE GOING.
THANKS FOR THE DRINK.

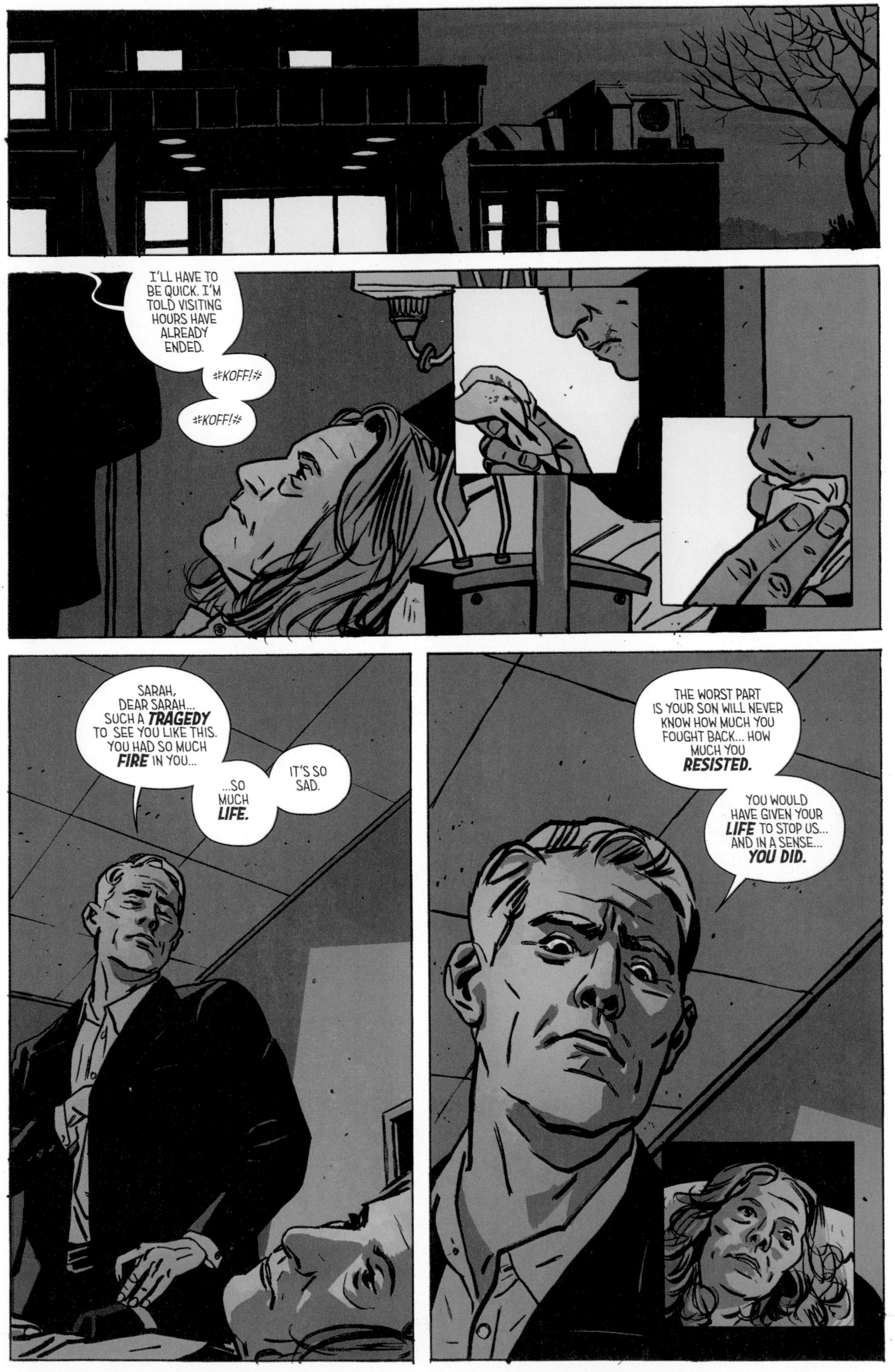

I'LL HAVE TO BE QUICK. I'M TOLD VISITING HOURS HAVE ALREADY ENDED.
KOFF!
KOFF!
SARAH, DEAR SARAH... SUCH A TRAGEDY TO SEE YOU LIKE THIS. YOU HAD SO MUCH FIRE IN YOU...
...SO MUCH LIFE.
IT'S SO SAD.
THE WORST PART IS YOUR SON WILL NEVER KNOW HOW MUCH YOU FOUGHT BACK... HOW MUCH YOU RESISTED.
YOU WOULD HAVE GIVEN YOUR LIFE TO STOP US... AND IN A SENSE... YOU DID.

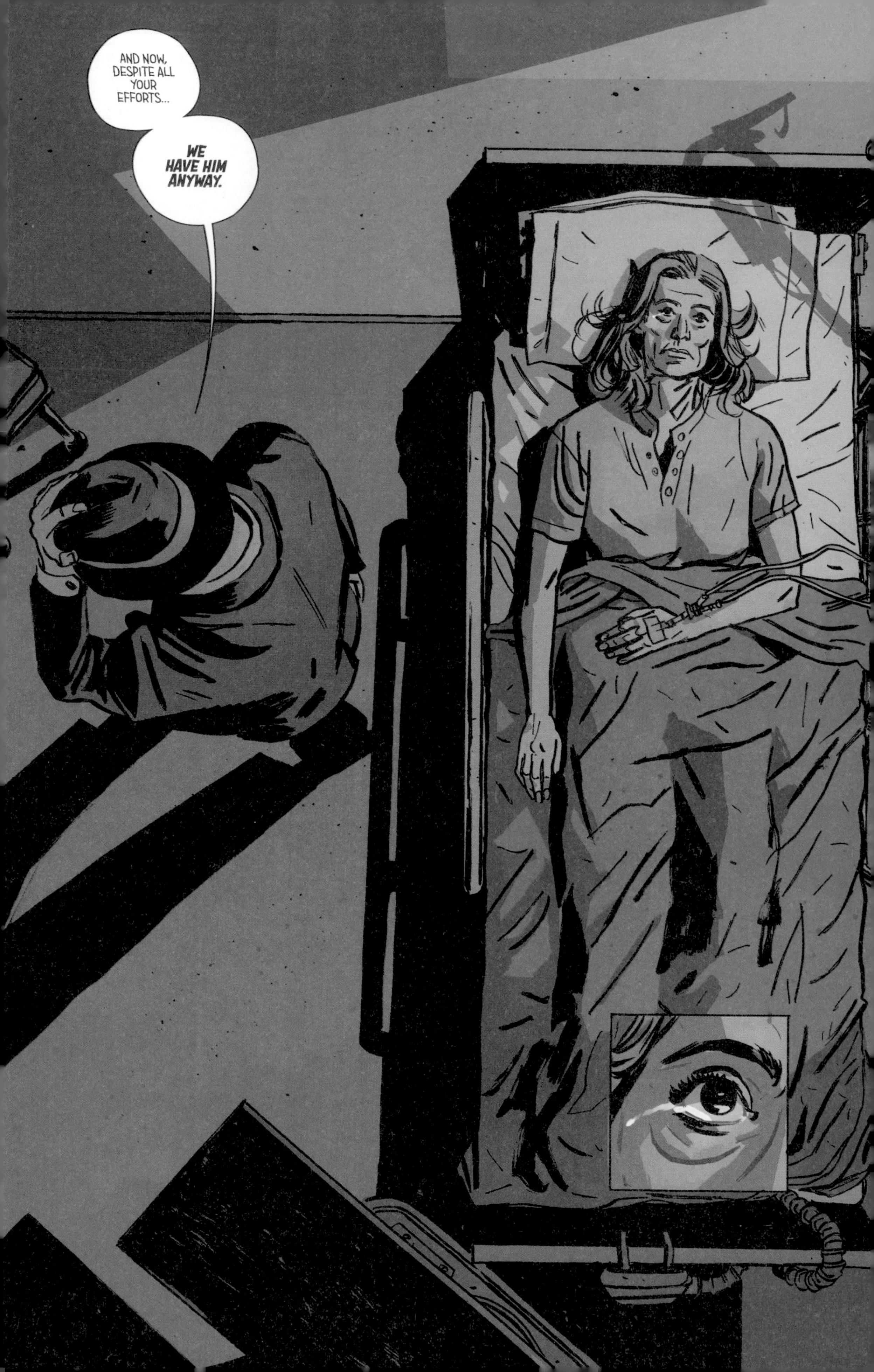
AND NOW, DESPITE ALL YOUR EFFORTS...
WE HAVE HIM ANYWAY.

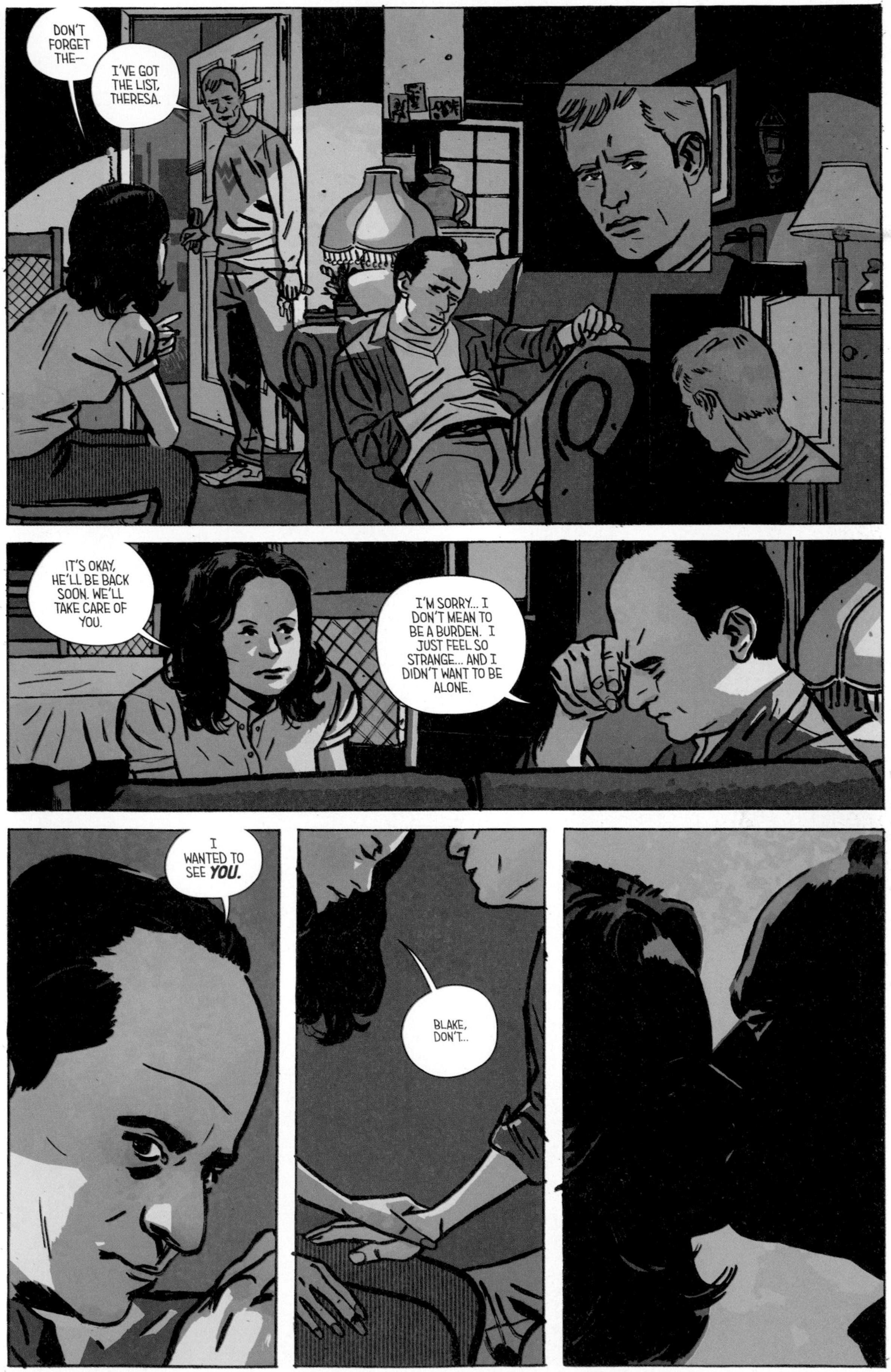
DON'T FORGET THE--
I'VE GOT THE LIST, THERESA.
IT'S OKAY, HE'LL BE BACK SOON. WE'LL TAKE CARE OF YOU.
I'M SORRY... I DON'T MEAN TO BE A BURDEN. I JUST FEEL SO STRANGE... AND I DIDN'T WANT TO BE ALONE.
I WANTED TO SEE *YOU.*
BLAKE, DON'T...

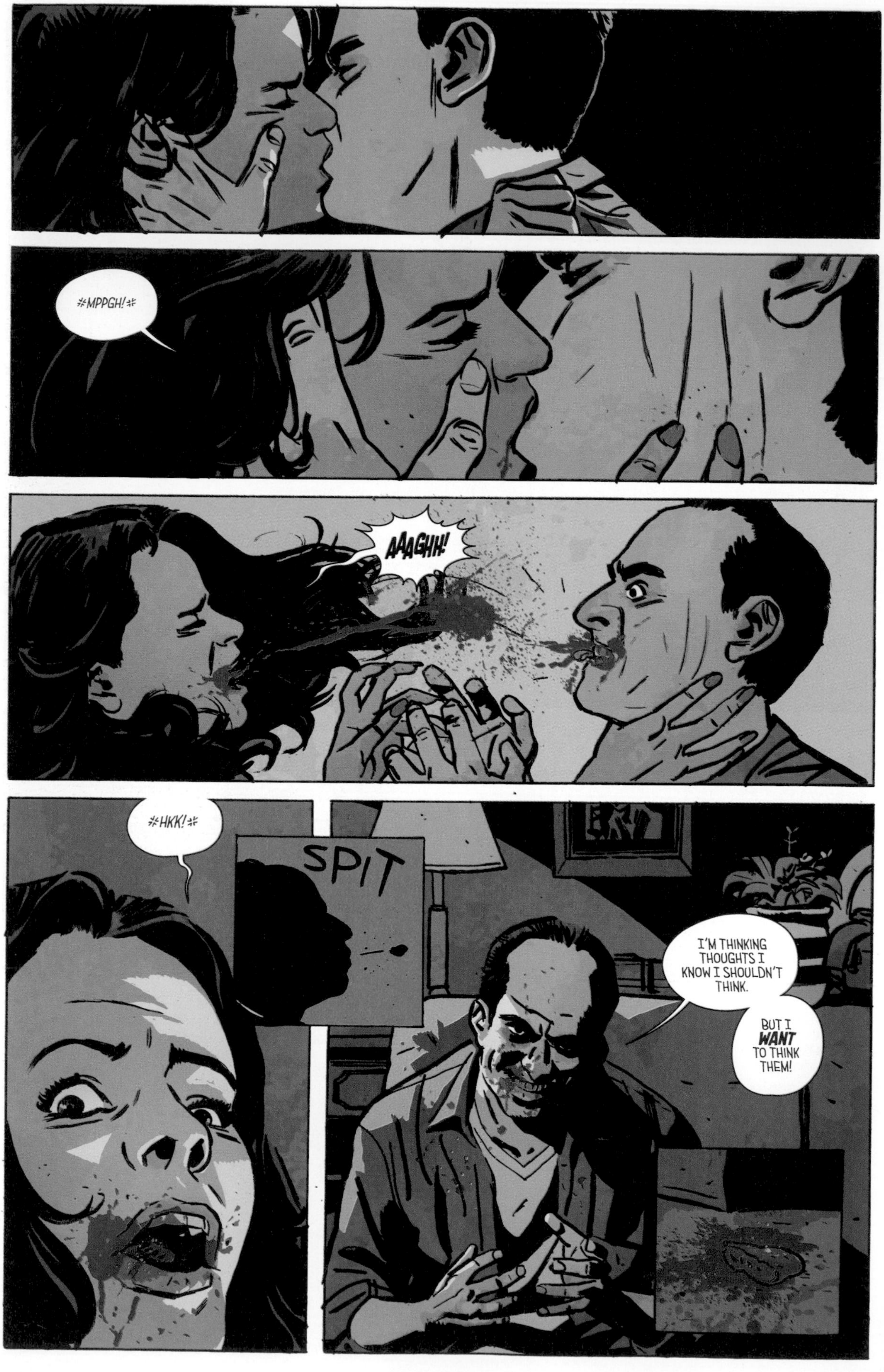

MPPGH!
AAAGHH!
HKK!
SPIT
I'M THINKING THOUGHTS I KNOW I SHOULDN'T THINK.
BUT I ***WANT*** TO THINK THEM!

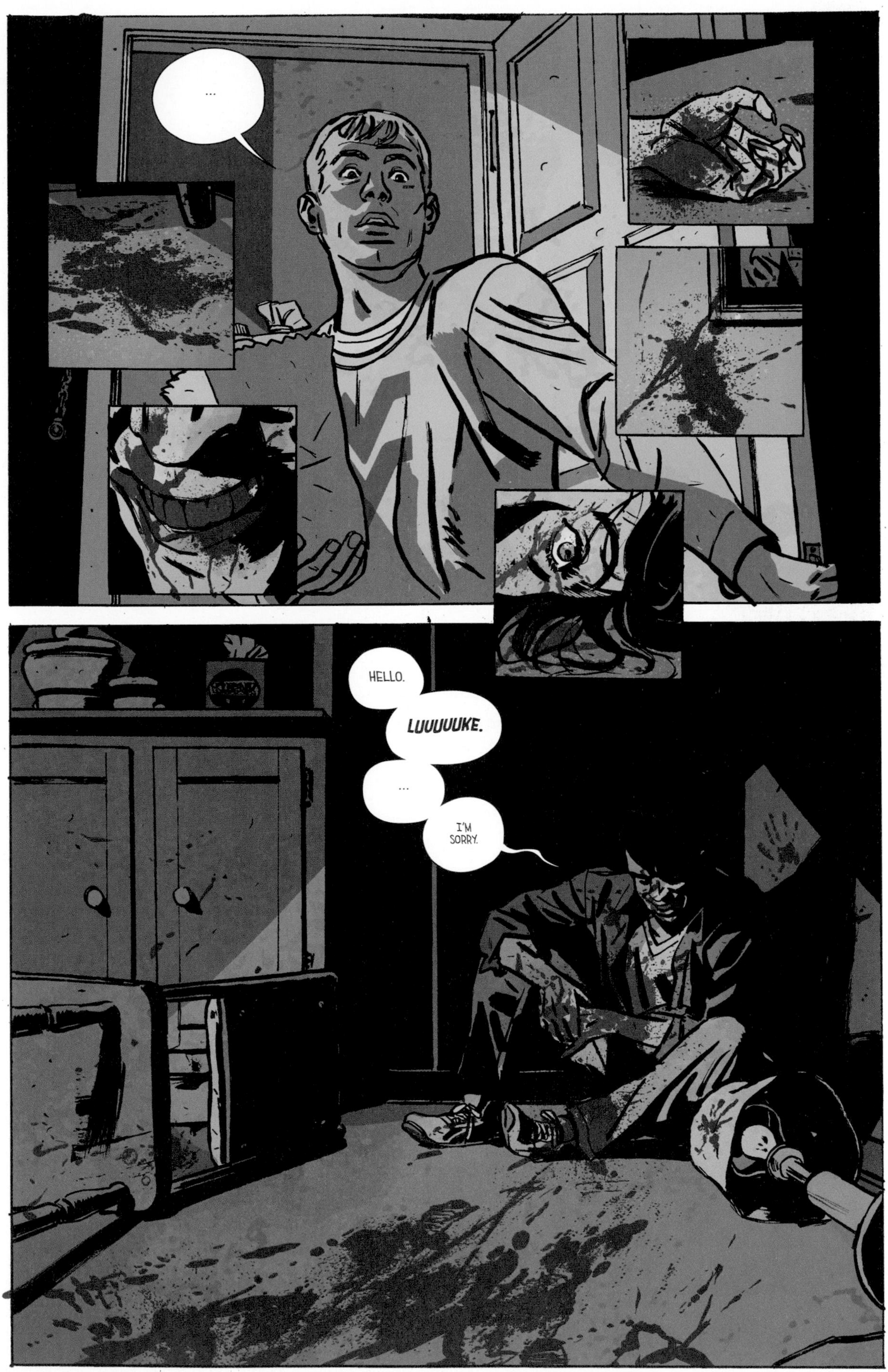
...
HELLO.
LUUUUUKE.
...
I'M SORRY.

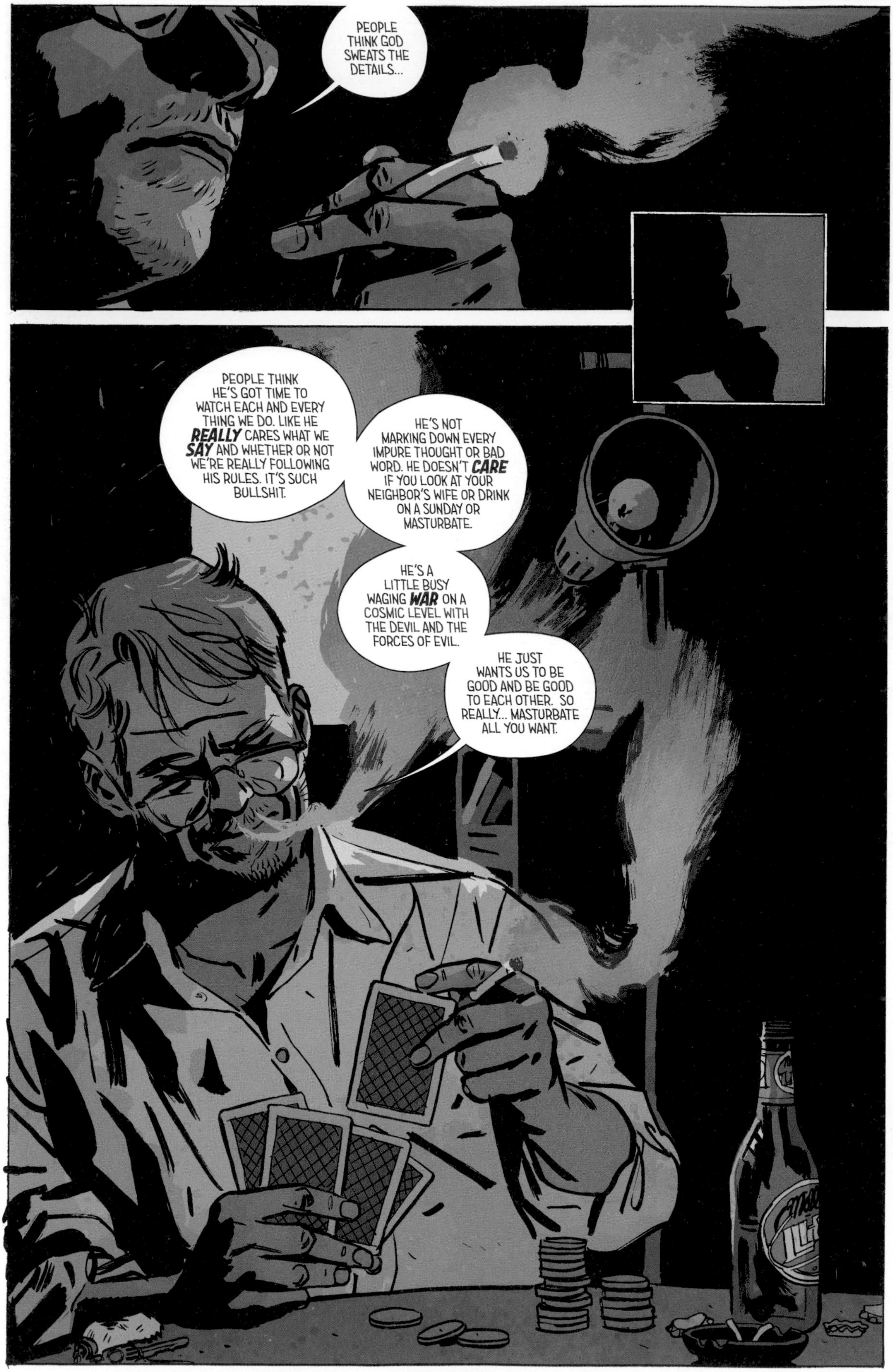

PEOPLE THINK GOD SWEATS THE DETAILS...
PEOPLE THINK HE'S GOT TIME TO WATCH EACH AND EVERY THING WE DO. LIKE HE **REALLY** CARES WHAT WE **SAY** AND WHETHER OR NOT WE'RE REALLY FOLLOWING HIS RULES. IT'S SUCH BULLSHIT.
HE'S NOT MARKING DOWN EVERY IMPURE THOUGHT OR BAD WORD. HE DOESN'T **CARE** IF YOU LOOK AT YOUR NEIGHBOR'S WIFE OR DRINK ON A SUNDAY OR MASTURBATE.
HE'S A LITTLE BUSY WAGING **WAR** ON A COSMIC LEVEL WITH THE DEVIL AND THE FORCES OF EVIL.
HE JUST WANTS US TO BE GOOD AND BE GOOD TO EACH OTHER. SO REALLY... MASTURBATE ALL YOU WANT.

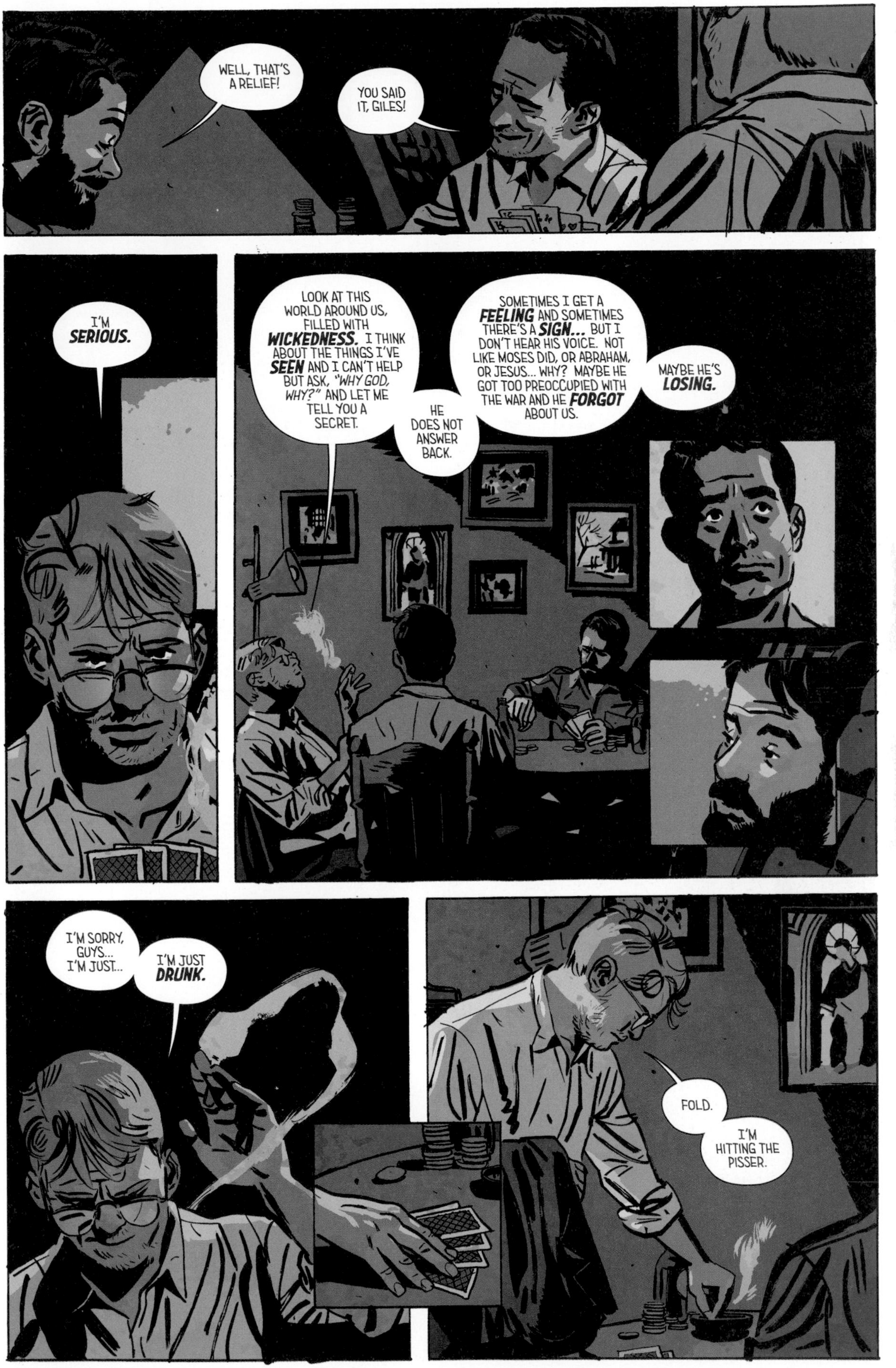

WELL, THAT'S A RELIEF!
YOU SAID IT, GILES!
I'M SERIOUS.
LOOK AT THIS WORLD AROUND US, FILLED WITH WICKEDNESS. I THINK ABOUT THE THINGS I'VE SEEN AND I CAN'T HELP BUT ASK, "WHY GOD, WHY?" AND LET ME TELL YOU A SECRET.
HE DOES NOT ANSWER BACK.
SOMETIMES I GET A FEELING AND SOMETIMES THERE'S A SIGN... BUT I DON'T HEAR HIS VOICE. NOT LIKE MOSES DID, OR ABRAHAM, OR JESUS... WHY? MAYBE HE GOT TOO PREOCCUPIED WITH THE WAR AND HE FORGOT ABOUT US.
MAYBE HE'S LOSING.
I'M SORRY, GUYS... I'M JUST...
I'M JUST DRUNK.
FOLD.
I'M HITTING THE PISSER.

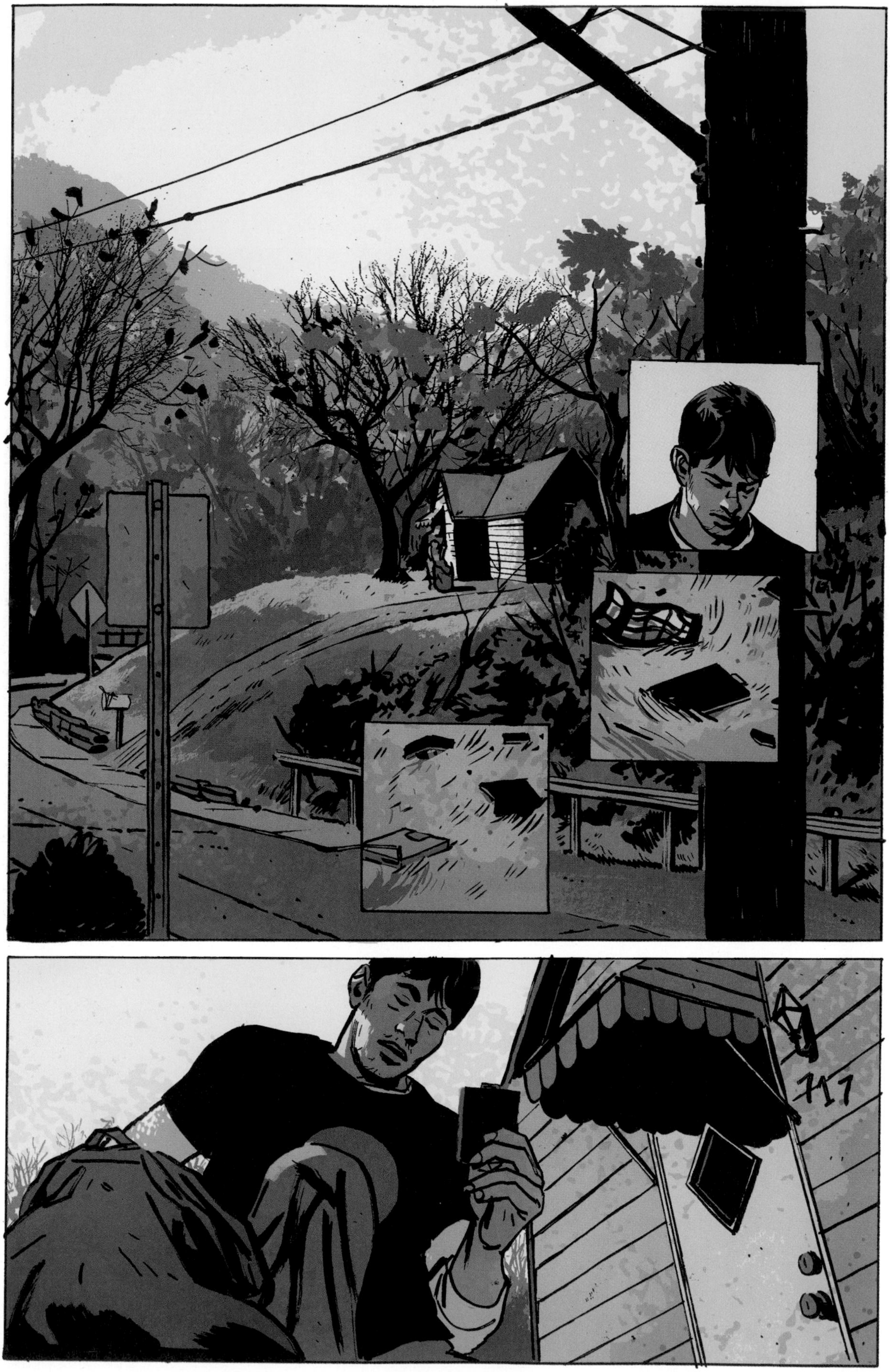
717

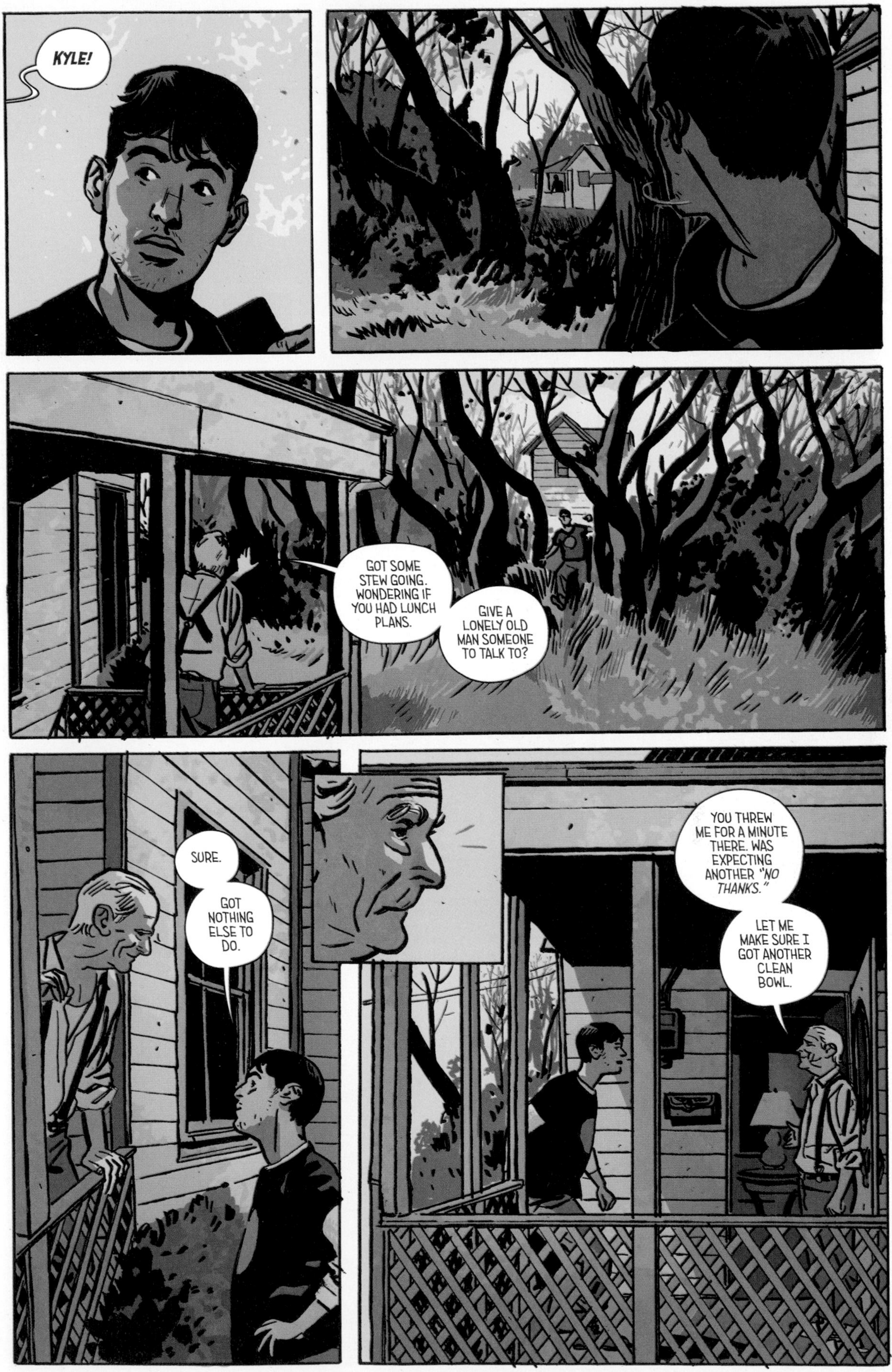
KYLE!
GOT SOME STEW GOING. WONDERING IF YOU HAD LUNCH PLANS.
GIVE A LONELY OLD MAN SOMEONE TO TALK TO?
SURE.
GOT NOTHING ELSE TO DO.
YOU THREW ME FOR A MINUTE THERE. WAS EXPECTING ANOTHER *"NO THANKS."*
LET ME MAKE SURE I GOT ANOTHER CLEAN BOWL.

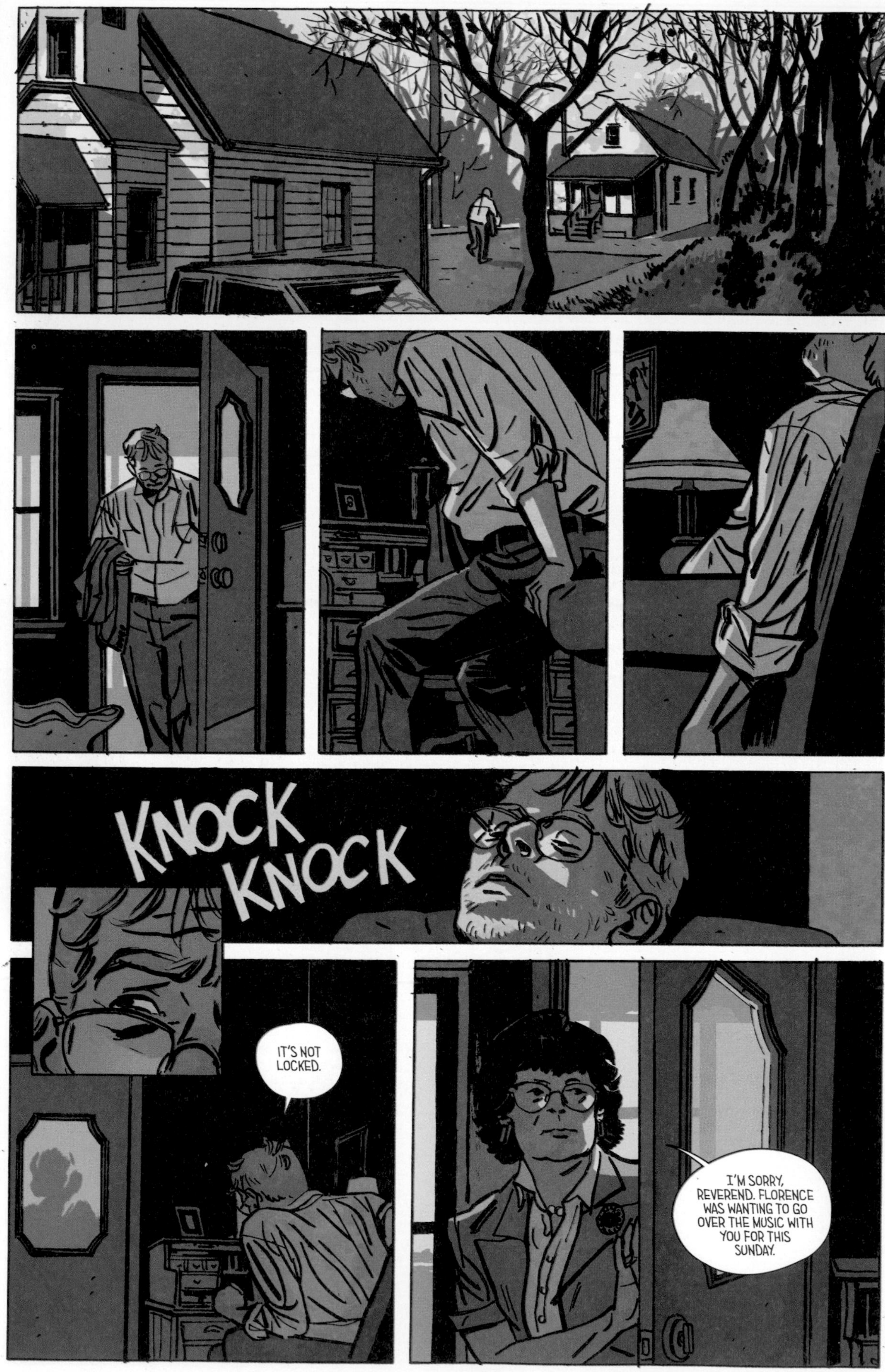
KNOCK KNOCK
IT'S NOT LOCKED.
I'M SORRY, REVEREND. FLORENCE WAS WANTING TO GO OVER THE MUSIC WITH YOU FOR THIS SUNDAY.

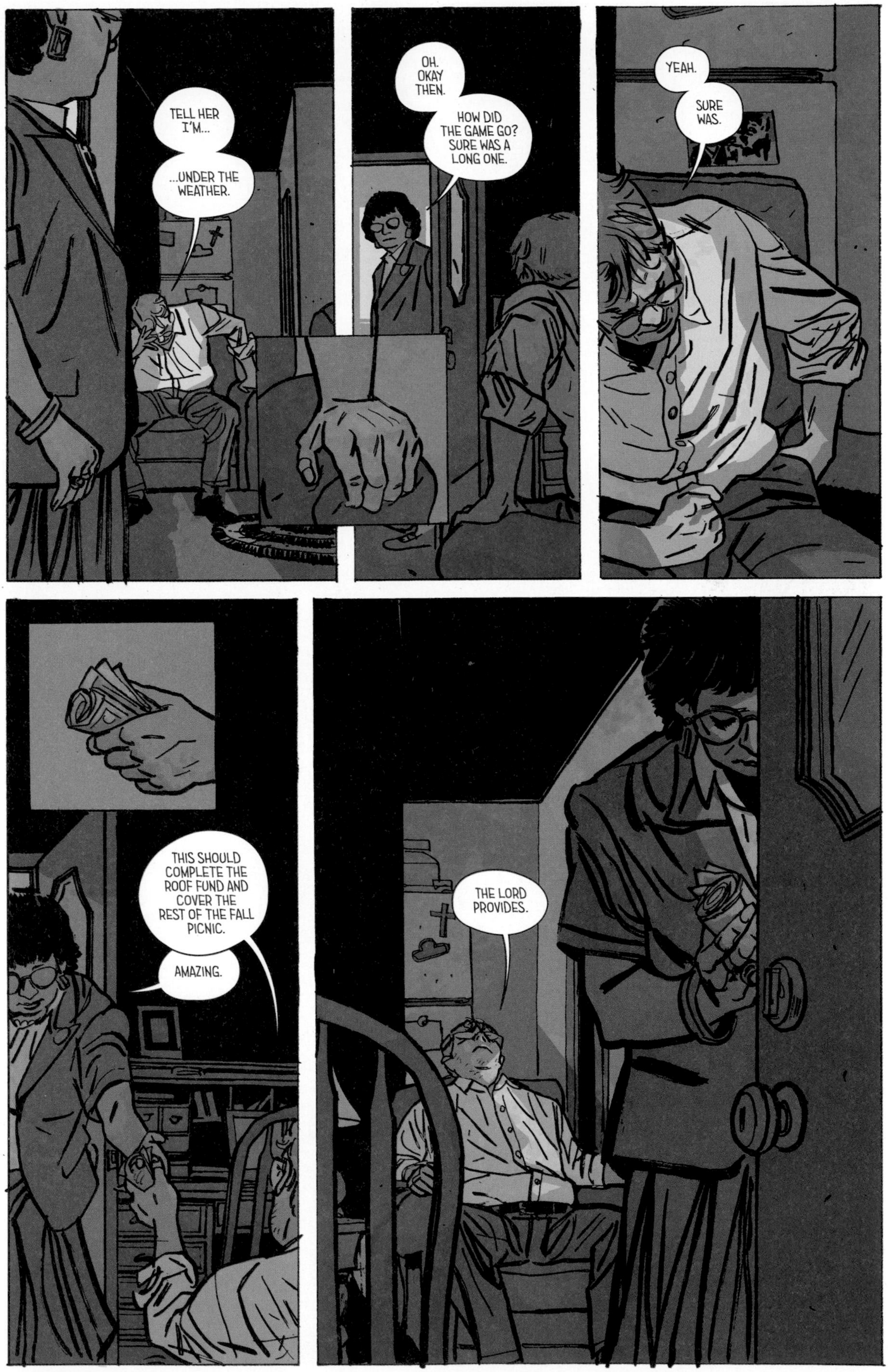
TELL HER I'M...
...UNDER THE WEATHER.
OH. OKAY THEN.
HOW DID THE GAME GO? SURE WAS A LONG ONE.
YEAH.
SURE WAS.
THIS SHOULD COMPLETE THE ROOF FUND AND COVER THE REST OF THE FALL PICNIC.
AMAZING.
THE LORD PROVIDES.

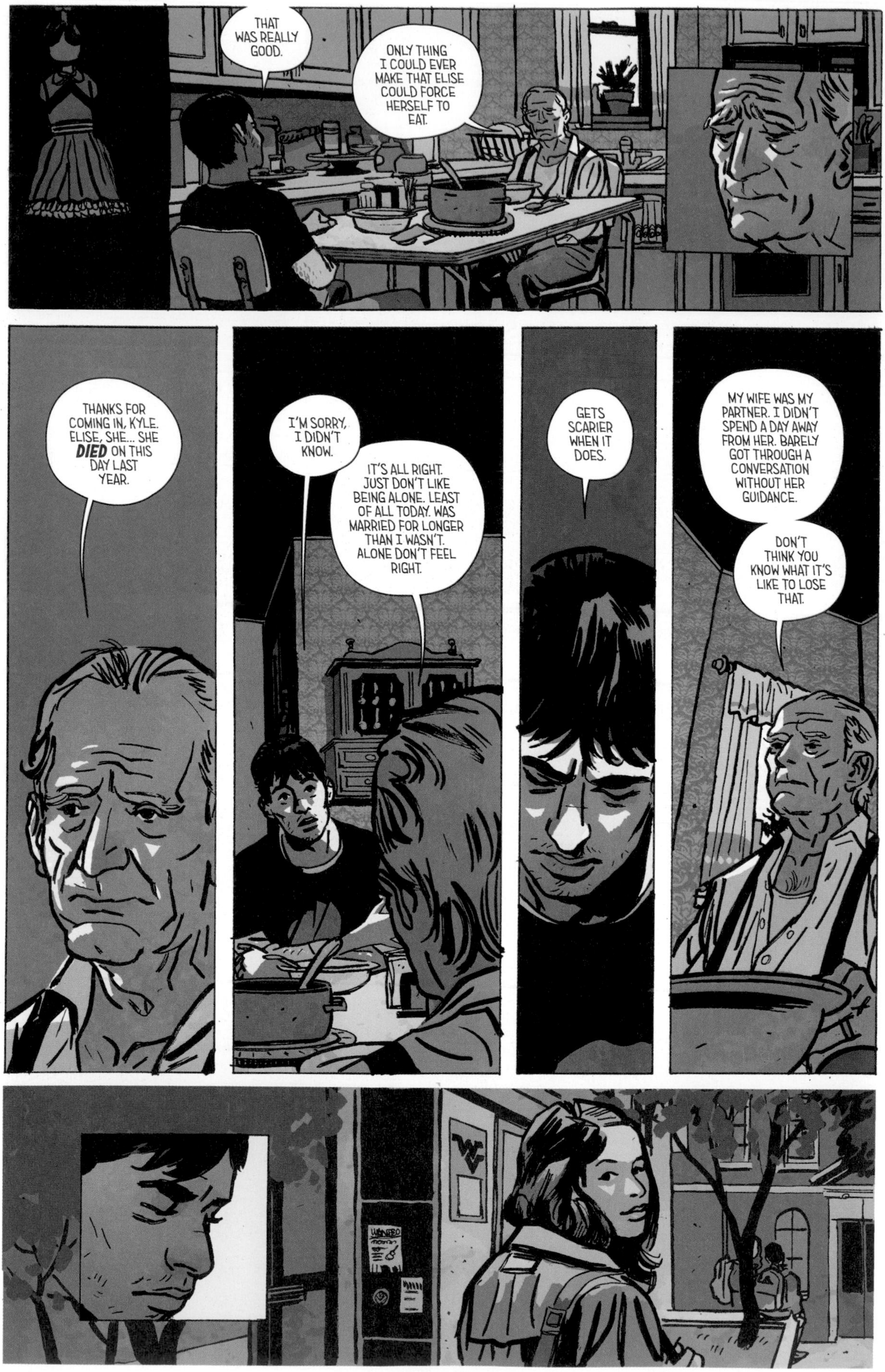
THAT WAS REALLY GOOD.
ONLY THING I COULD EVER MAKE THAT ELISE COULD FORCE HERSELF TO EAT.
THANKS FOR COMING IN, KYLE. ELISE, SHE... SHE **DIED** ON THIS DAY LAST YEAR.
I'M SORRY, I DIDN'T KNOW.
IT'S ALL RIGHT. JUST DON'T LIKE BEING ALONE. LEAST OF ALL TODAY. WAS MARRIED FOR LONGER THAN I WASN'T. ALONE DON'T FEEL RIGHT.
GETS SCARIER WHEN IT DOES.
MY WIFE WAS MY PARTNER. I DIDN'T SPEND A DAY AWAY FROM HER. BARELY GOT THROUGH A CONVERSATION WITHOUT HER GUIDANCE.
DON'T THINK YOU KNOW WHAT IT'S LIKE TO LOSE THAT.

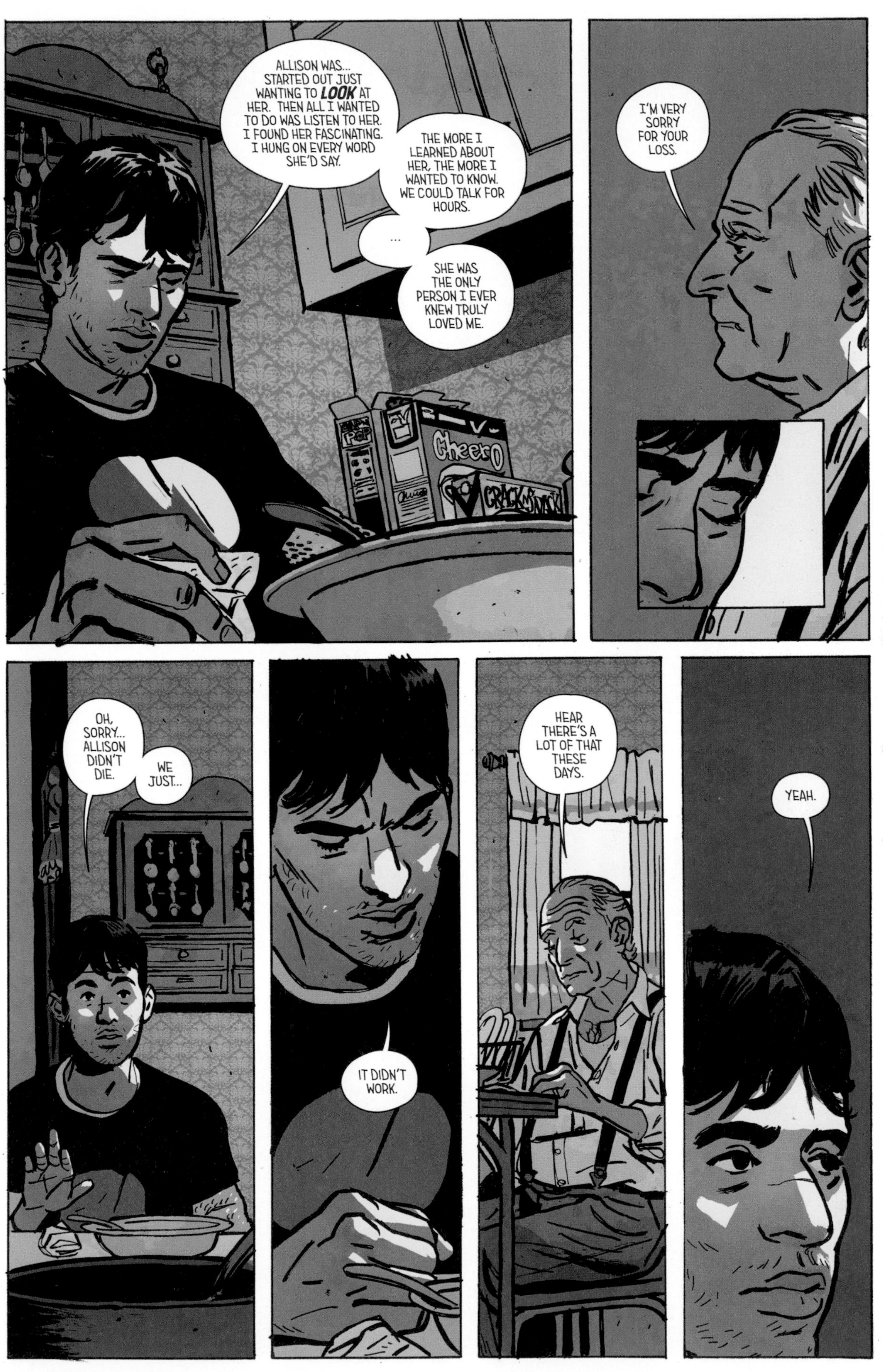
ALLISON WAS... STARTED OUT JUST WANTING TO LOOK AT HER. THEN ALL I WANTED TO DO WAS LISTEN TO HER. I FOUND HER FASCINATING. I HUNG ON EVERY WORD SHE'D SAY.
THE MORE I LEARNED ABOUT HER, THE MORE I WANTED TO KNOW. WE COULD TALK FOR HOURS.
...
SHE WAS THE ONLY PERSON I EVER KNEW TRULY LOVED ME.
I'M VERY SORRY FOR YOUR LOSS.
OH, SORRY... ALLISON DIDN'T DIE.
WE JUST...
IT DIDN'T WORK.
HEAR THERE'S A LOT OF THAT THESE DAYS.
YEAH.

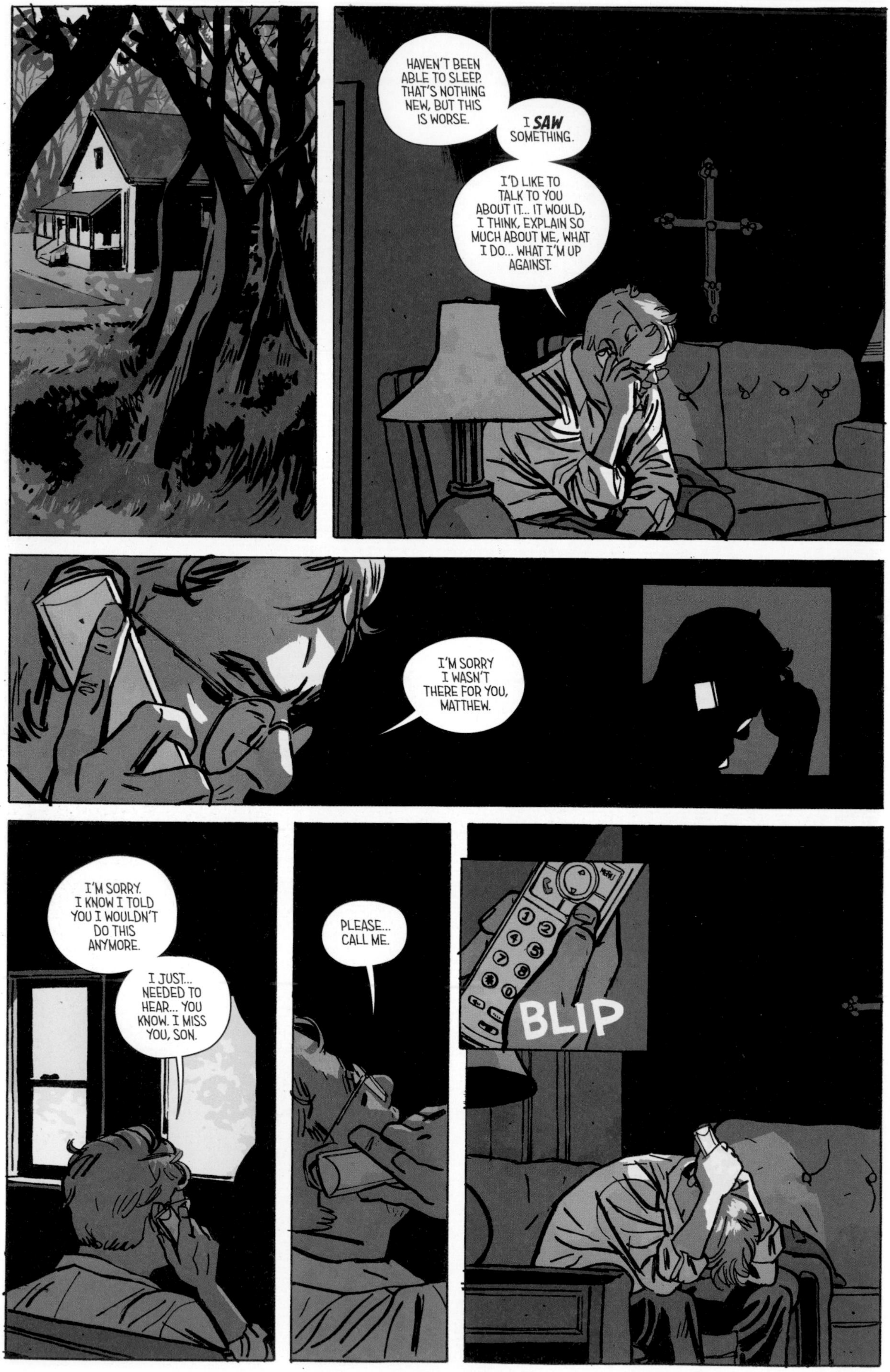
HAVEN'T BEEN ABLE TO SLEEP. THAT'S NOTHING NEW, BUT THIS IS WORSE.
I SAW SOMETHING.
I'D LIKE TO TALK TO YOU ABOUT IT... IT WOULD, I THINK, EXPLAIN SO MUCH ABOUT ME, WHAT I DO... WHAT I'M UP AGAINST.
I'M SORRY I WASN'T THERE FOR YOU, MATTHEW.
I'M SORRY. I KNOW I TOLD YOU I WOULDN'T DO THIS ANYMORE.
I JUST... NEEDED TO HEAR... YOU KNOW. I MISS YOU, SON.
PLEASE... CALL ME.
MENU
BLIP

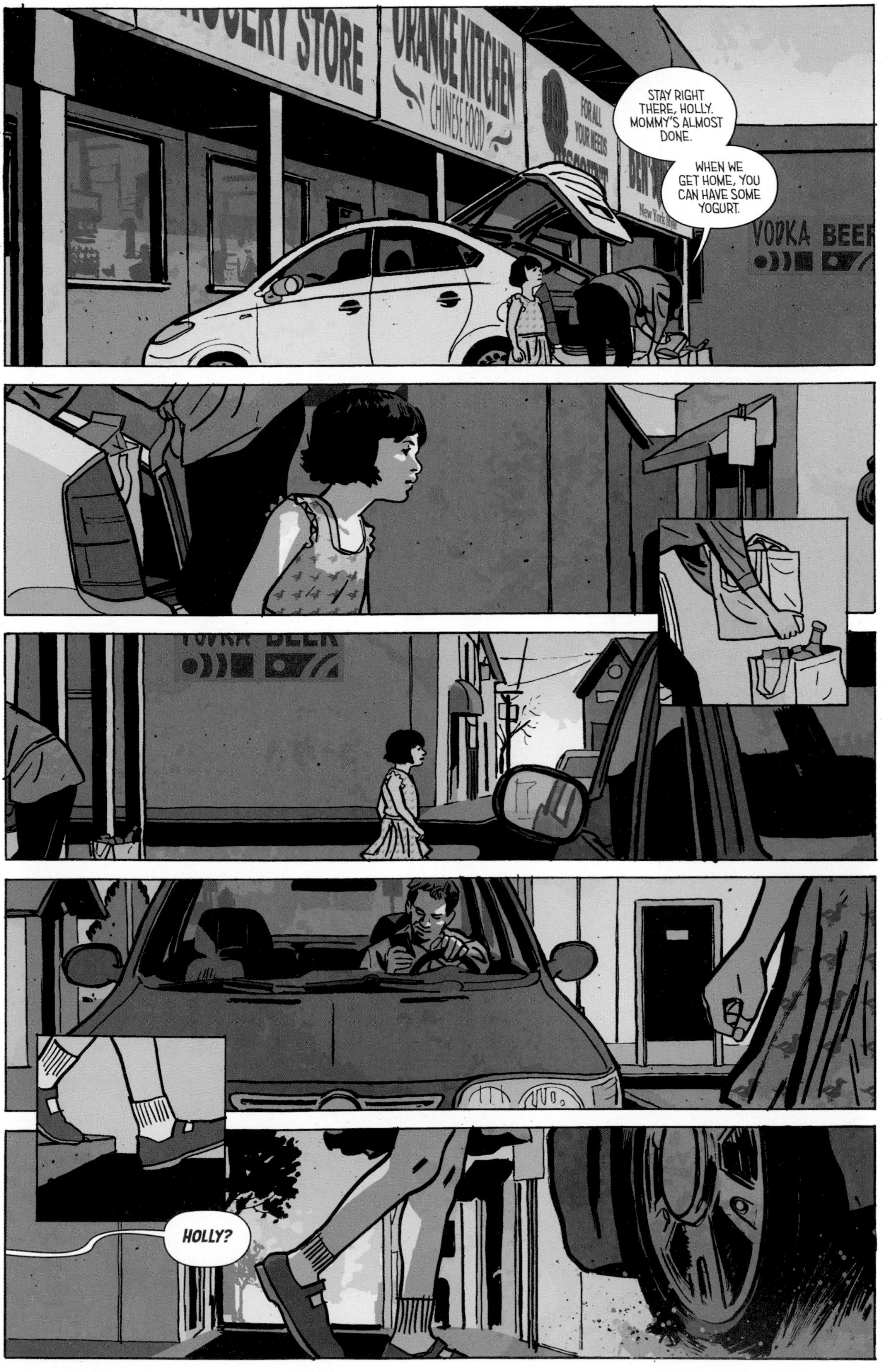

ROCERY STORE
ORANGE KITCHEN
CHINESE FOOD
99¢
FOR ALL YOUR NEEDS
DISCOUNT
New York Style
STAY RIGHT THERE, HOLLY. MOMMY'S ALMOST DONE.
WHEN WE GET HOME, YOU CAN HAVE SOME YOGURT.
VODKA BEER
HOLLY?

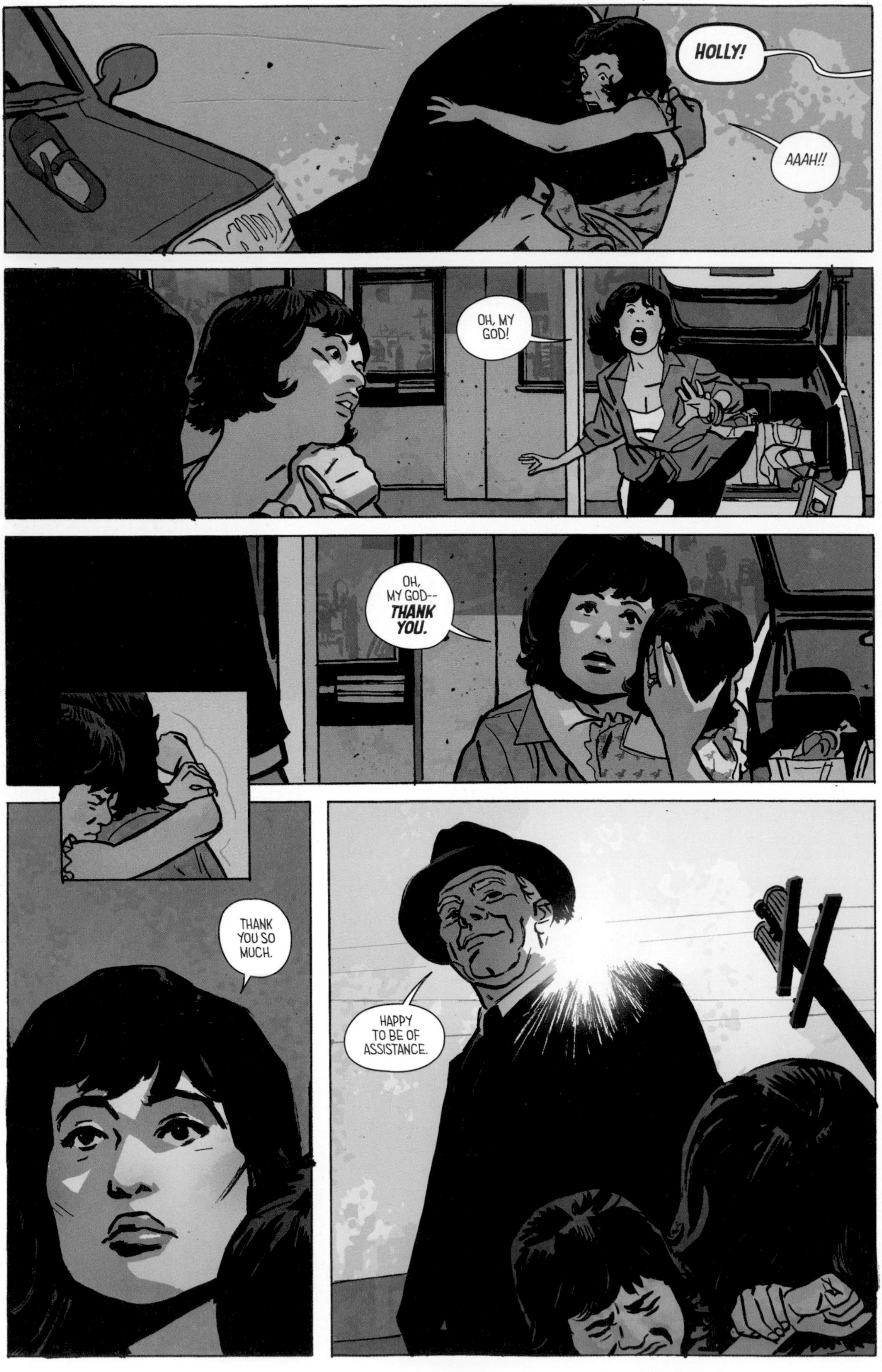
HOLLY!
AAAH!!
OH, MY GOD!
OH, MY GOD-- THANK YOU.
THANK YOU SO MUCH.
HAPPY TO BE OF ASSISTANCE.

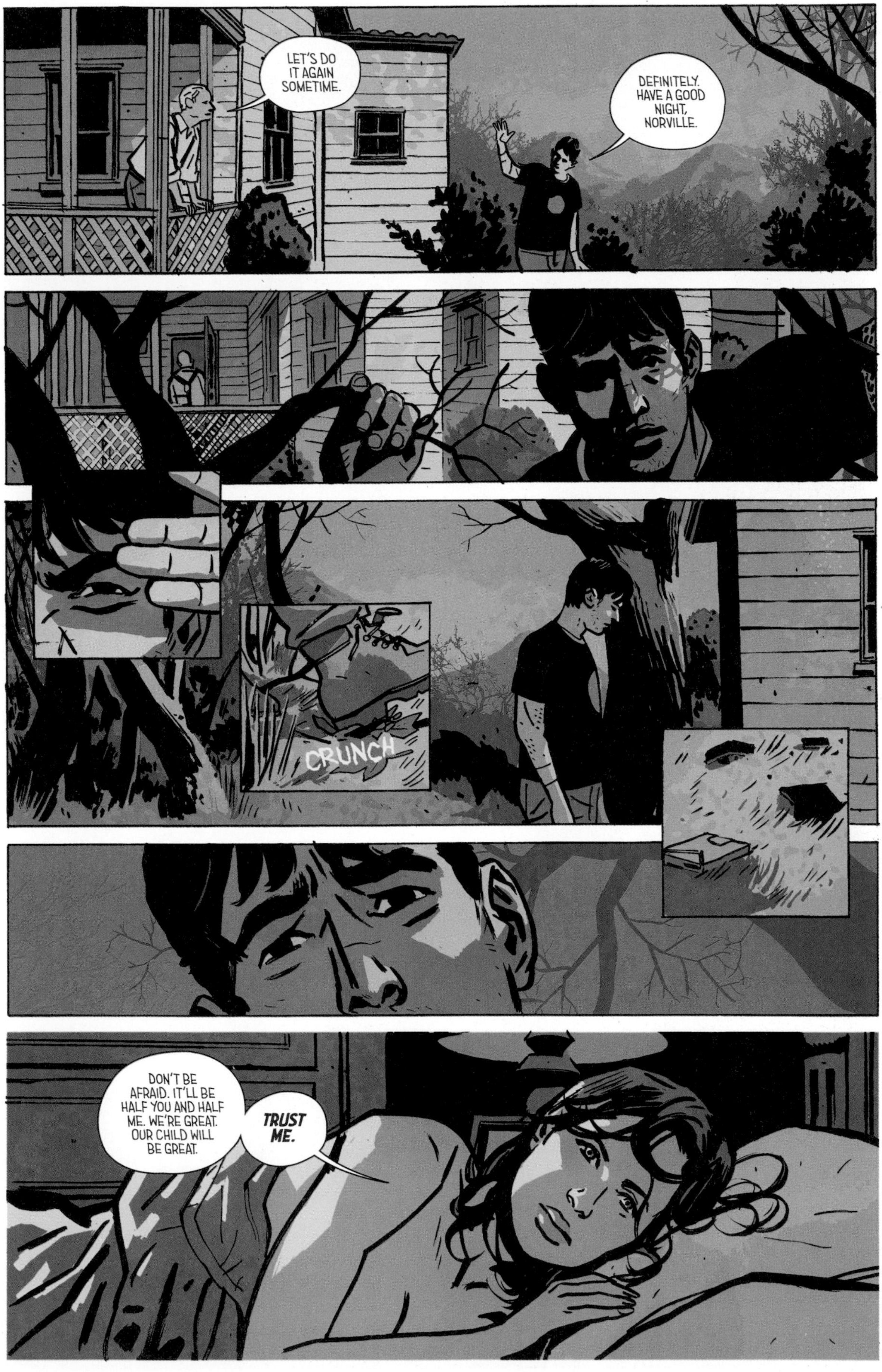
LET'S DO IT AGAIN SOMETIME.
DEFINITELY. HAVE A GOOD NIGHT, NORVILLE.
CRUNCH
DON'T BE AFRAID. IT'LL BE HALF YOU AND HALF ME. WE'RE GREAT. OUR CHILD WILL BE GREAT.
TRUST ME.

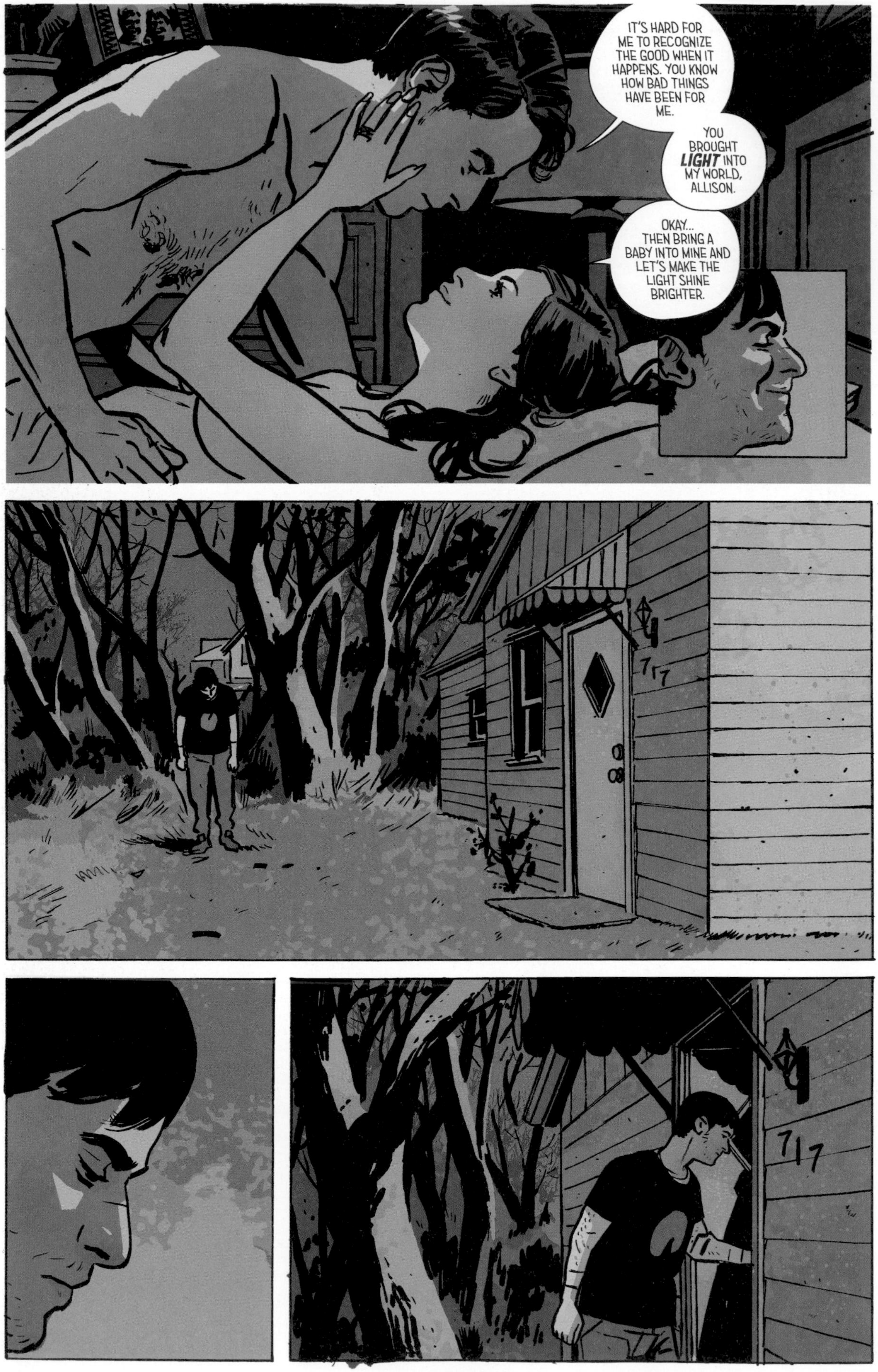
IT'S HARD FOR ME TO RECOGNIZE THE GOOD WHEN IT HAPPENS. YOU KNOW HOW BAD THINGS HAVE BEEN FOR ME.
YOU BROUGHT **LIGHT** INTO MY WORLD, ALLISON.
OKAY... THEN BRING A BABY INTO MINE AND LET'S MAKE THE LIGHT SHINE BRIGHTER.
717
717

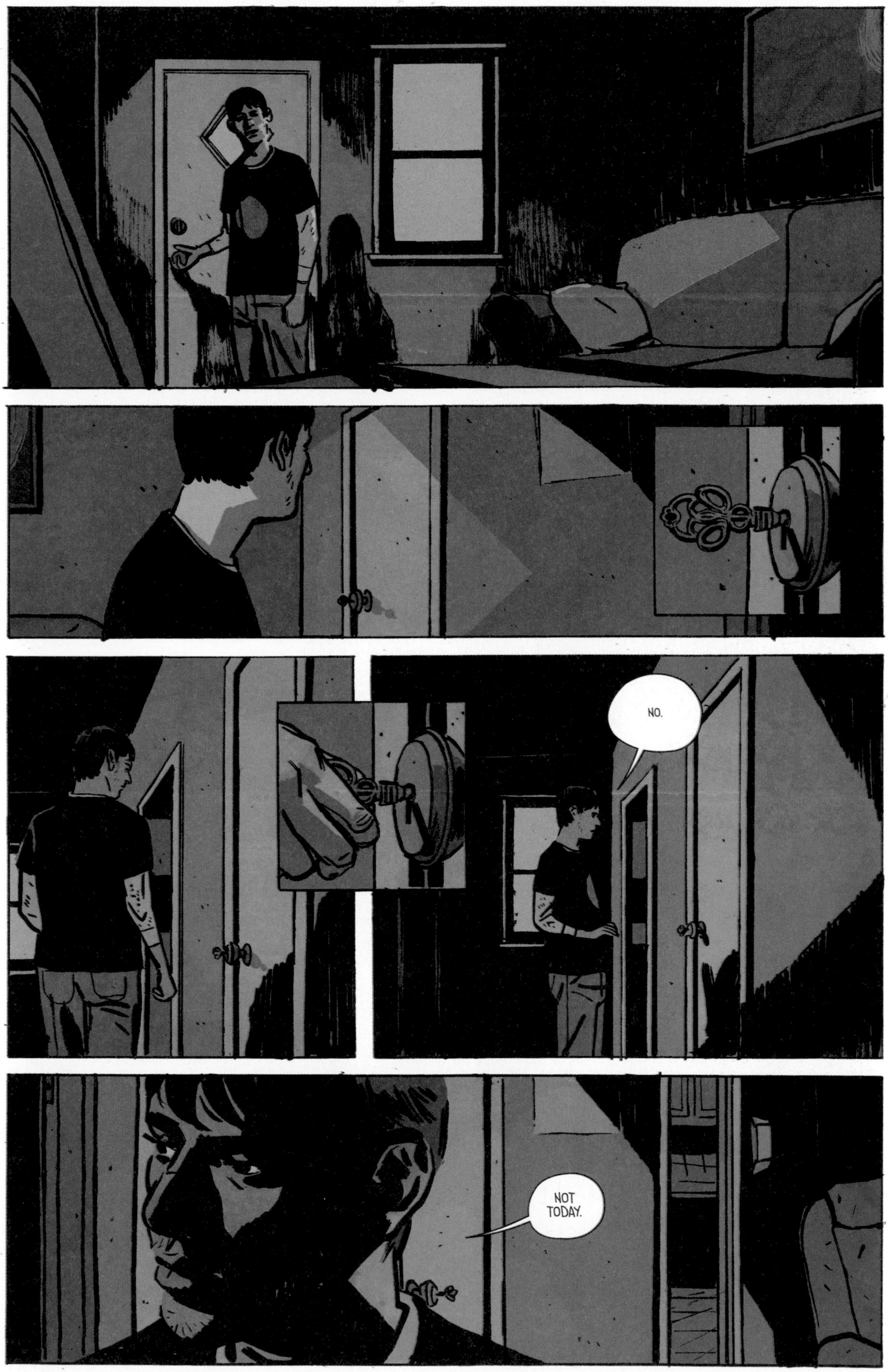
NO.
NOT TODAY.

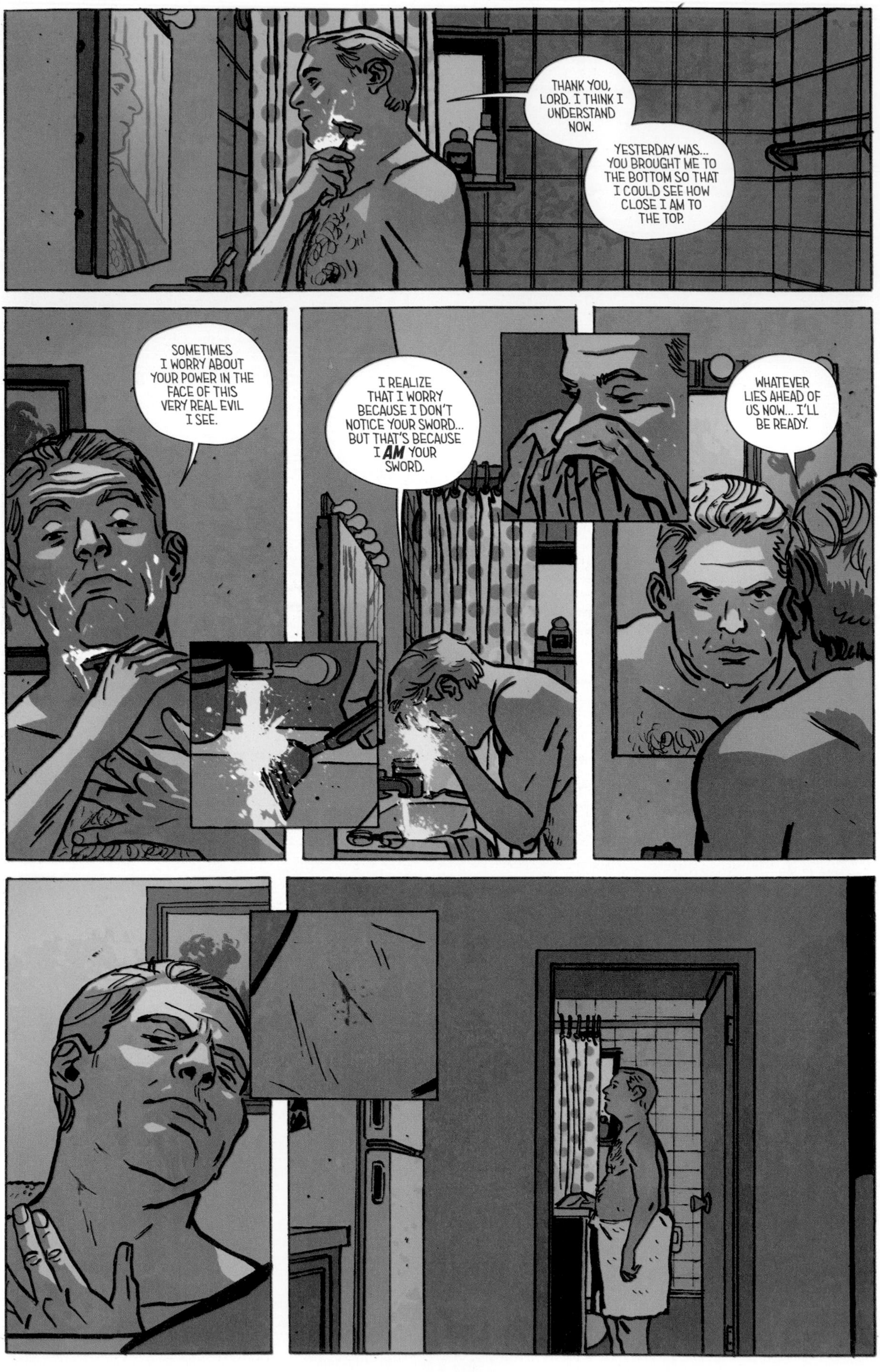
THANK YOU, LORD. I THINK I UNDERSTAND NOW.
YESTERDAY WAS... YOU BROUGHT ME TO THE BOTTOM SO THAT I COULD SEE HOW CLOSE I AM TO THE TOP.
SOMETIMES I WORRY ABOUT YOUR POWER IN THE FACE OF THIS VERY REAL EVIL I SEE.
I REALIZE THAT I WORRY BECAUSE I DON'T NOTICE YOUR SWORD... BUT THAT'S BECAUSE I AM YOUR SWORD.
WHATEVER LIES AHEAD OF US NOW... I'LL BE READY.

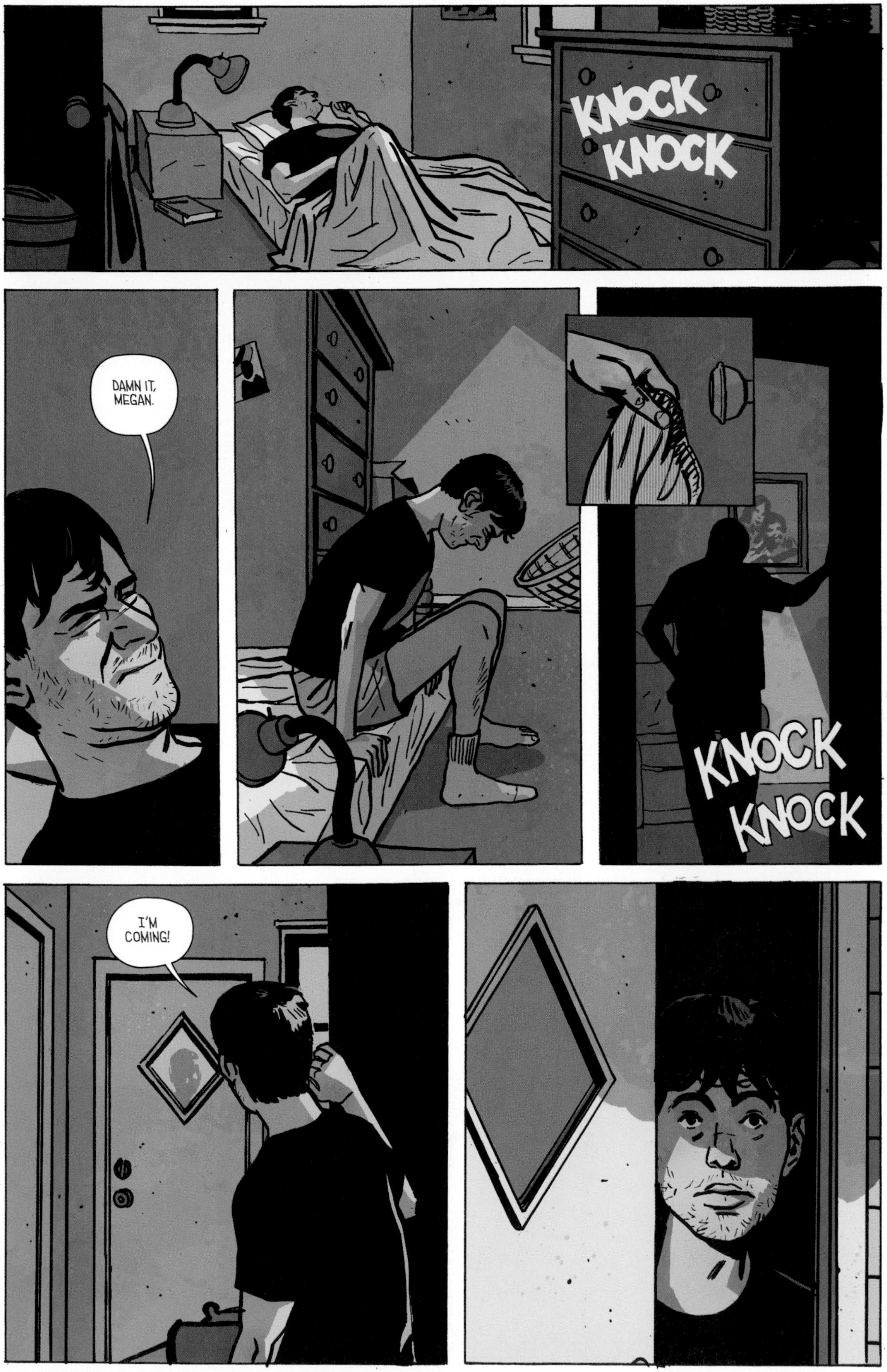
KNOCK KNOCK
DAMN IT, MEGAN.
KNOCK KNOCK
I'M COMING!

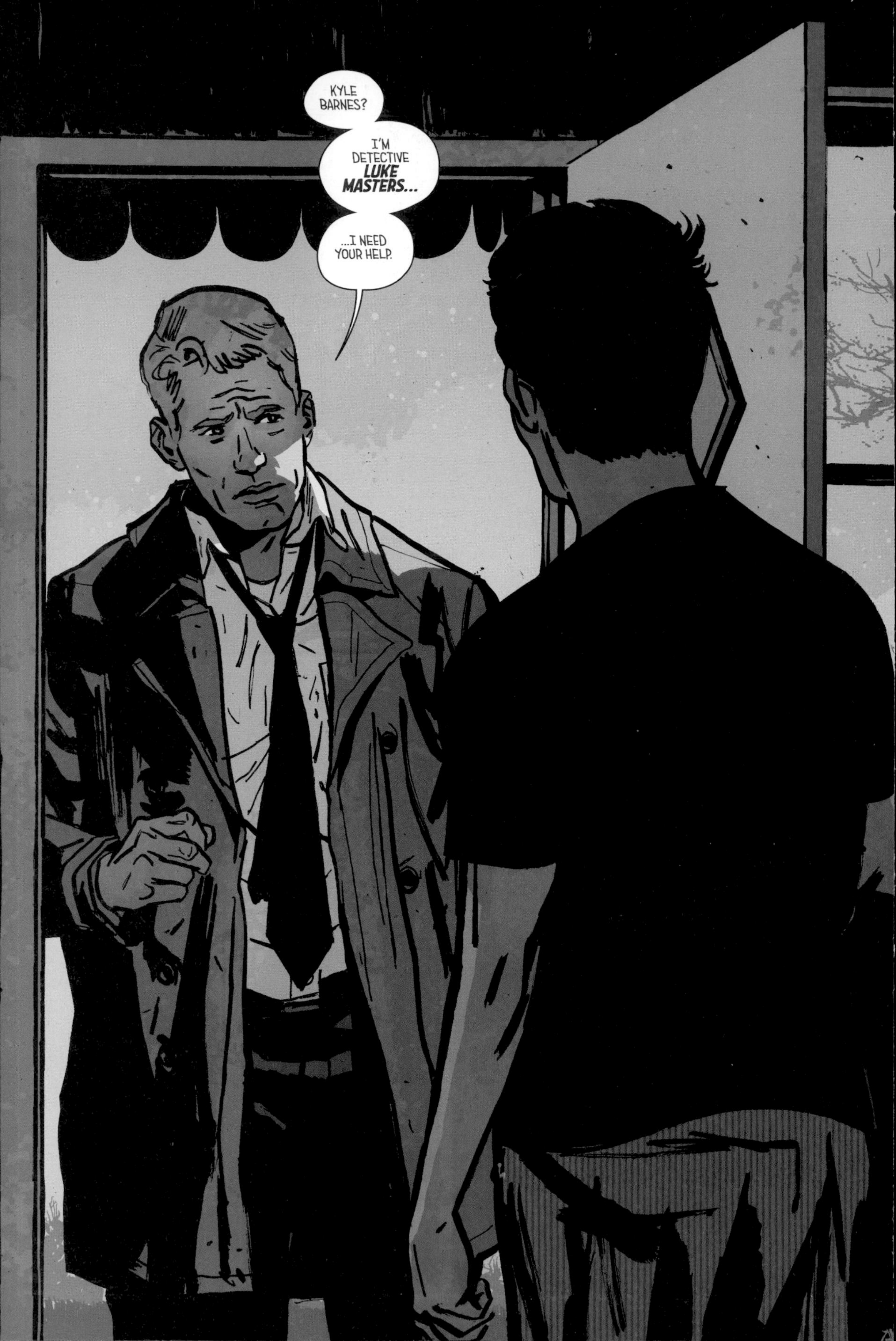
KYLE BARNES?
I'M DETECTIVE LUKE MASTERS...
...I NEED YOUR HELP.

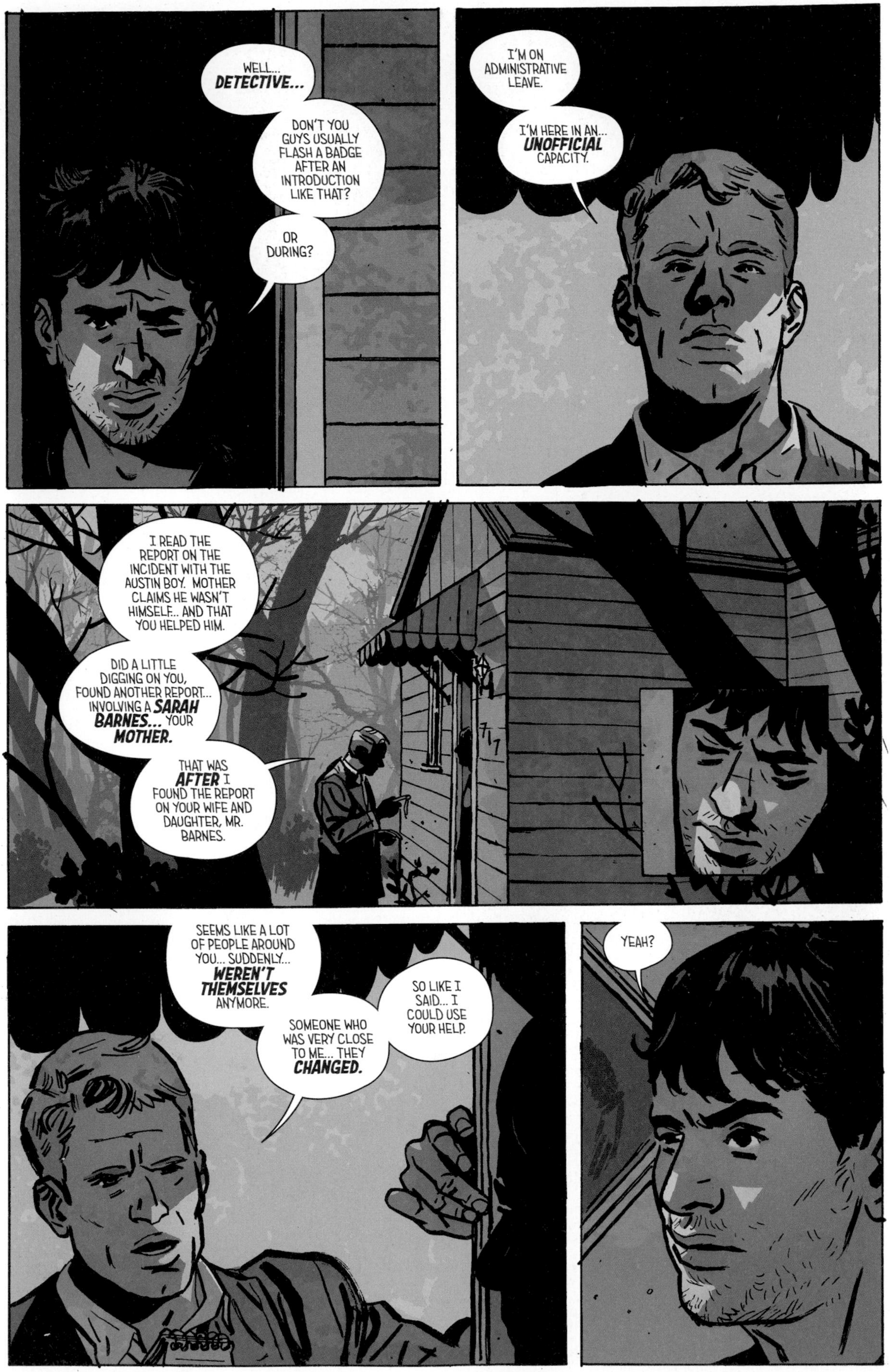
WELL... DETECTIVE...
DON'T YOU GUYS USUALLY FLASH A BADGE AFTER AN INTRODUCTION LIKE THAT?
OR DURING?
I'M ON ADMINISTRATIVE LEAVE.
I'M HERE IN AN... UNOFFICIAL CAPACITY.
I READ THE REPORT ON THE INCIDENT WITH THE AUSTIN BOY. MOTHER CLAIMS HE WASN'T HIMSELF... AND THAT YOU HELPED HIM.
DID A LITTLE DIGGING ON YOU, FOUND ANOTHER REPORT... INVOLVING A SARAH BARNES... YOUR MOTHER.
THAT WAS AFTER I FOUND THE REPORT ON YOUR WIFE AND DAUGHTER, MR. BARNES.
SEEMS LIKE A LOT OF PEOPLE AROUND YOU... SUDDENLY... WEREN'T THEMSELVES ANYMORE.
SOMEONE WHO WAS VERY CLOSE TO ME... THEY CHANGED.
SO LIKE I SAID... I COULD USE YOUR HELP.
YEAH?

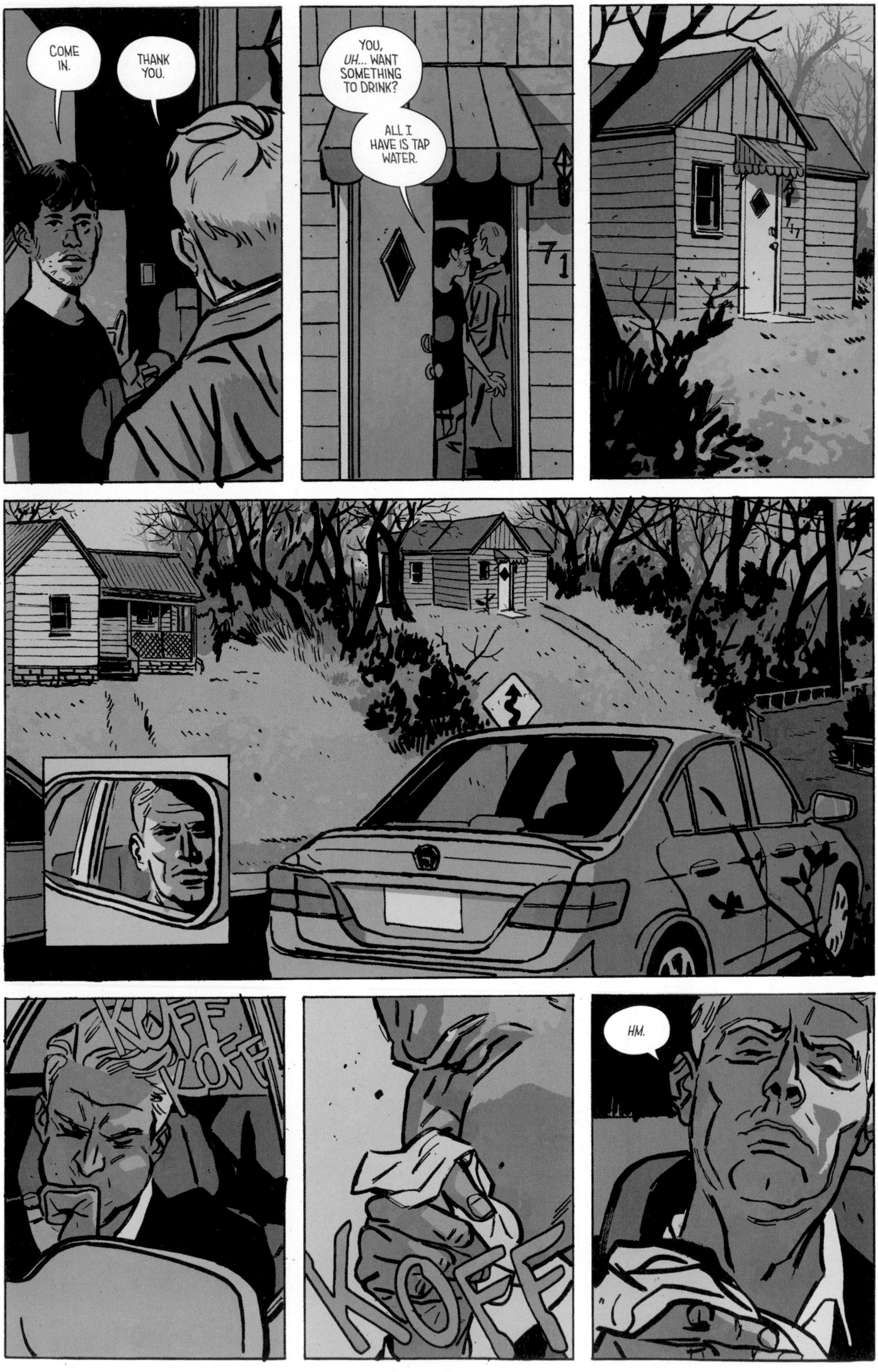
COME IN.
THANK YOU.
YOU, UH... WANT SOMETHING TO DRINK?
ALL I HAVE IS TAP WATER.
71
KOFF KOFF
KOFF
HM.

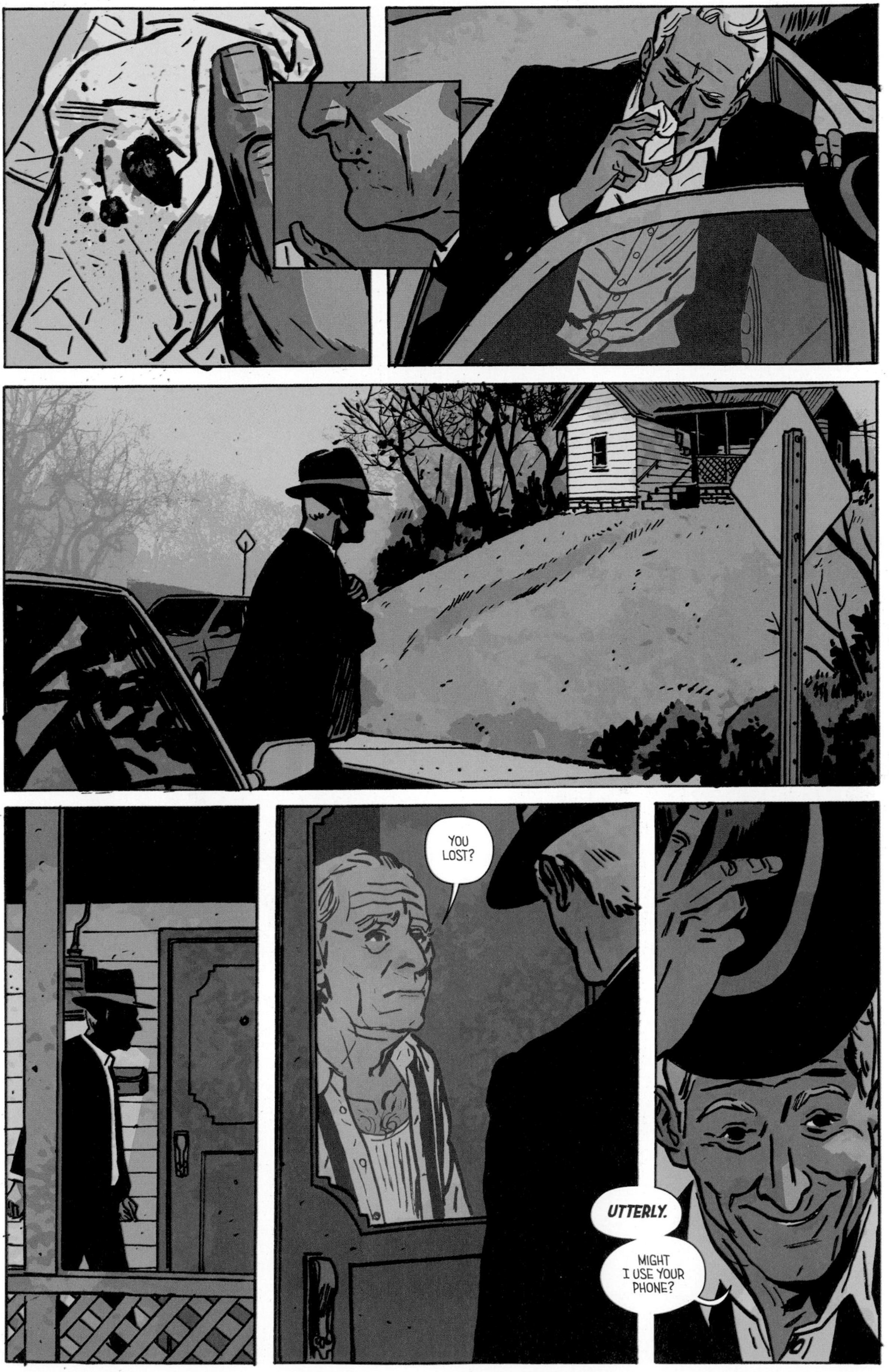
YOU LOST?
UTTERLY.
MIGHT I USE YOUR PHONE?

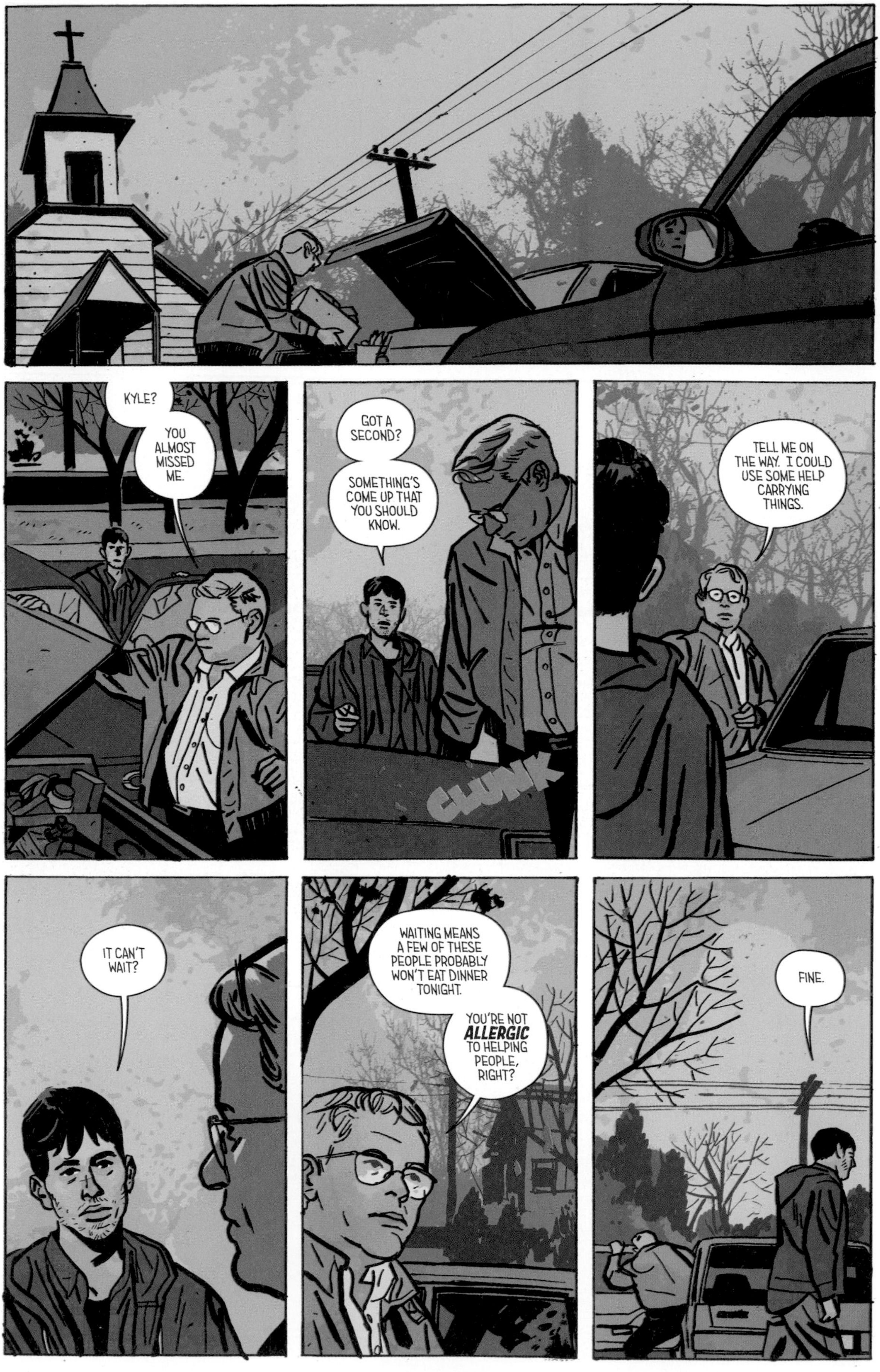
KYLE?
YOU ALMOST MISSED ME.
GOT A SECOND?
SOMETHING'S COME UP THAT YOU SHOULD KNOW.
CLUNK
TELL ME ON THE WAY. I COULD USE SOME HELP CARRYING THINGS.
IT CAN'T WAIT?
WAITING MEANS A FEW OF THESE PEOPLE PROBABLY WON'T EAT DINNER TONIGHT.
YOU'RE NOT ALLERGIC TO HELPING PEOPLE, RIGHT?
FINE.

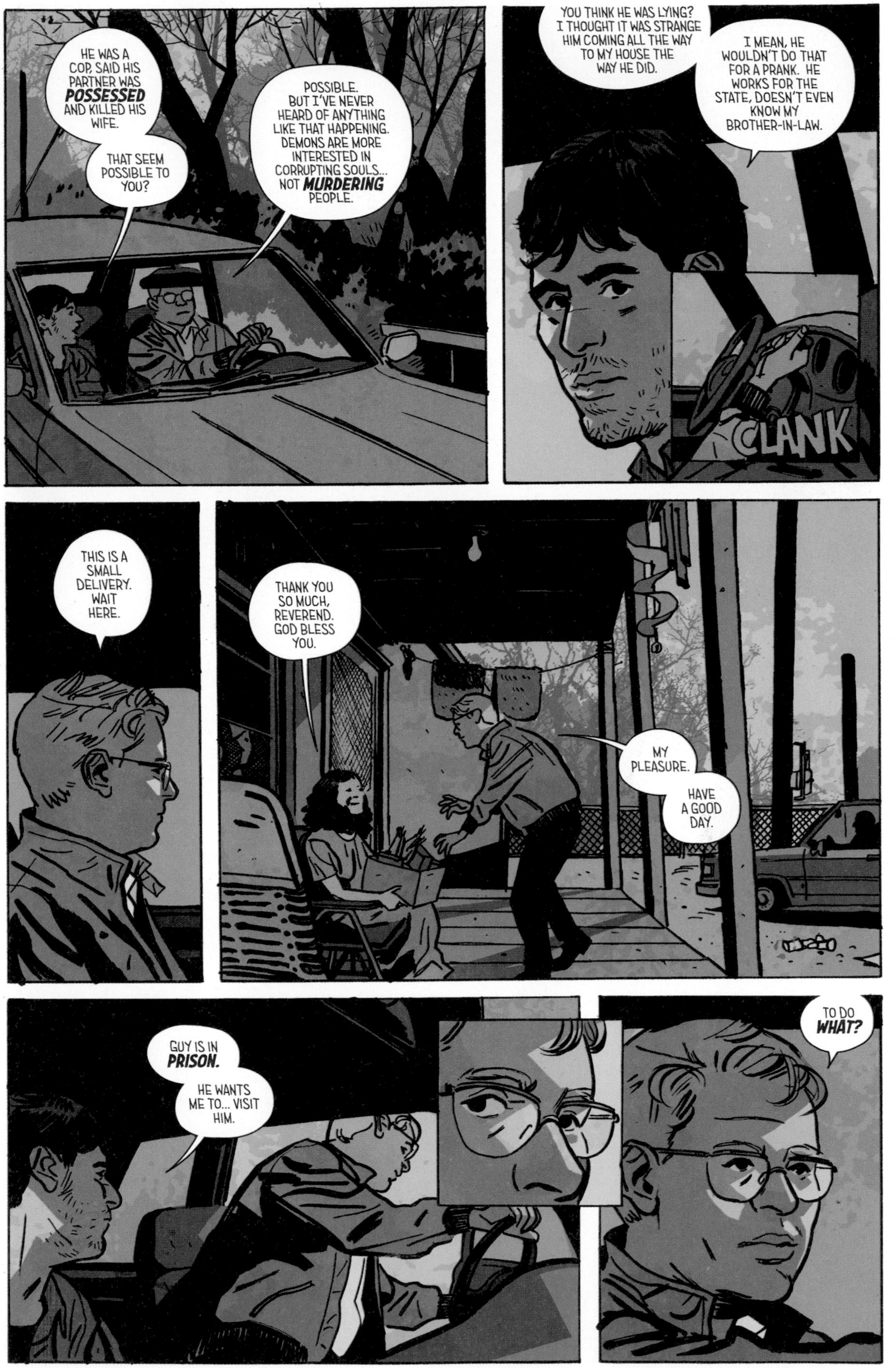
HE WAS A COP, SAID HIS PARTNER WAS ***POSSESSED*** AND KILLED HIS WIFE.
THAT SEEM POSSIBLE TO YOU?
POSSIBLE. BUT I'VE NEVER HEARD OF ANYTHING LIKE THAT HAPPENING. DEMONS ARE MORE INTERESTED IN CORRUPTING SOULS... NOT ***MURDERING*** PEOPLE.
YOU THINK HE WAS LYING? I THOUGHT IT WAS STRANGE HIM COMING ALL THE WAY TO MY HOUSE THE WAY HE DID.
I MEAN, HE WOULDN'T DO THAT FOR A PRANK. HE WORKS FOR THE STATE, DOESN'T EVEN KNOW MY BROTHER-IN-LAW.
CLANK
THIS IS A SMALL DELIVERY. WAIT HERE.
THANK YOU SO MUCH, REVEREND. GOD BLESS YOU.
MY PLEASURE.
HAVE A GOOD DAY.
GUY IS IN ***PRISON.***
HE WANTS ME TO... VISIT HIM.
TO DO ***WHAT?***

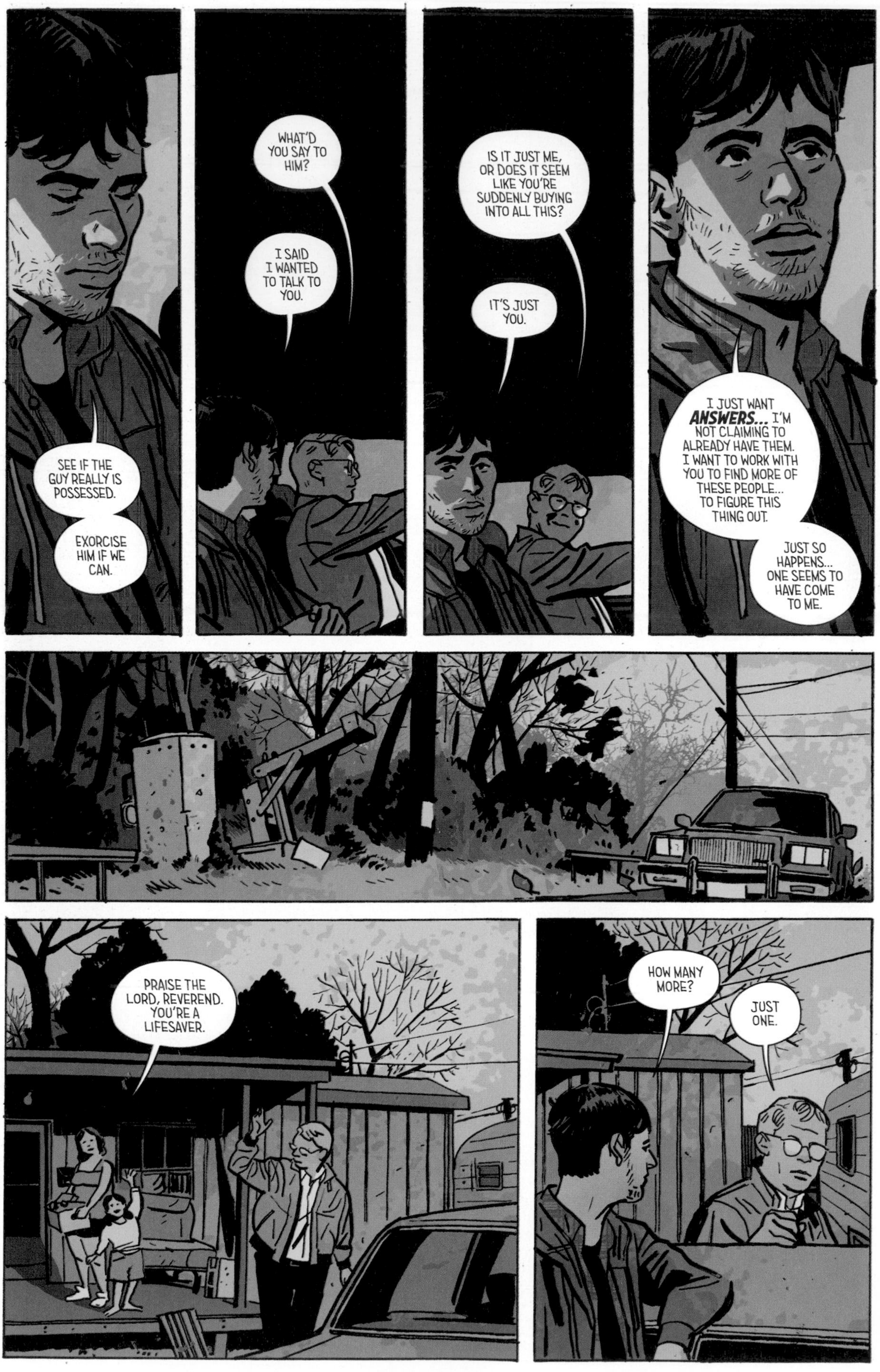
SEE IF THE GUY REALLY IS POSSESSED.
EXORCISE HIM IF WE CAN.
WHAT'D YOU SAY TO HIM?
I SAID I WANTED TO TALK TO YOU.
IS IT JUST ME, OR DOES IT SEEM LIKE YOU'RE SUDDENLY BUYING INTO ALL THIS?
IT'S JUST YOU.
I JUST WANT ANSWERS... I'M NOT CLAIMING TO ALREADY HAVE THEM. I WANT TO WORK WITH YOU TO FIND MORE OF THESE PEOPLE... TO FIGURE THIS THING OUT.
JUST SO HAPPENS... ONE SEEMS TO HAVE COME TO ME.
PRAISE THE LORD, REVEREND. YOU'RE A LIFESAVER.
HOW MANY MORE?
JUST ONE.

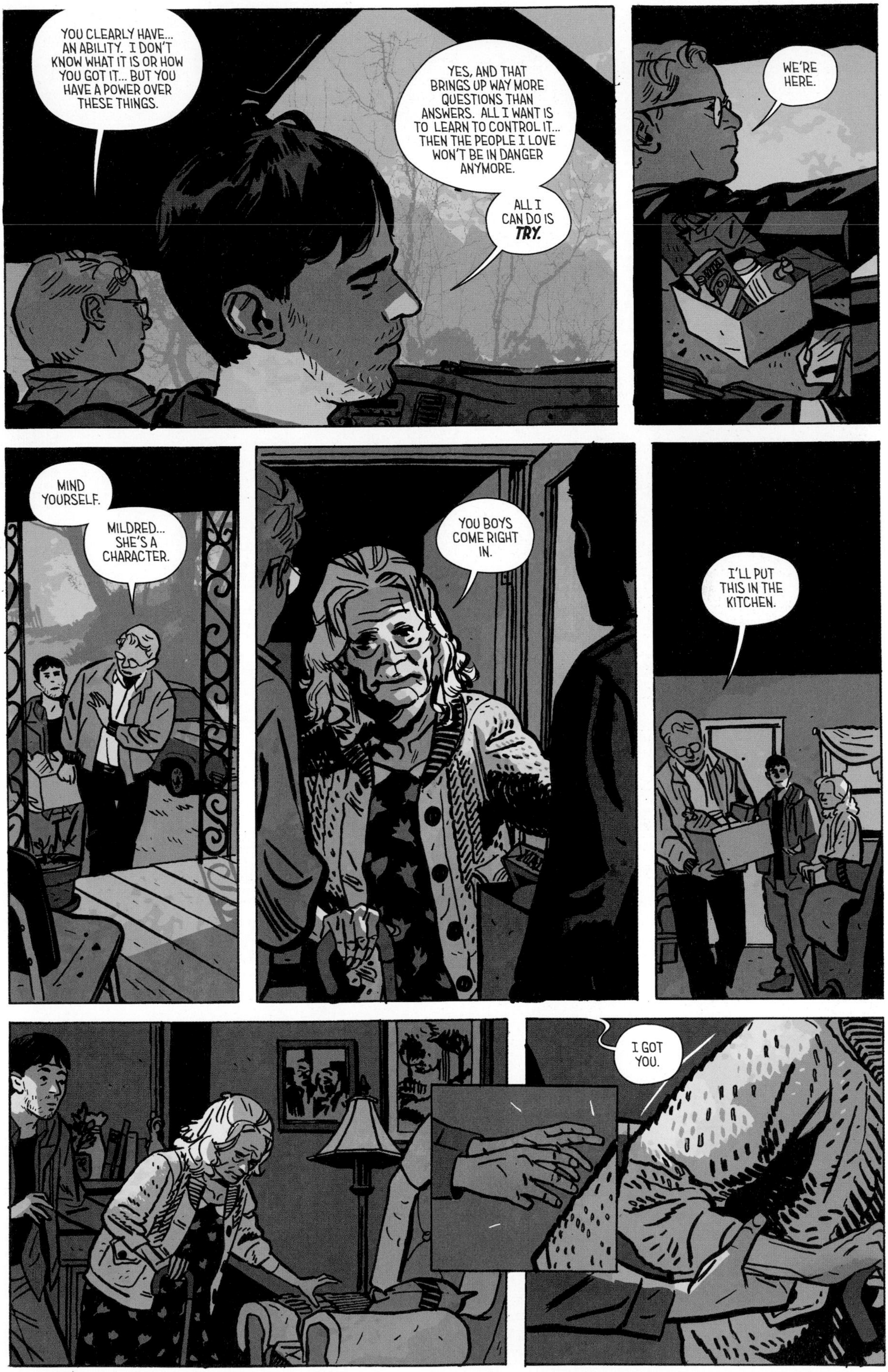
YOU CLEARLY HAVE... AN ABILITY. I DON'T KNOW WHAT IT IS OR HOW YOU GOT IT... BUT YOU HAVE A POWER OVER THESE THINGS.
YES, AND THAT BRINGS UP WAY MORE QUESTIONS THAN ANSWERS. ALL I WANT IS TO LEARN TO CONTROL IT... THEN THE PEOPLE I LOVE WON'T BE IN DANGER ANYMORE.
ALL I CAN DO IS *TRY.*
WE'RE HERE.
MIND YOURSELF.
MILDRED... SHE'S A CHARACTER.
YOU BOYS COME RIGHT IN.
I'LL PUT THIS IN THE KITCHEN.
I GOT YOU.

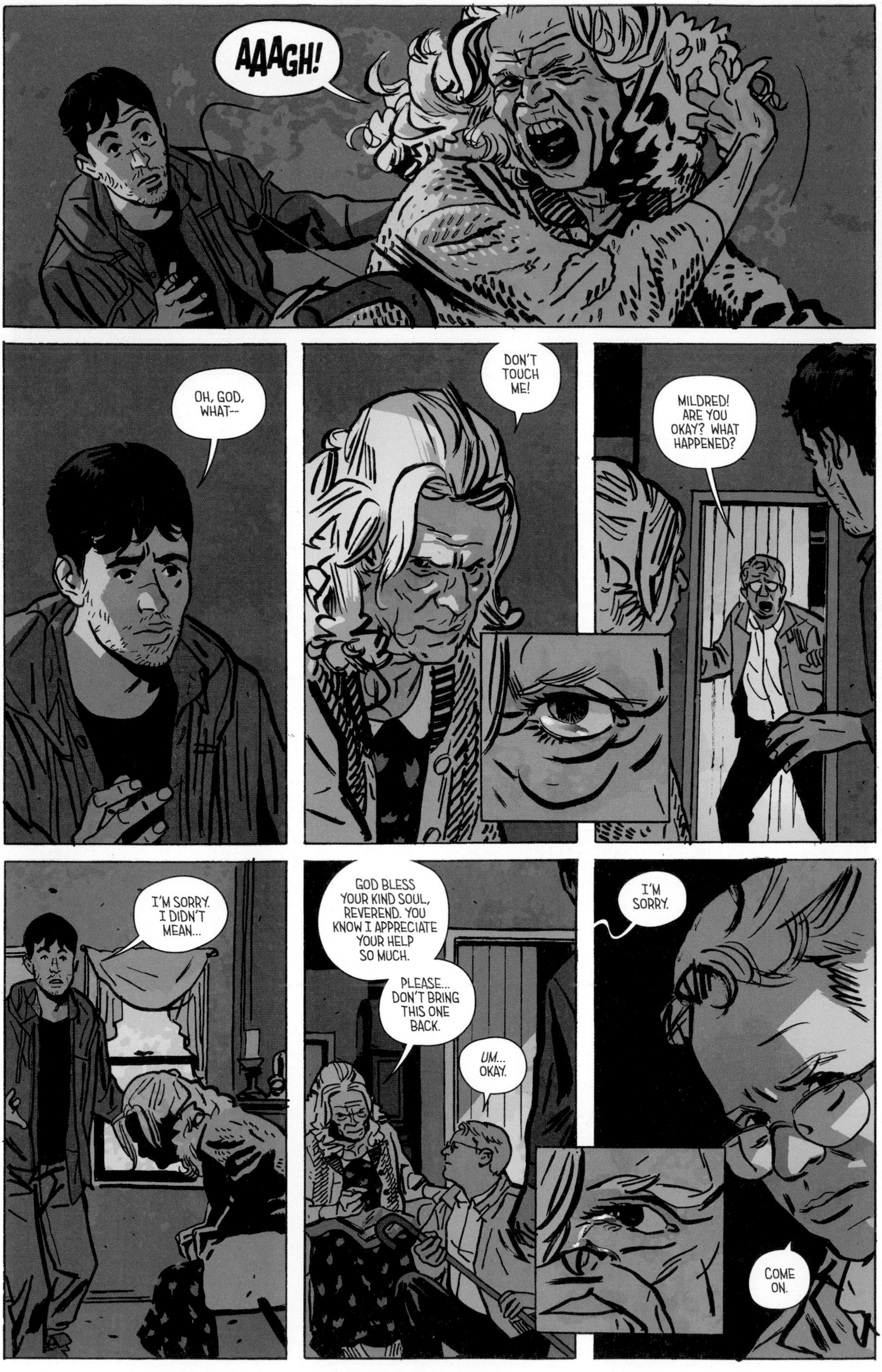
AAAGH!
OH, GOD, WHAT--
DON'T TOUCH ME!
MILDRED! ARE YOU OKAY? WHAT HAPPENED?
I'M SORRY. I DIDN'T MEAN...
GOD BLESS YOUR KIND SOUL, REVEREND. YOU KNOW I APPRECIATE YOUR HELP SO MUCH.
PLEASE... DON'T BRING THIS ONE BACK.
UM... OKAY.
I'M SORRY.
COME ON.

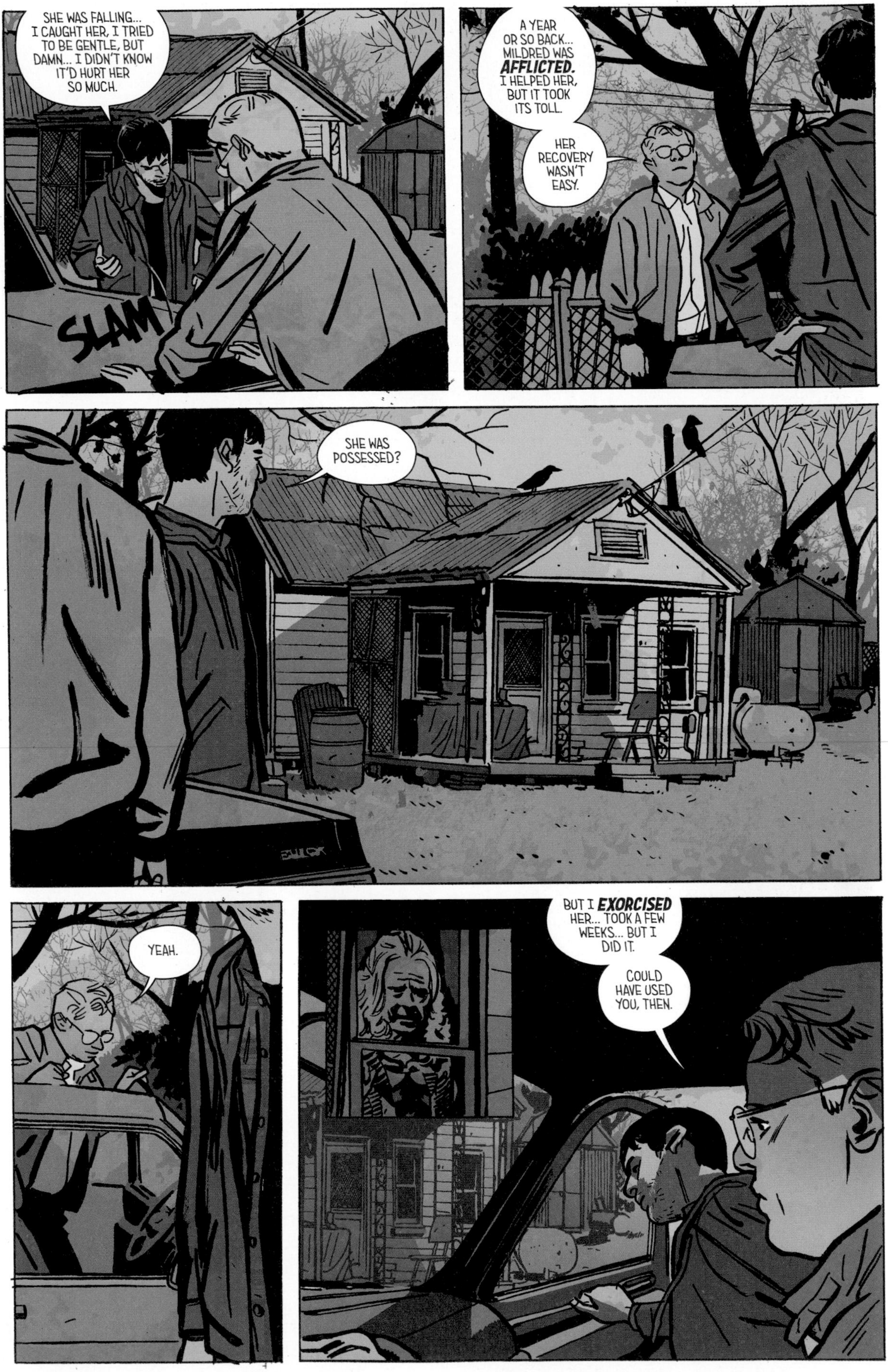
SHE WAS FALLING... I CAUGHT HER, I TRIED TO BE GENTLE, BUT DAMN... I DIDN'T KNOW IT'D HURT HER SO MUCH.
SLAM
A YEAR OR SO BACK... MILDRED WAS AFFLICTED. I HELPED HER, BUT IT TOOK ITS TOLL.
HER RECOVERY WASN'T EASY.
SHE WAS POSSESSED?
YEAH.
BUT I EXORCISED HER... TOOK A FEW WEEKS... BUT I DID IT.
COULD HAVE USED YOU, THEN.

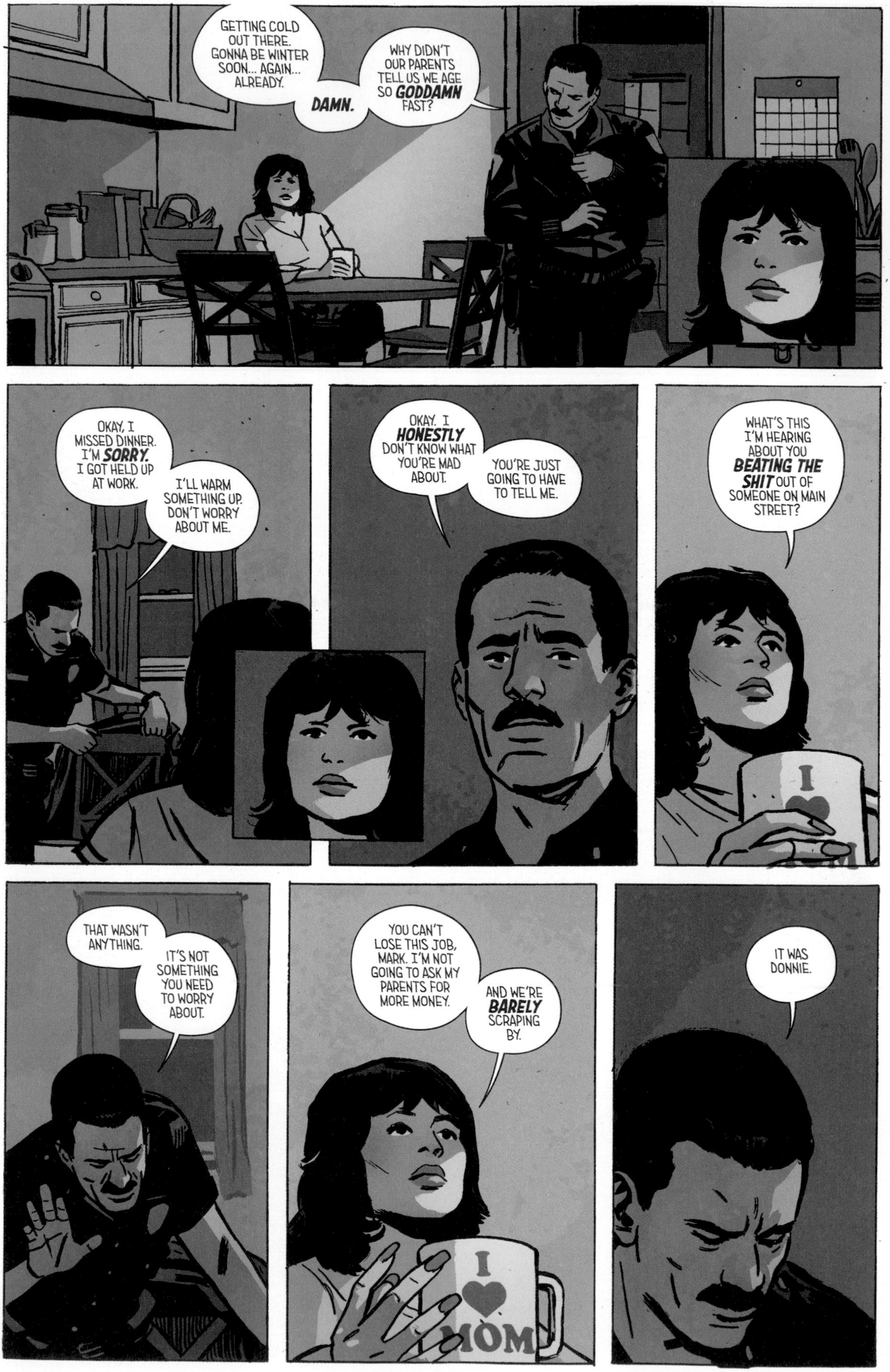
GETTING COLD OUT THERE. GONNA BE WINTER SOON... AGAIN... ALREADY.
DAMN.
WHY DIDN'T OUR PARENTS TELL US WE AGE SO GODDAMN FAST?
OKAY, I MISSED DINNER. I'M SORRY. I GOT HELD UP AT WORK.
I'LL WARM SOMETHING UP. DON'T WORRY ABOUT ME.
OKAY. I HONESTLY DON'T KNOW WHAT YOU'RE MAD ABOUT.
YOU'RE JUST GOING TO HAVE TO TELL ME.
WHAT'S THIS I'M HEARING ABOUT YOU BEATING THE SHIT OUT OF SOMEONE ON MAIN STREET?
THAT WASN'T ANYTHING.
IT'S NOT SOMETHING YOU NEED TO WORRY ABOUT.
YOU CAN'T LOSE THIS JOB, MARK. I'M NOT GOING TO ASK MY PARENTS FOR MORE MONEY.
AND WE'RE BARELY SCRAPING BY.
I ♥ MOM
IT WAS DONNIE.

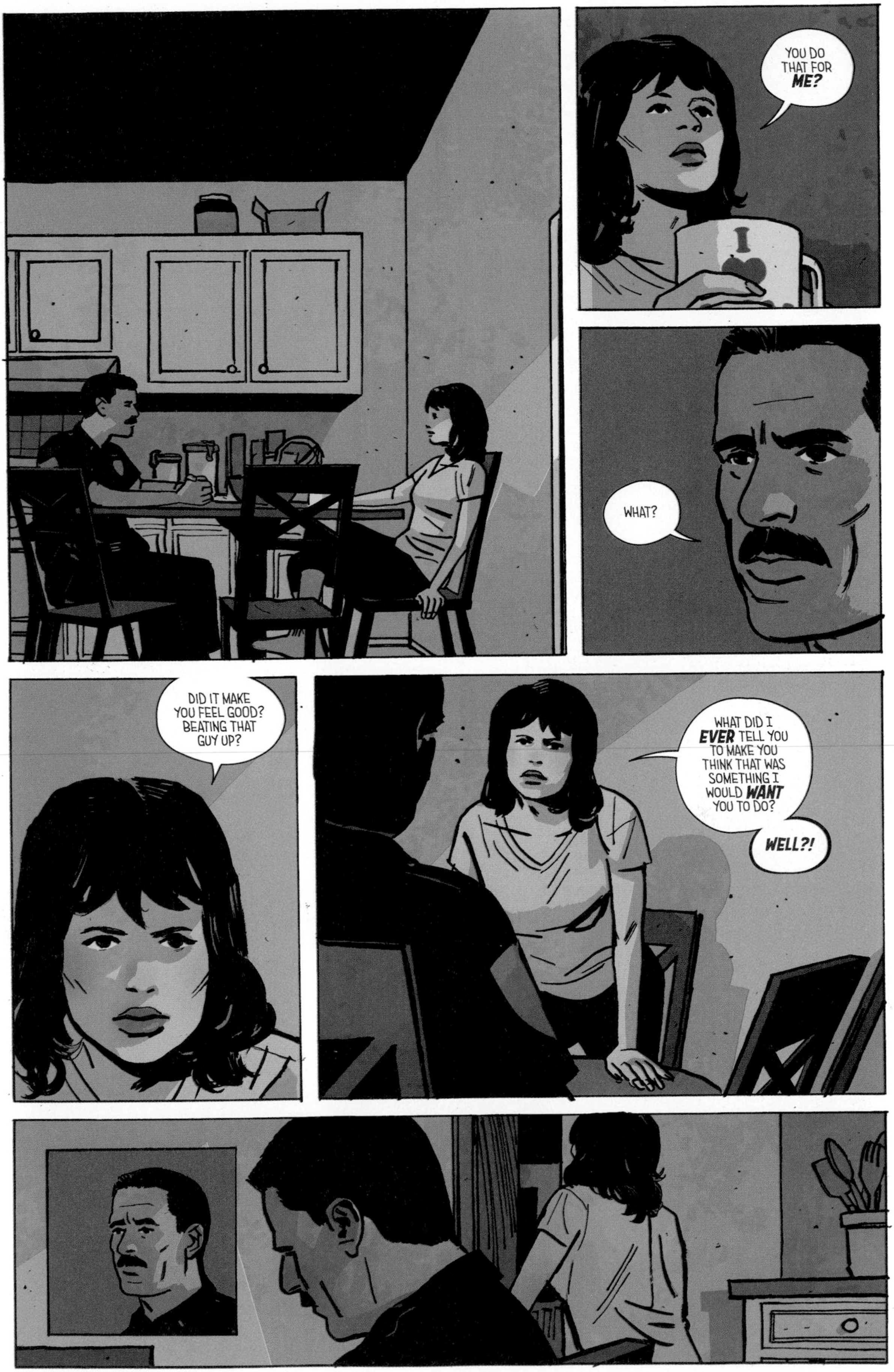
YOU DO THAT FOR **ME?**
WHAT?
DID IT MAKE YOU FEEL GOOD? BEATING THAT GUY UP?
WHAT DID I **EVER** TELL YOU TO MAKE YOU THINK THAT WAS SOMETHING I WOULD **WANT** YOU TO DO?
WELL?!

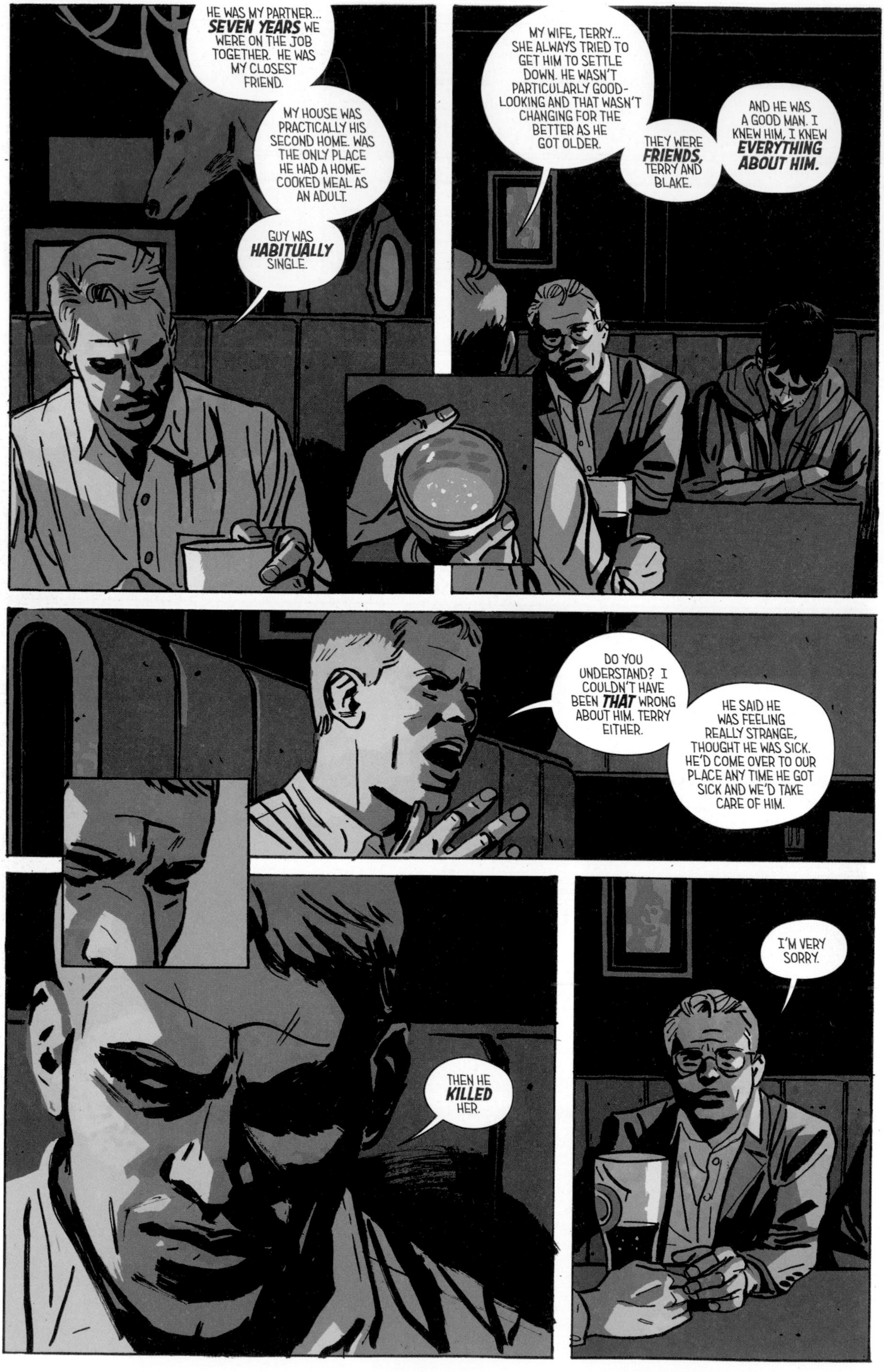
HE WAS MY PARTNER... SEVEN YEARS WE WERE ON THE JOB TOGETHER. HE WAS MY CLOSEST FRIEND.
MY HOUSE WAS PRACTICALLY HIS SECOND HOME. WAS THE ONLY PLACE HE HAD A HOME-COOKED MEAL AS AN ADULT.
GUY WAS HABITUALLY SINGLE.
MY WIFE, TERRY... SHE ALWAYS TRIED TO GET HIM TO SETTLE DOWN. HE WASN'T PARTICULARLY GOOD-LOOKING AND THAT WASN'T CHANGING FOR THE BETTER AS HE GOT OLDER.
THEY WERE FRIENDS, TERRY AND BLAKE.
AND HE WAS A GOOD MAN. I KNEW HIM, I KNEW EVERYTHING ABOUT HIM.
DO YOU UNDERSTAND? I COULDN'T HAVE BEEN THAT WRONG ABOUT HIM. TERRY EITHER.
HE SAID HE WAS FEELING REALLY STRANGE, THOUGHT HE WAS SICK. HE'D COME OVER TO OUR PLACE ANY TIME HE GOT SICK AND WE'D TAKE CARE OF HIM.
THEN HE KILLED HER.
I'M VERY SORRY.

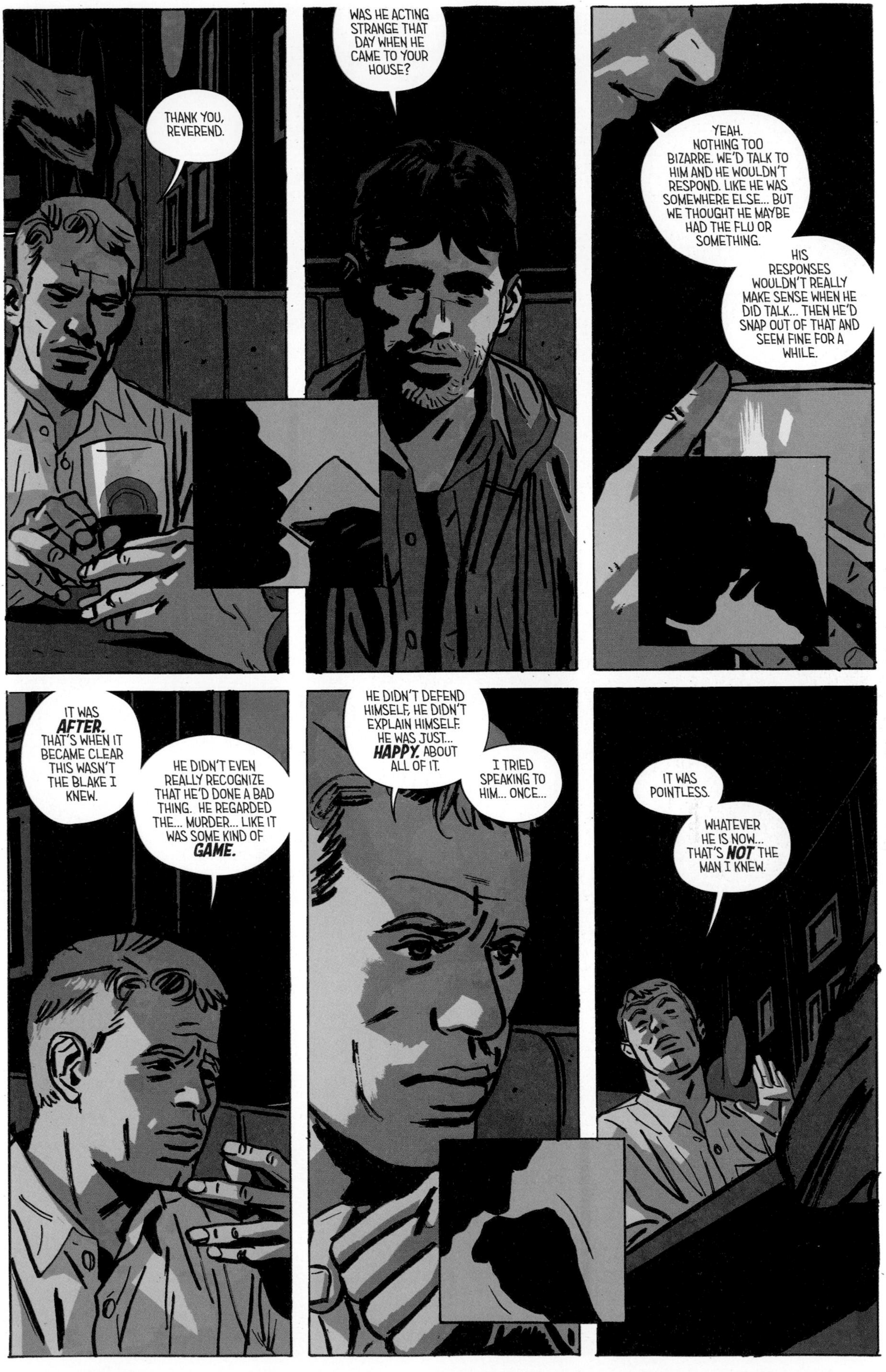
THANK YOU, REVEREND.
WAS HE ACTING STRANGE THAT DAY WHEN HE CAME TO YOUR HOUSE?
YEAH. NOTHING TOO BIZARRE. WE'D TALK TO HIM AND HE WOULDN'T RESPOND. LIKE HE WAS SOMEWHERE ELSE... BUT WE THOUGHT HE MAYBE HAD THE FLU OR SOMETHING.
HIS RESPONSES WOULDN'T REALLY MAKE SENSE WHEN HE DID TALK... THEN HE'D SNAP OUT OF THAT AND SEEM FINE FOR A WHILE.
IT WAS **AFTER.** THAT'S WHEN IT BECAME CLEAR THIS WASN'T THE BLAKE I KNEW.
HE DIDN'T EVEN REALLY RECOGNIZE THAT HE'D DONE A BAD THING. HE REGARDED THE... MURDER... LIKE IT WAS SOME KIND OF **GAME.**
HE DIDN'T DEFEND HIMSELF, HE DIDN'T EXPLAIN HIMSELF. HE WAS JUST... **HAPPY.** ABOUT ALL OF IT.
I TRIED SPEAKING TO HIM... ONCE...
IT WAS POINTLESS.
WHATEVER HE IS NOW... THAT'S **NOT** THE MAN I KNEW.

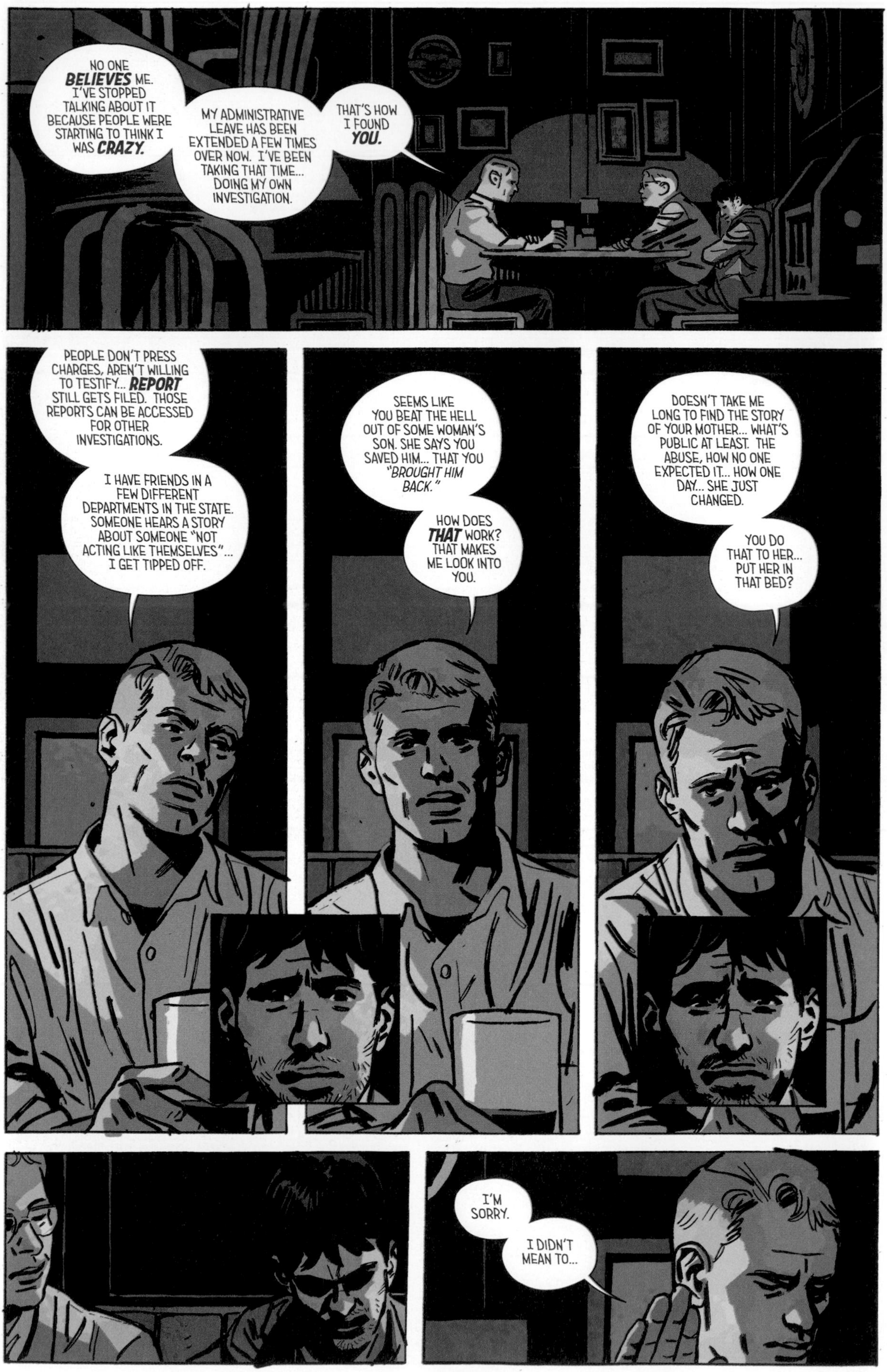
NO ONE BELIEVES ME. I'VE STOPPED TALKING ABOUT IT BECAUSE PEOPLE WERE STARTING TO THINK I WAS CRAZY.
MY ADMINISTRATIVE LEAVE HAS BEEN EXTENDED A FEW TIMES OVER NOW. I'VE BEEN TAKING THAT TIME... DOING MY OWN INVESTIGATION.
THAT'S HOW I FOUND YOU.
PEOPLE DON'T PRESS CHARGES, AREN'T WILLING TO TESTIFY... REPORT STILL GETS FILED. THOSE REPORTS CAN BE ACCESSED FOR OTHER INVESTIGATIONS.
I HAVE FRIENDS IN A FEW DIFFERENT DEPARTMENTS IN THE STATE. SOMEONE HEARS A STORY ABOUT SOMEONE "NOT ACTING LIKE THEMSELVES"... I GET TIPPED OFF.
SEEMS LIKE YOU BEAT THE HELL OUT OF SOME WOMAN'S SON. SHE SAYS YOU SAVED HIM... THAT YOU "BROUGHT HIM BACK."
HOW DOES THAT WORK? THAT MAKES ME LOOK INTO YOU.
DOESN'T TAKE ME LONG TO FIND THE STORY OF YOUR MOTHER... WHAT'S PUBLIC AT LEAST. THE ABUSE, HOW NO ONE EXPECTED IT... HOW ONE DAY... SHE JUST CHANGED.
YOU DO THAT TO HER... PUT HER IN THAT BED?
I'M SORRY.
I DIDN'T MEAN TO...

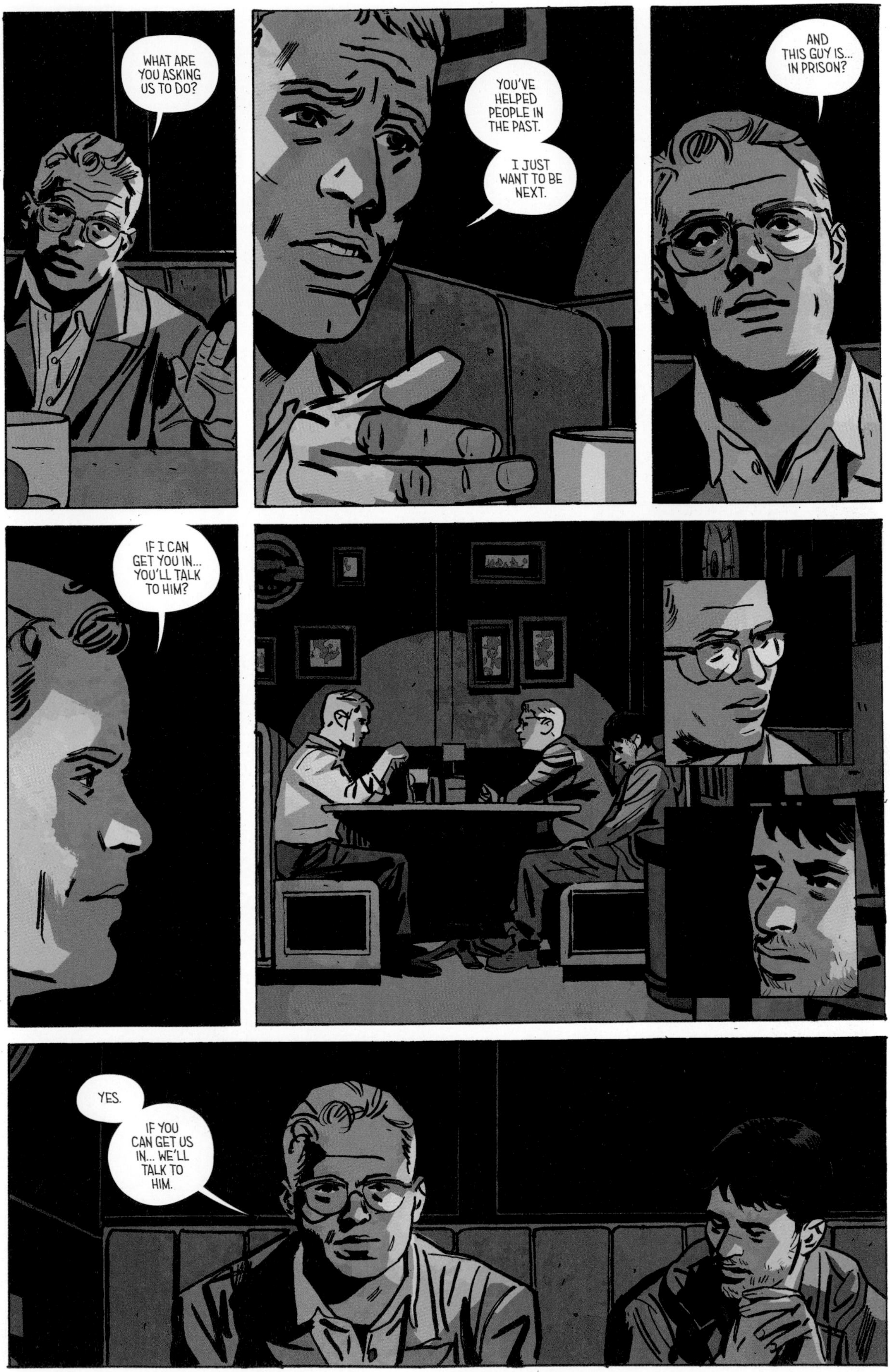
WHAT ARE YOU ASKING US TO DO?
YOU'VE HELPED PEOPLE IN THE PAST.
I JUST WANT TO BE NEXT.
AND THIS GUY IS... IN PRISON?
IF I CAN GET YOU IN... YOU'LL TALK TO HIM?
YES.
IF YOU CAN GET US IN... WE'LL TALK TO HIM.

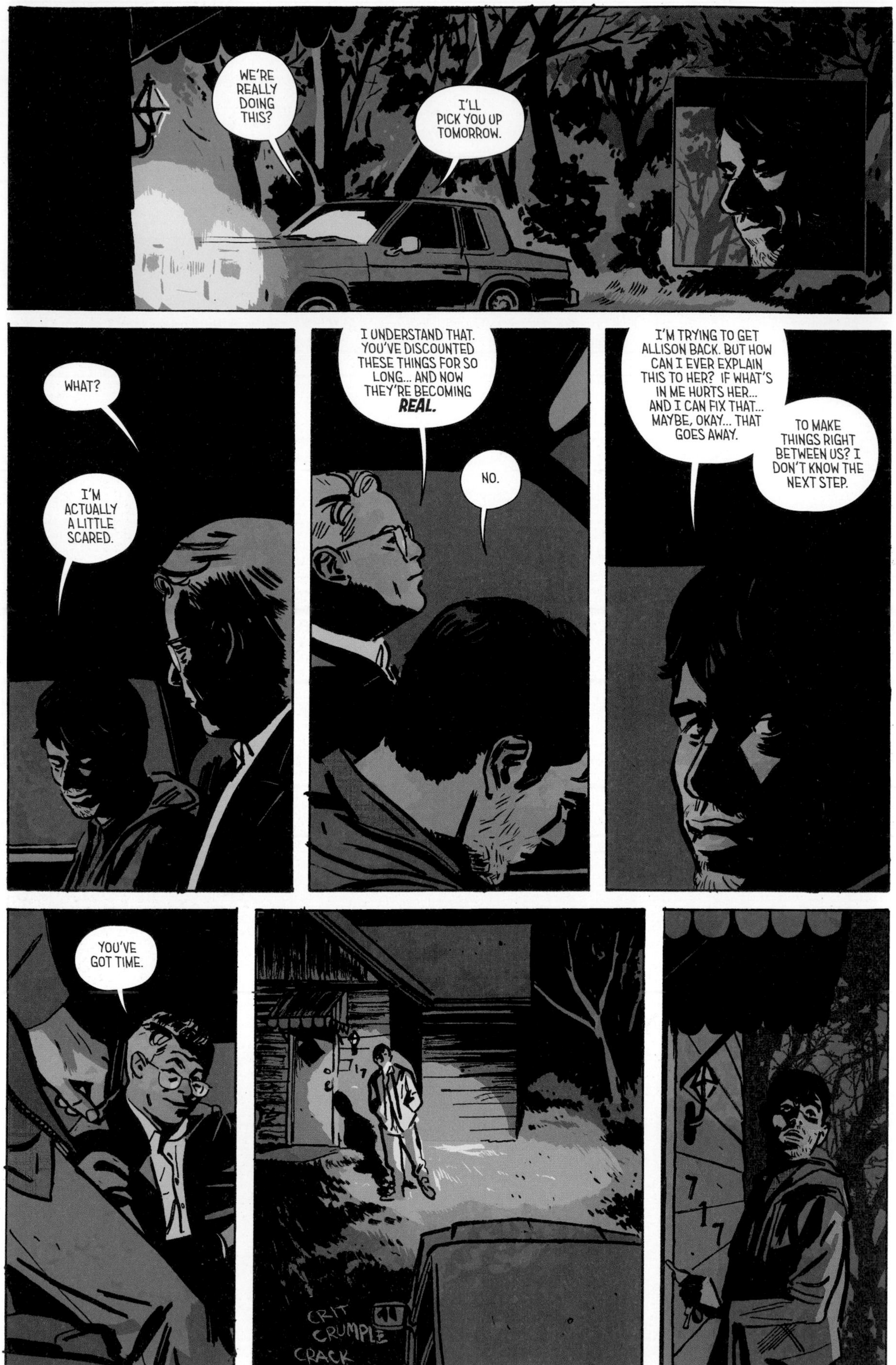
WE'RE REALLY DOING THIS?
I'LL PICK YOU UP TOMORROW.
WHAT?
I'M ACTUALLY A LITTLE SCARED.
I UNDERSTAND THAT. YOU'VE DISCOUNTED THESE THINGS FOR SO LONG... AND NOW THEY'RE BECOMING REAL.
NO.
I'M TRYING TO GET ALLISON BACK. BUT HOW CAN I EVER EXPLAIN THIS TO HER? IF WHAT'S IN ME HURTS HER... AND I CAN FIX THAT... MAYBE, OKAY... THAT GOES AWAY.
TO MAKE THINGS RIGHT BETWEEN US? I DON'T KNOW THE NEXT STEP.
YOU'VE GOT TIME.
CRIT
CRUMPLE
CRACK

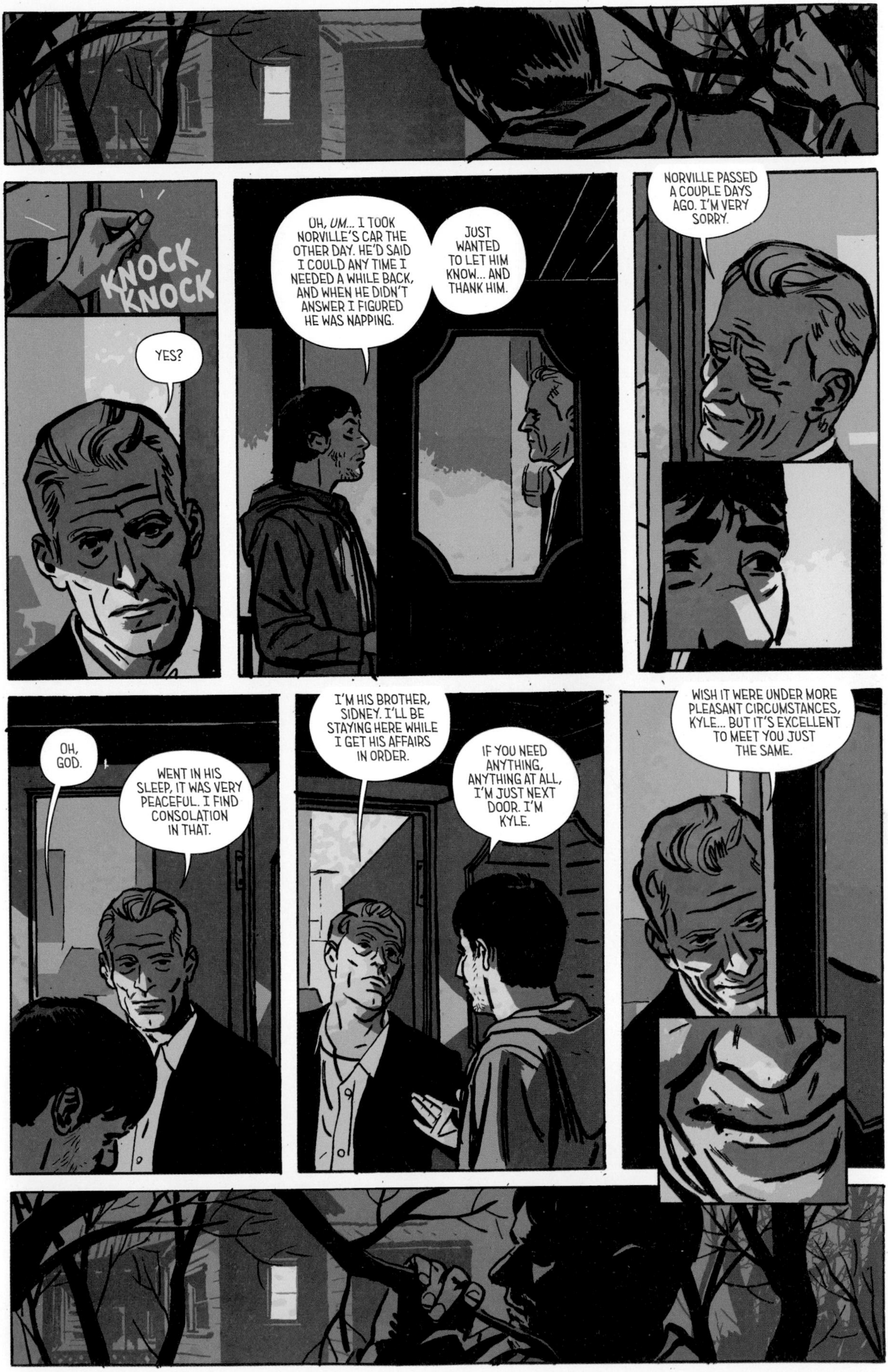
KNOCK KNOCK
YES?
OH, UM... I TOOK NORVILLE'S CAR THE OTHER DAY. HE'D SAID I COULD ANY TIME I NEEDED A WHILE BACK, AND WHEN HE DIDN'T ANSWER I FIGURED HE WAS NAPPING.
JUST WANTED TO LET HIM KNOW... AND THANK HIM.
NORVILLE PASSED A COUPLE DAYS AGO. I'M VERY SORRY.
OH, GOD.
WENT IN HIS SLEEP, IT WAS VERY PEACEFUL. I FIND CONSOLATION IN THAT.
I'M HIS BROTHER, SIDNEY. I'LL BE STAYING HERE WHILE I GET HIS AFFAIRS IN ORDER.
IF YOU NEED ANYTHING, ANYTHING AT ALL, I'M JUST NEXT DOOR. I'M KYLE.
WISH IT WERE UNDER MORE PLEASANT CIRCUMSTANCES, KYLE... BUT IT'S EXCELLENT TO MEET YOU JUST THE SAME.

JUST GOING TO TALK?

NEVER HURTS TO BE PREPARED.

WEST VIRGINIA STATE PRISON

WE NEED TO SIGN IN.

THANKS AGAIN FOR AGREEING TO DO THIS.

STOP
NO LIQUIDS
NO WEAPONS
NO SHARP OBJECTS
BEYOND THIS POINT

MORNING, REVEREND.

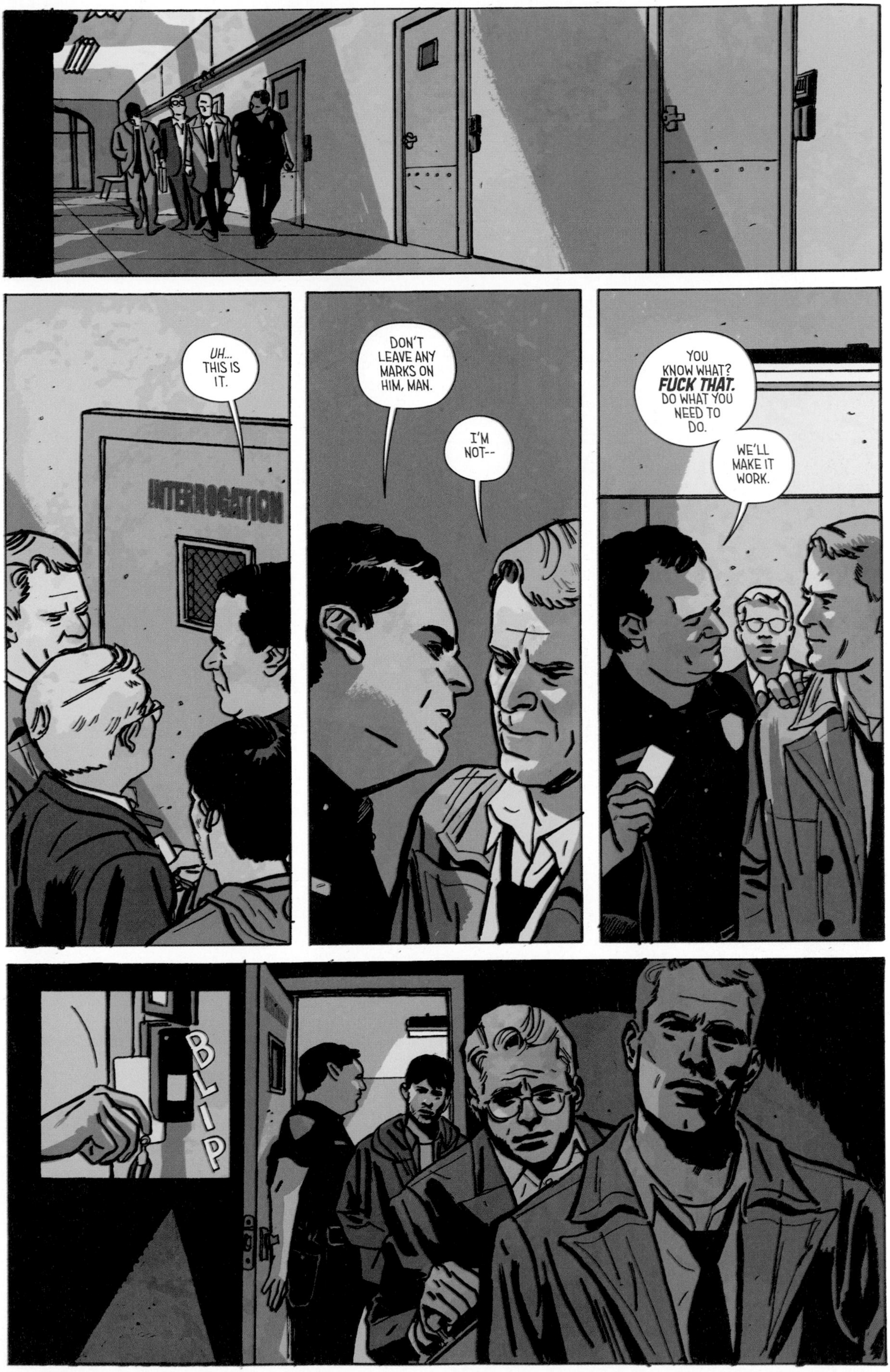
UH... THIS IS IT.
INTERROGATION
DON'T LEAVE ANY MARKS ON HIM, MAN.
I'M NOT--
YOU KNOW WHAT? FUCK THAT. DO WHAT YOU NEED TO DO.
WE'LL MAKE IT WORK.
BLIP

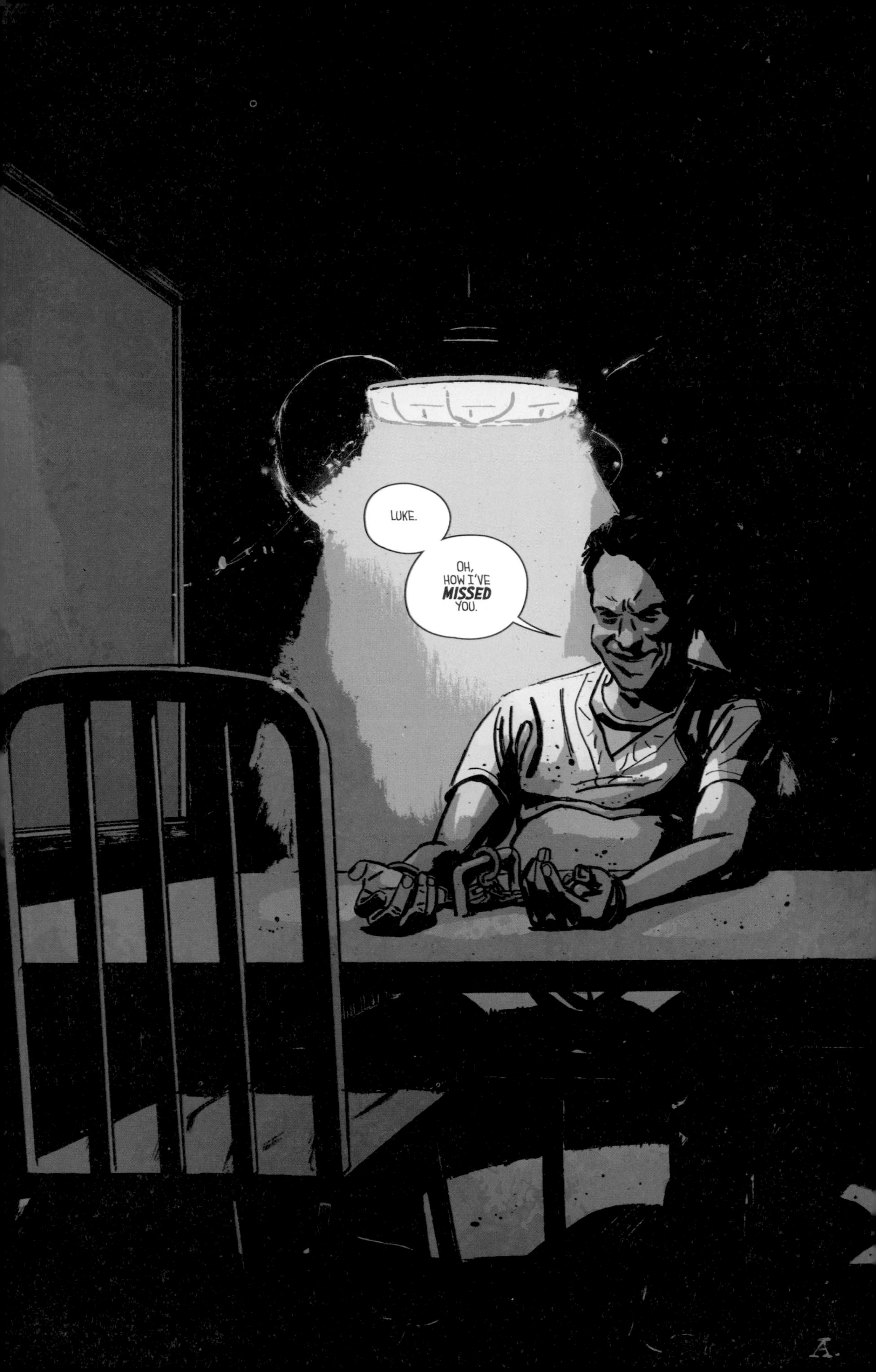
LUKE.
OH, HOW I'VE MISSED YOU.

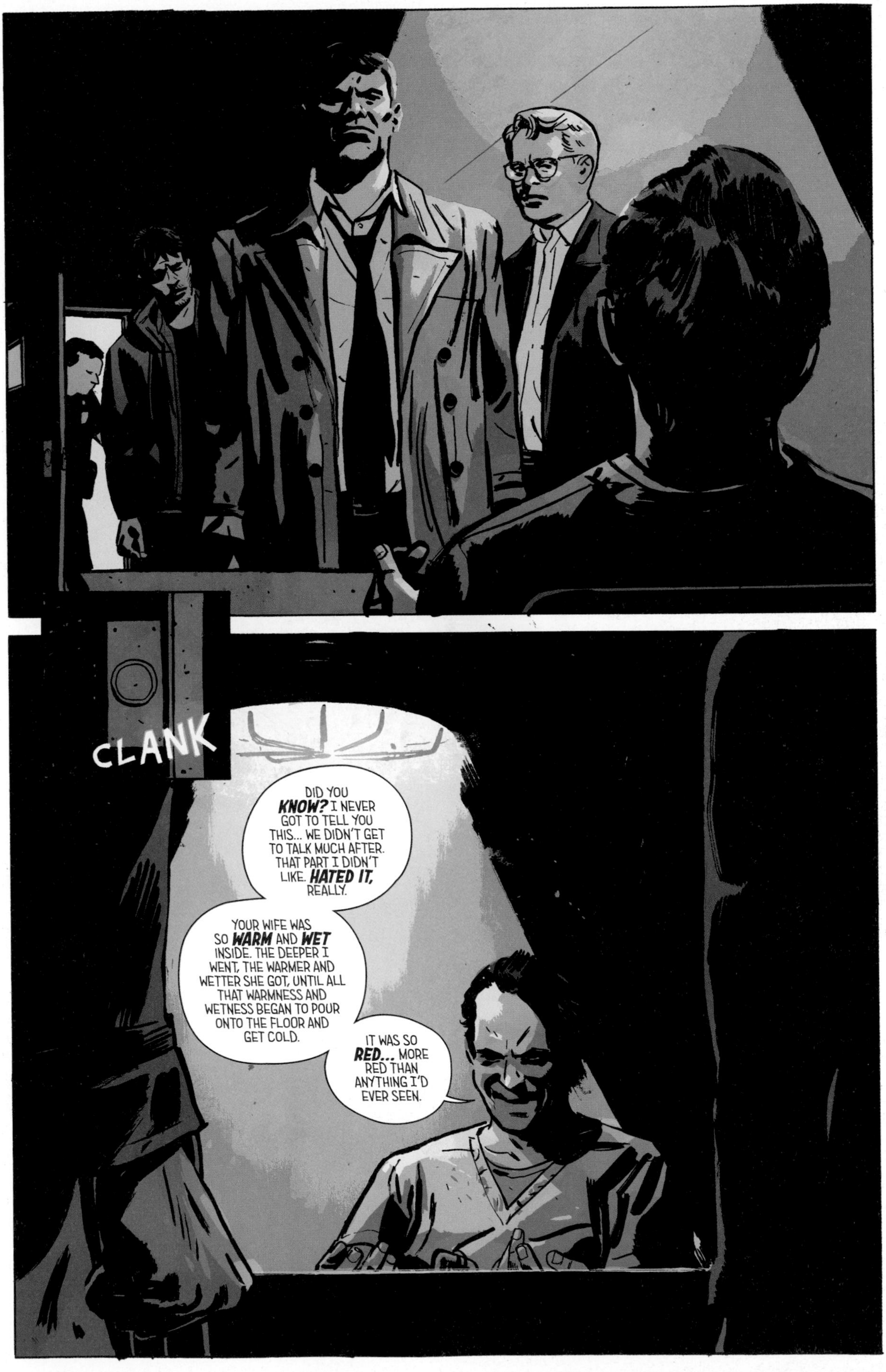
CLANK
DID YOU KNOW? I NEVER GOT TO TELL YOU THIS... WE DIDN'T GET TO TALK MUCH AFTER. THAT PART I DIDN'T LIKE. HATED IT, REALLY.
YOUR WIFE WAS SO WARM AND WET INSIDE. THE DEEPER I WENT, THE WARMER AND WETTER SHE GOT, UNTIL ALL THAT WARMNESS AND WETNESS BEGAN TO POUR ONTO THE FLOOR AND GET COLD.
IT WAS SO RED... MORE RED THAN ANYTHING I'D EVER SEEN.

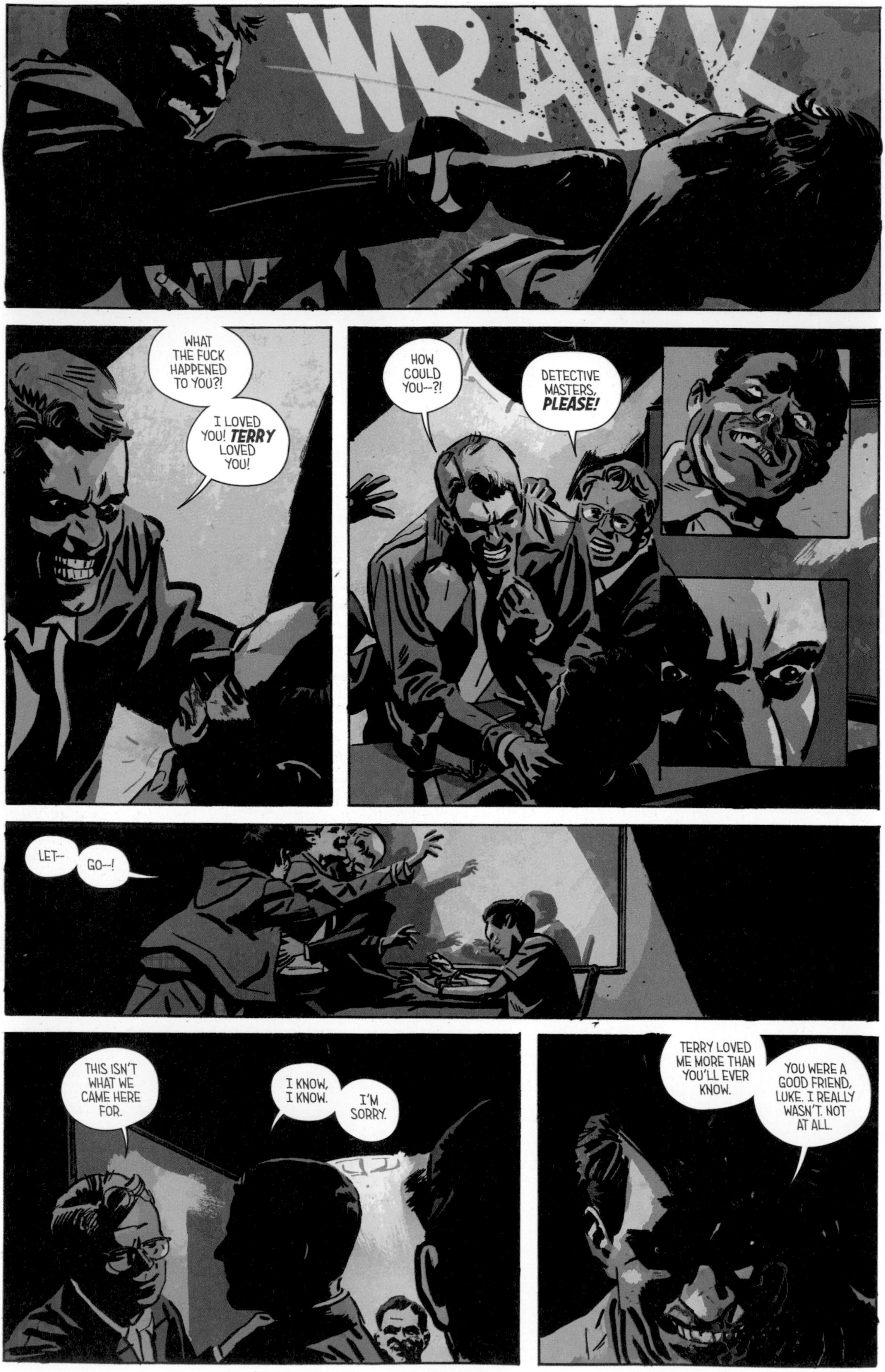
WRAKK
WHAT THE FUCK HAPPENED TO YOU?!
I LOVED YOU! TERRY LOVED YOU!
HOW COULD YOU--?!
DETECTIVE MASTERS, PLEASE!
LET--
GO--!
THIS ISN'T WHAT WE CAME HERE FOR.
I KNOW, I KNOW.
I'M SORRY.
TERRY LOVED ME MORE THAN YOU'LL EVER KNOW.
YOU WERE A GOOD FRIEND, LUKE. I REALLY WASN'T. NOT AT ALL.

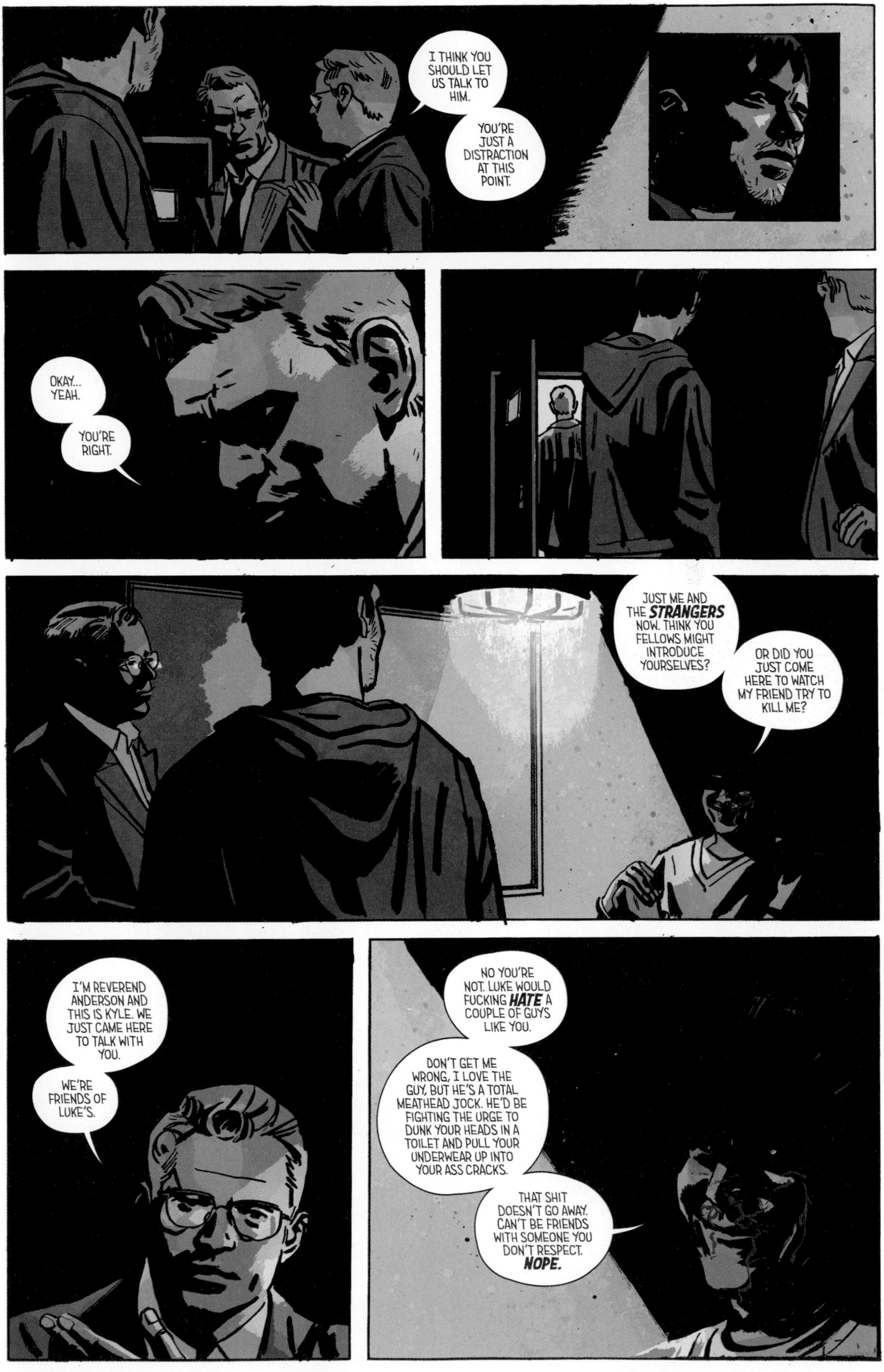
I THINK YOU SHOULD LET US TALK TO HIM.
YOU'RE JUST A DISTRACTION AT THIS POINT.
OKAY... YEAH.
YOU'RE RIGHT.
JUST ME AND THE STRANGERS NOW. THINK YOU FELLOWS MIGHT INTRODUCE YOURSELVES?
OR DID YOU JUST COME HERE TO WATCH MY FRIEND TRY TO KILL ME?
I'M REVEREND ANDERSON AND THIS IS KYLE. WE JUST CAME HERE TO TALK WITH YOU.
WE'RE FRIENDS OF LUKE'S.
NO YOU'RE NOT. LUKE WOULD FUCKING HATE A COUPLE OF GUYS LIKE YOU.
DON'T GET ME WRONG, I LOVE THE GUY, BUT HE'S A TOTAL MEATHEAD JOCK. HE'D BE FIGHTING THE URGE TO DUNK YOUR HEADS IN A TOILET AND PULL YOUR UNDERWEAR UP INTO YOUR ASS CRACKS.
THAT SHIT DOESN'T GO AWAY. CAN'T BE FRIENDS WITH SOMEONE YOU DON'T RESPECT. NOPE.

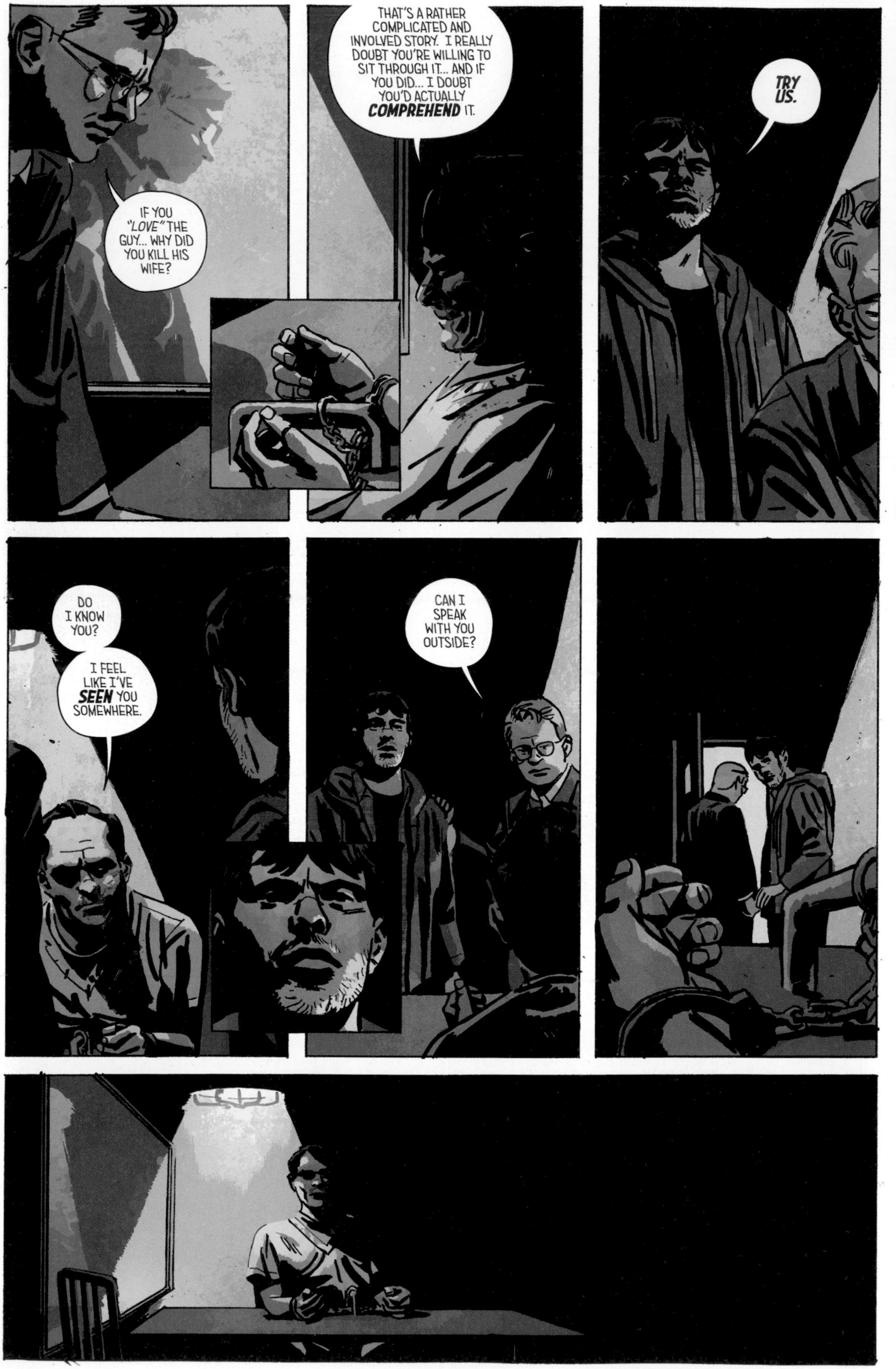
IF YOU "LOVE" THE GUY... WHY DID YOU KILL HIS WIFE?
THAT'S A RATHER COMPLICATED AND INVOLVED STORY. I REALLY DOUBT YOU'RE WILLING TO SIT THROUGH IT... AND IF YOU DID... I DOUBT YOU'D ACTUALLY COMPREHEND IT.
TRY US.
DO I KNOW YOU?
I FEEL LIKE I'VE SEEN YOU SOMEWHERE.
CAN I SPEAK WITH YOU OUTSIDE?

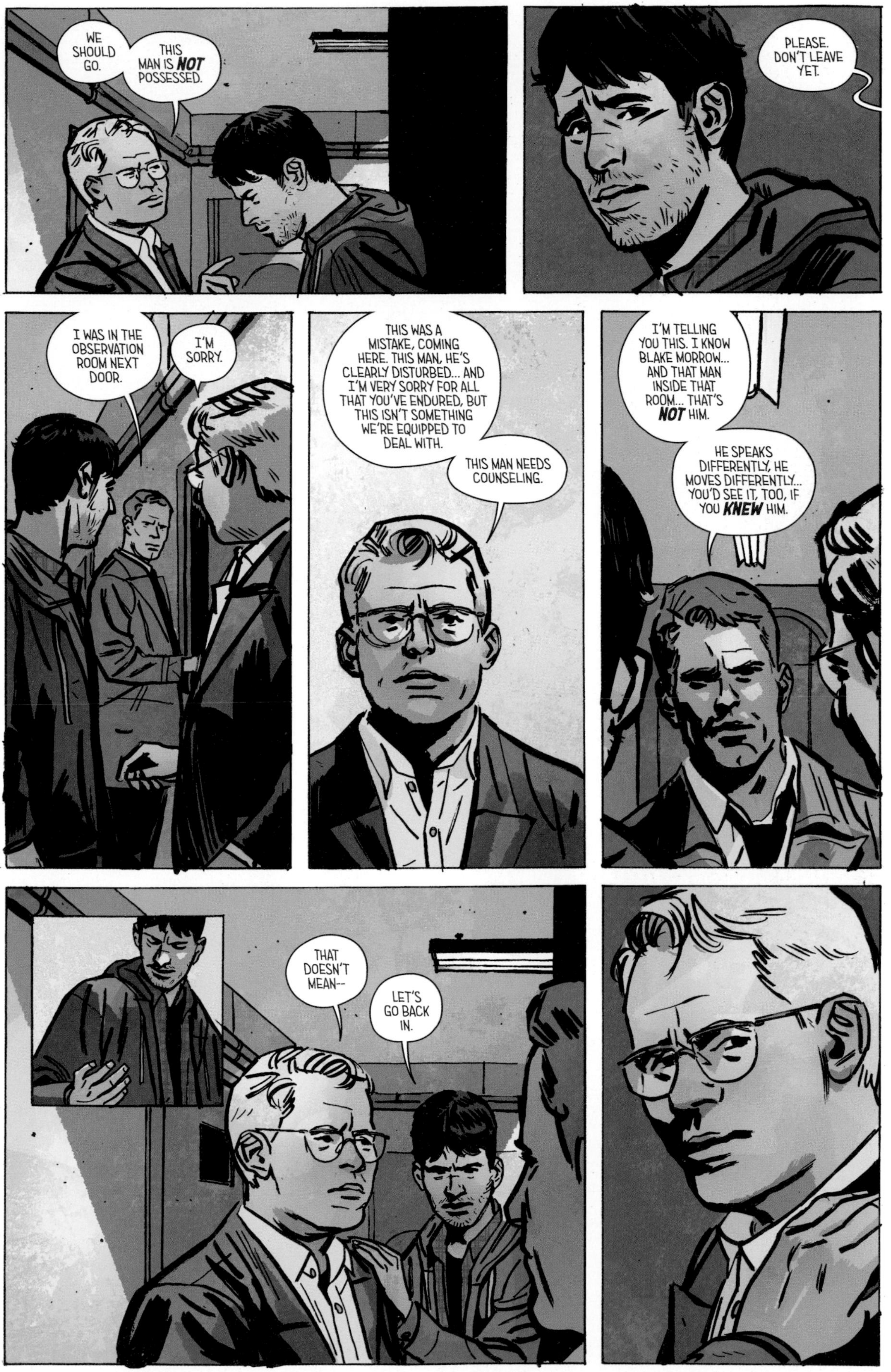
WE SHOULD GO.
THIS MAN IS **NOT** POSSESSED.
PLEASE. DON'T LEAVE YET.
I WAS IN THE OBSERVATION ROOM NEXT DOOR.
I'M SORRY.
THIS WAS A MISTAKE, COMING HERE. THIS MAN, HE'S CLEARLY DISTURBED... AND I'M VERY SORRY FOR ALL THAT YOU'VE ENDURED, BUT THIS ISN'T SOMETHING WE'RE EQUIPPED TO DEAL WITH.
THIS MAN NEEDS COUNSELING.
I'M TELLING YOU THIS. I KNOW BLAKE MORROW... AND THAT MAN INSIDE THAT ROOM... THAT'S **NOT** HIM.
HE SPEAKS DIFFERENTLY, HE MOVES DIFFERENTLY... YOU'D SEE IT, TOO, IF YOU **KNEW** HIM.
THAT DOESN'T MEAN--
LET'S GO BACK IN.

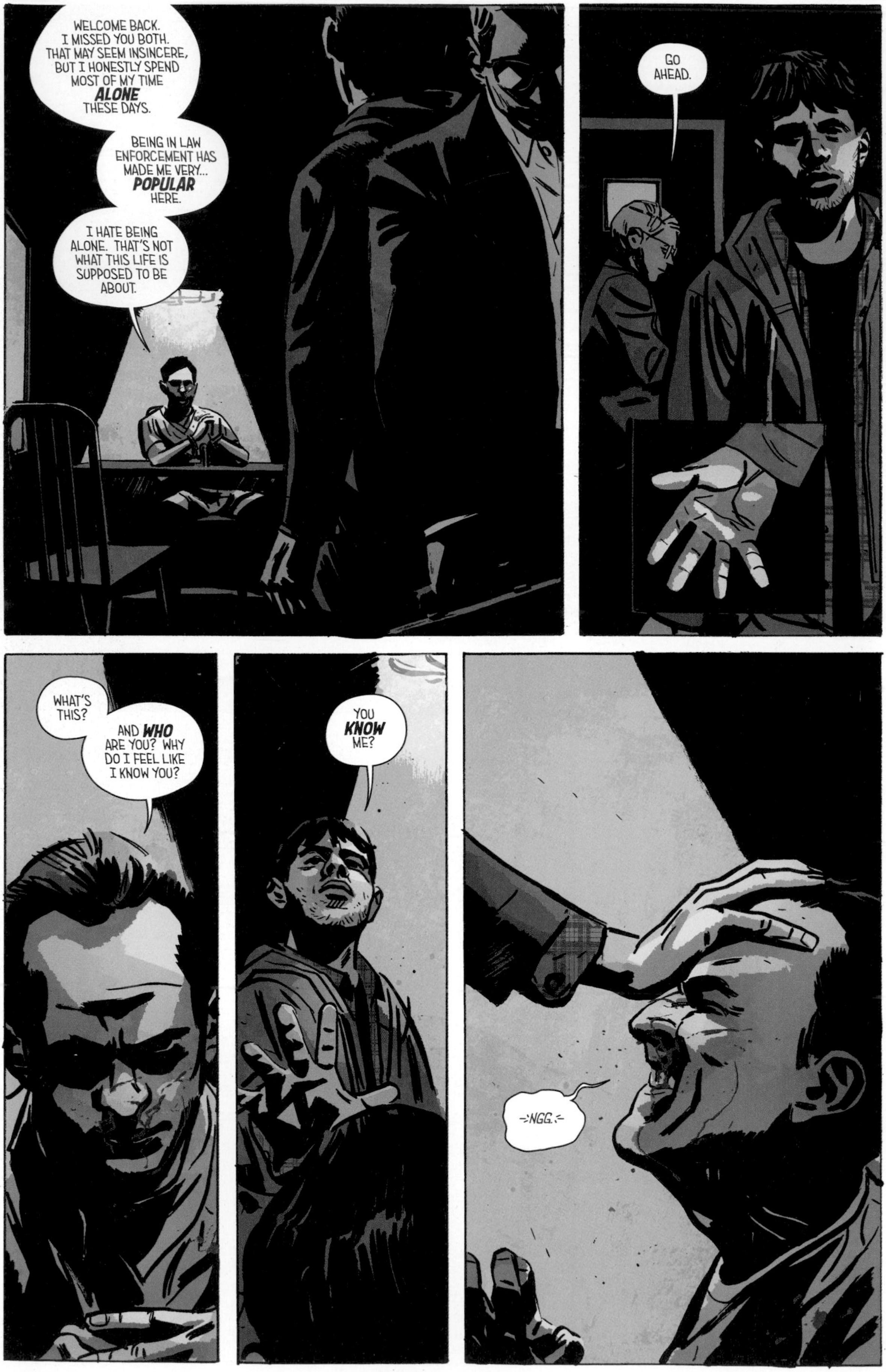
WELCOME BACK. I MISSED YOU BOTH. THAT MAY SEEM INSINCERE, BUT I HONESTLY SPEND MOST OF MY TIME ALONE THESE DAYS.
BEING IN LAW ENFORCEMENT HAS MADE ME VERY... POPULAR HERE.
I HATE BEING ALONE. THAT'S NOT WHAT THIS LIFE IS SUPPOSED TO BE ABOUT.
GO AHEAD.
WHAT'S THIS?
AND WHO ARE YOU? WHY DO I FEEL LIKE I KNOW YOU?
YOU KNOW ME?
NGG.

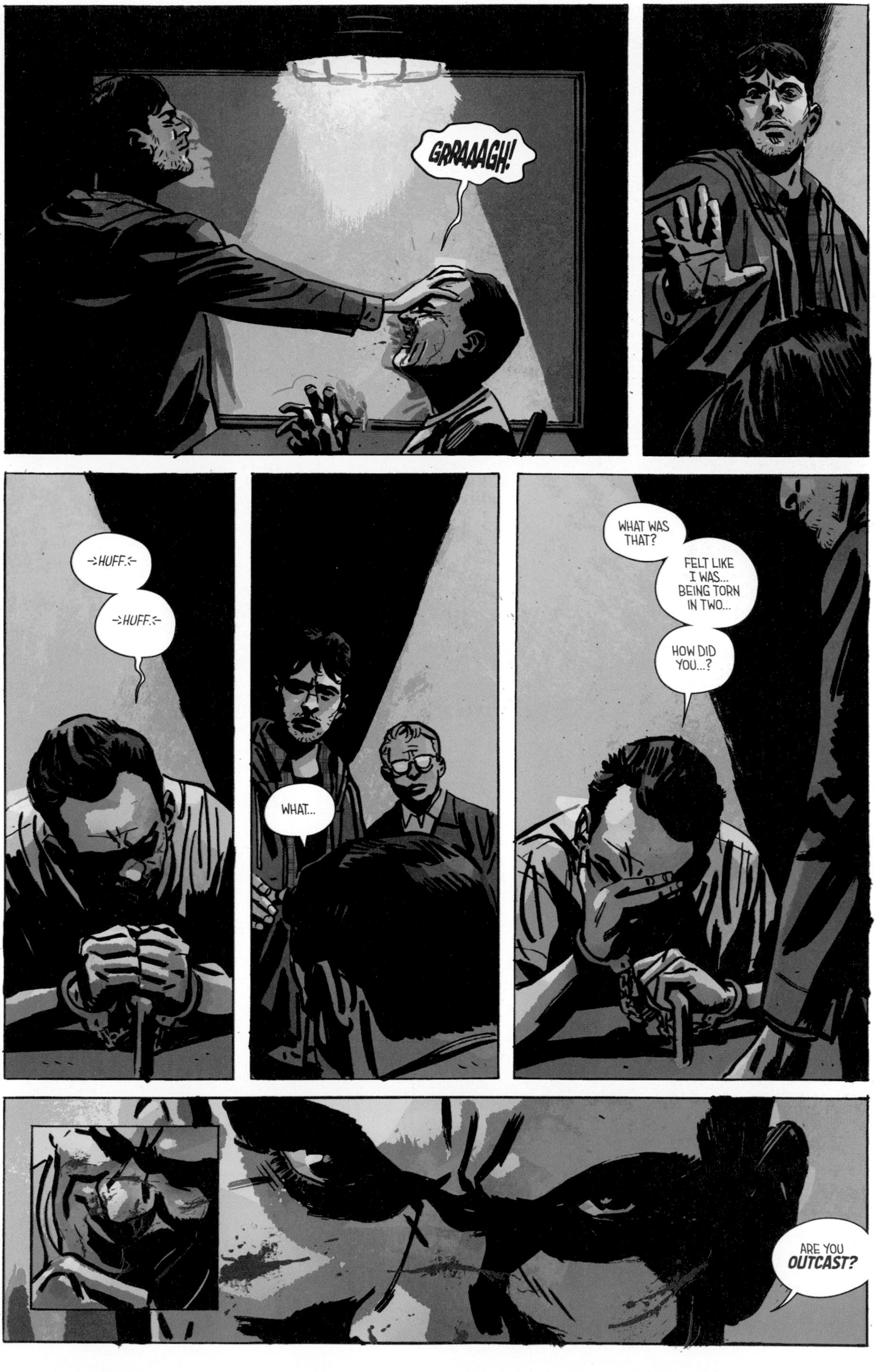
GRRAAAGH!
HUFF.
HUFF.
WHAT...
WHAT WAS THAT?
FELT LIKE I WAS... BEING TORN IN TWO...
HOW DID YOU...?
ARE YOU *OUTCAST?*

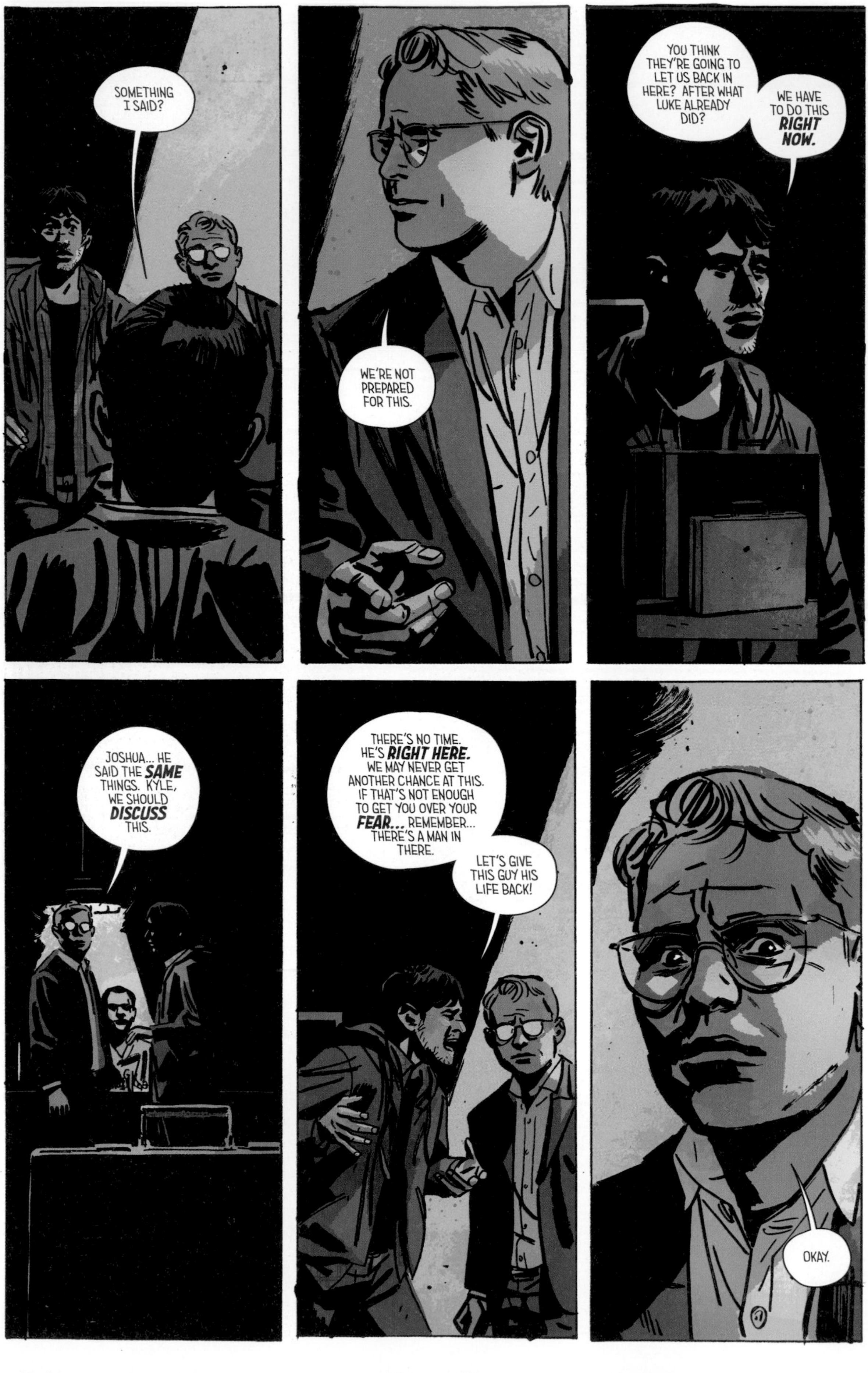
SOMETHING I SAID?
WE'RE NOT PREPARED FOR THIS.
YOU THINK THEY'RE GOING TO LET US BACK IN HERE? AFTER WHAT LUKE ALREADY DID?
WE HAVE TO DO THIS **RIGHT NOW.**
JOSHUA... HE SAID THE **SAME** THINGS. KYLE, WE SHOULD **DISCUSS** THIS.
THERE'S NO TIME. HE'S **RIGHT HERE.** WE MAY NEVER GET ANOTHER CHANCE AT THIS. IF THAT'S NOT ENOUGH TO GET YOU OVER YOUR **FEAR...** REMEMBER... THERE'S A MAN IN THERE.
LET'S GIVE THIS GUY HIS LIFE BACK!
OKAY.

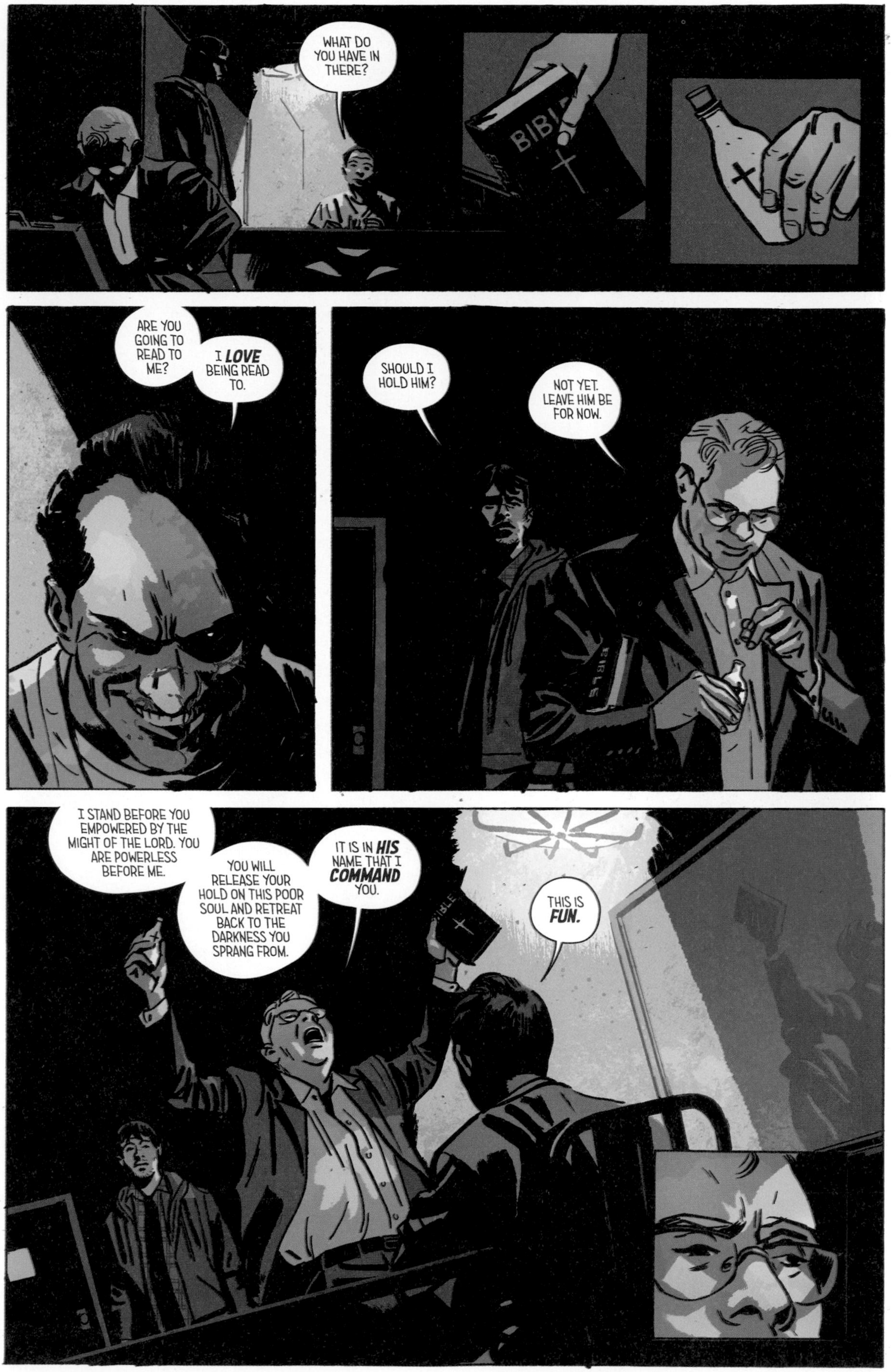
WHAT DO YOU HAVE IN THERE?
BIBLE
ARE YOU GOING TO READ TO ME?
I LOVE BEING READ TO.
SHOULD I HOLD HIM?
NOT YET. LEAVE HIM BE FOR NOW.
BIBLE
I STAND BEFORE YOU EMPOWERED BY THE MIGHT OF THE LORD. YOU ARE POWERLESS BEFORE ME.
YOU WILL RELEASE YOUR HOLD ON THIS POOR SOUL AND RETREAT BACK TO THE DARKNESS YOU SPRANG FROM.
IT IS IN HIS NAME THAT I COMMAND YOU.
BIBLE
THIS IS FUN.

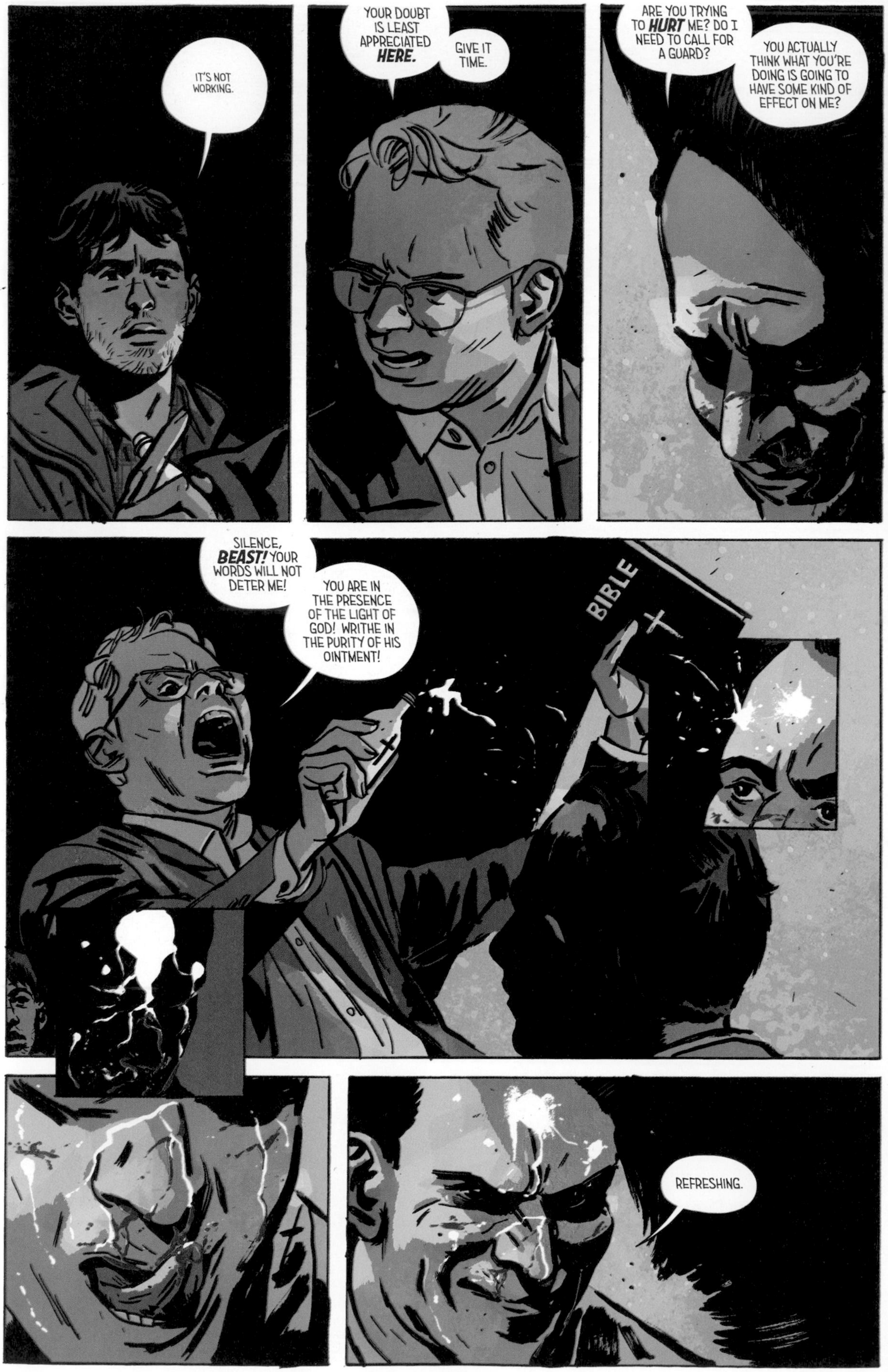
IT'S NOT WORKING.
YOUR DOUBT IS LEAST APPRECIATED HERE.
GIVE IT TIME.
ARE YOU TRYING TO HURT ME? DO I NEED TO CALL FOR A GUARD?
YOU ACTUALLY THINK WHAT YOU'RE DOING IS GOING TO HAVE SOME KIND OF EFFECT ON ME?
SILENCE, BEAST! YOUR WORDS WILL NOT DETER ME!
YOU ARE IN THE PRESENCE OF THE LIGHT OF GOD! WRITHE IN THE PURITY OF HIS OINTMENT!
BIBLE
REFRESHING.

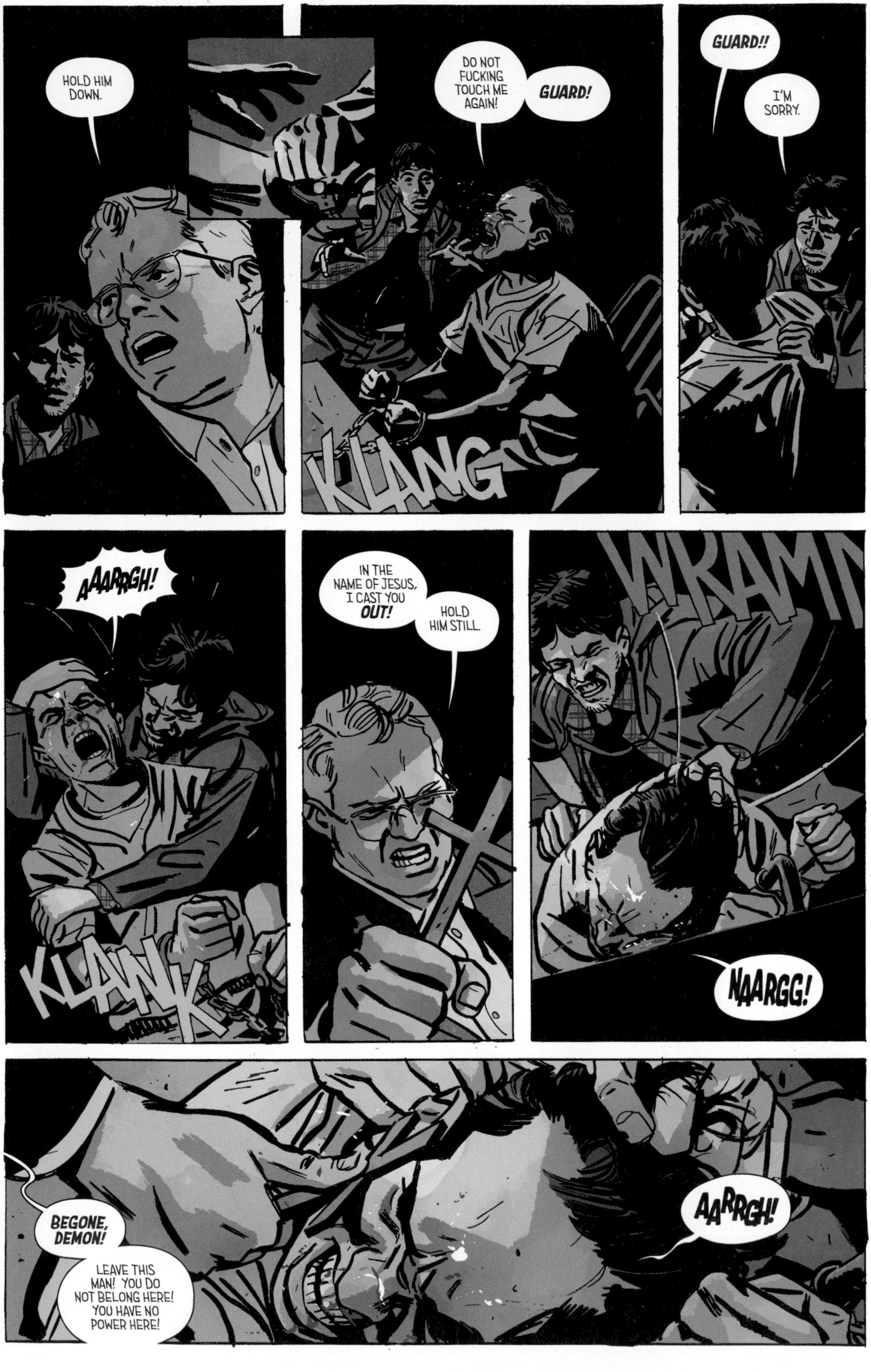
HOLD HIM DOWN.
DO NOT FUCKING TOUCH ME AGAIN!
GUARD!
KLANG
GUARD!!
I'M SORRY.
AAARRGH!
KLANK
IN THE NAME OF JESUS, I CAST YOU OUT!
HOLD HIM STILL.
WRAMM
NAARGG!
BEGONE, DEMON!
LEAVE THIS MAN! YOU DO NOT BELONG HERE! YOU HAVE NO POWER HERE!
AARRGH!

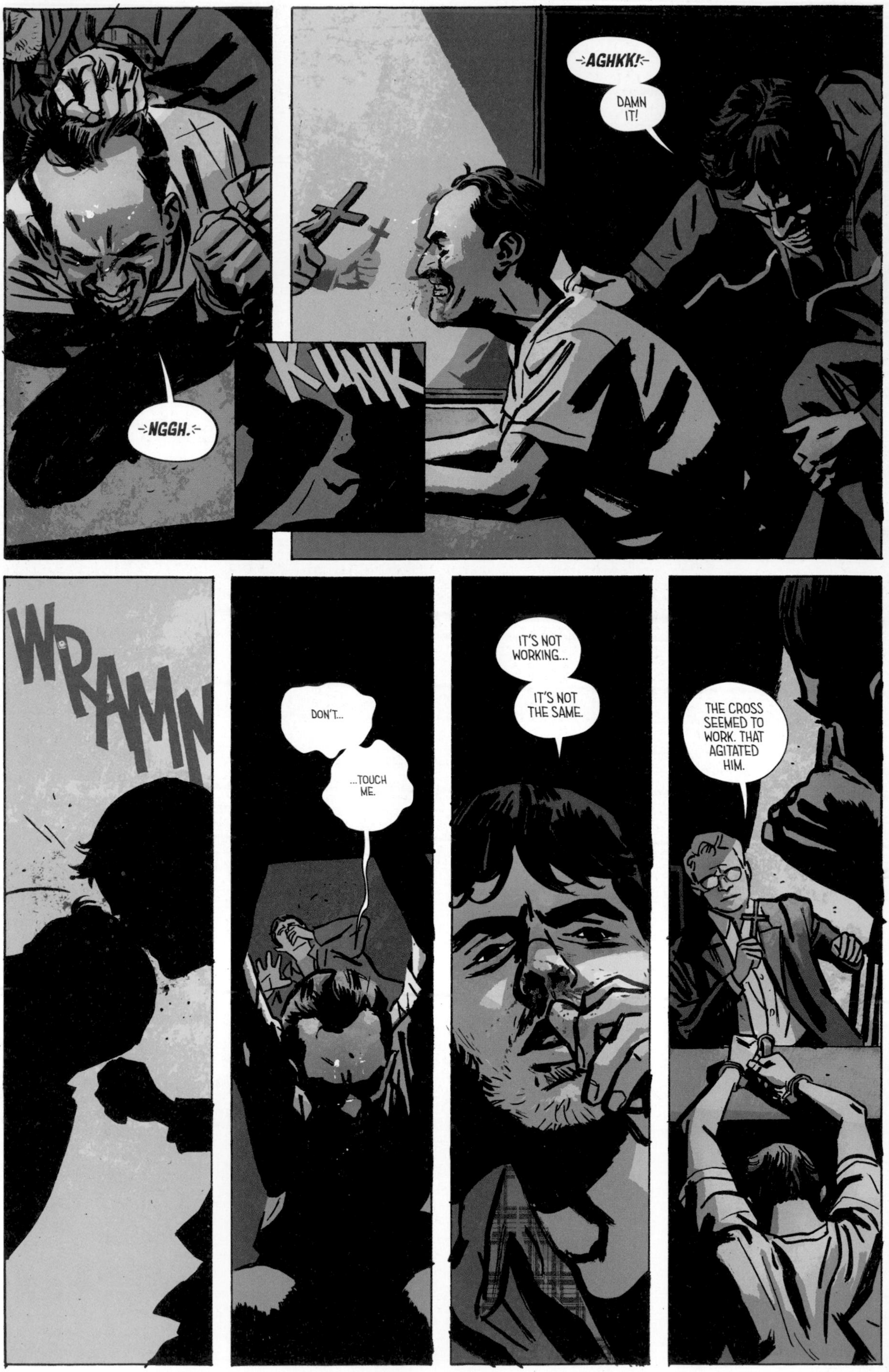
-NGGH.-
KUNK
-AGHKK!-
DAMN IT!
WRAMM
DON'T...
...TOUCH ME.
IT'S NOT WORKING...
IT'S NOT THE SAME.
THE CROSS SEEMED TO WORK. THAT AGITATED HIM.

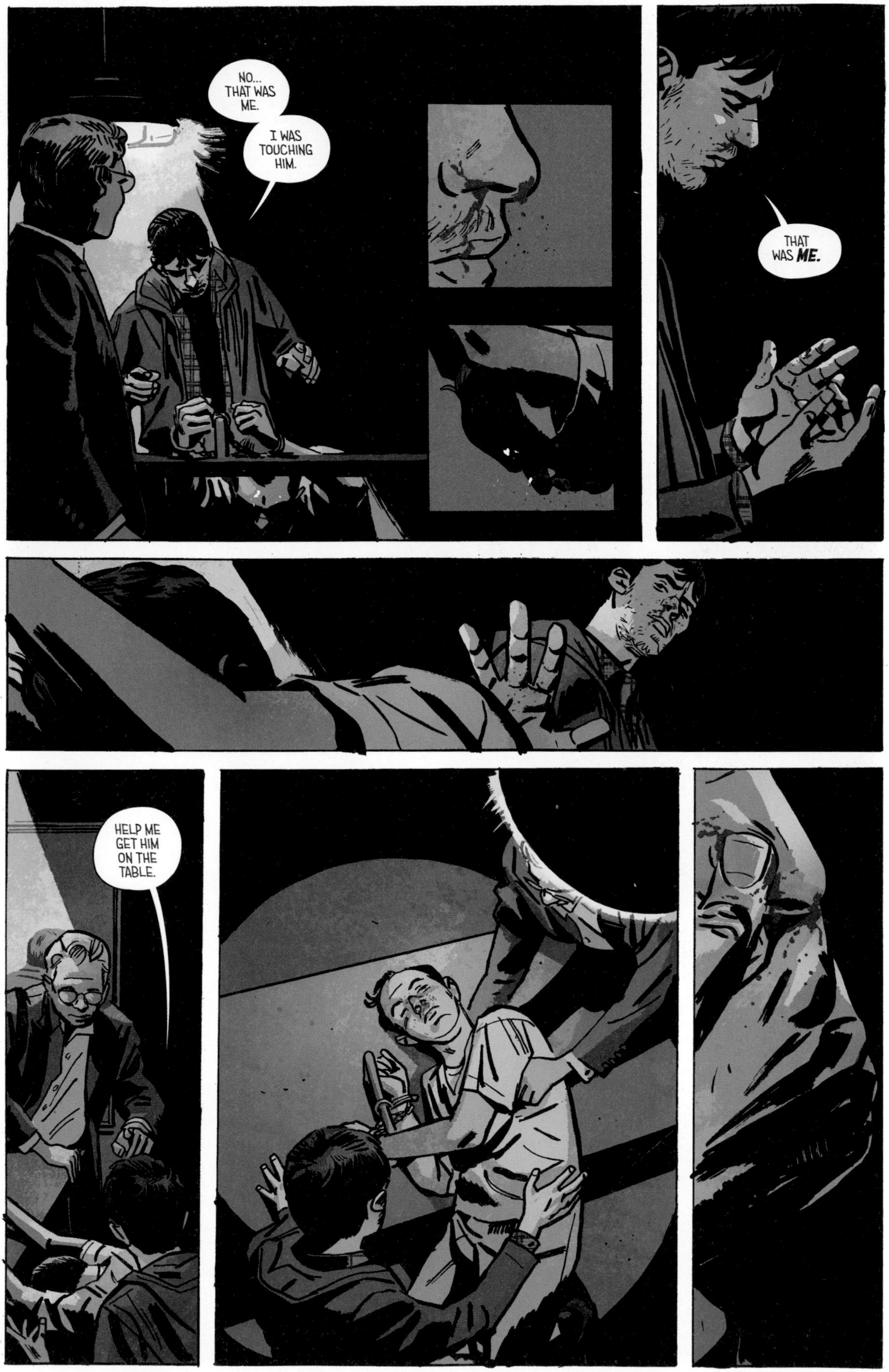
NO... THAT WAS ME.
I WAS TOUCHING HIM.
THAT WAS ***ME.***
HELP ME GET HIM ON THE TABLE.

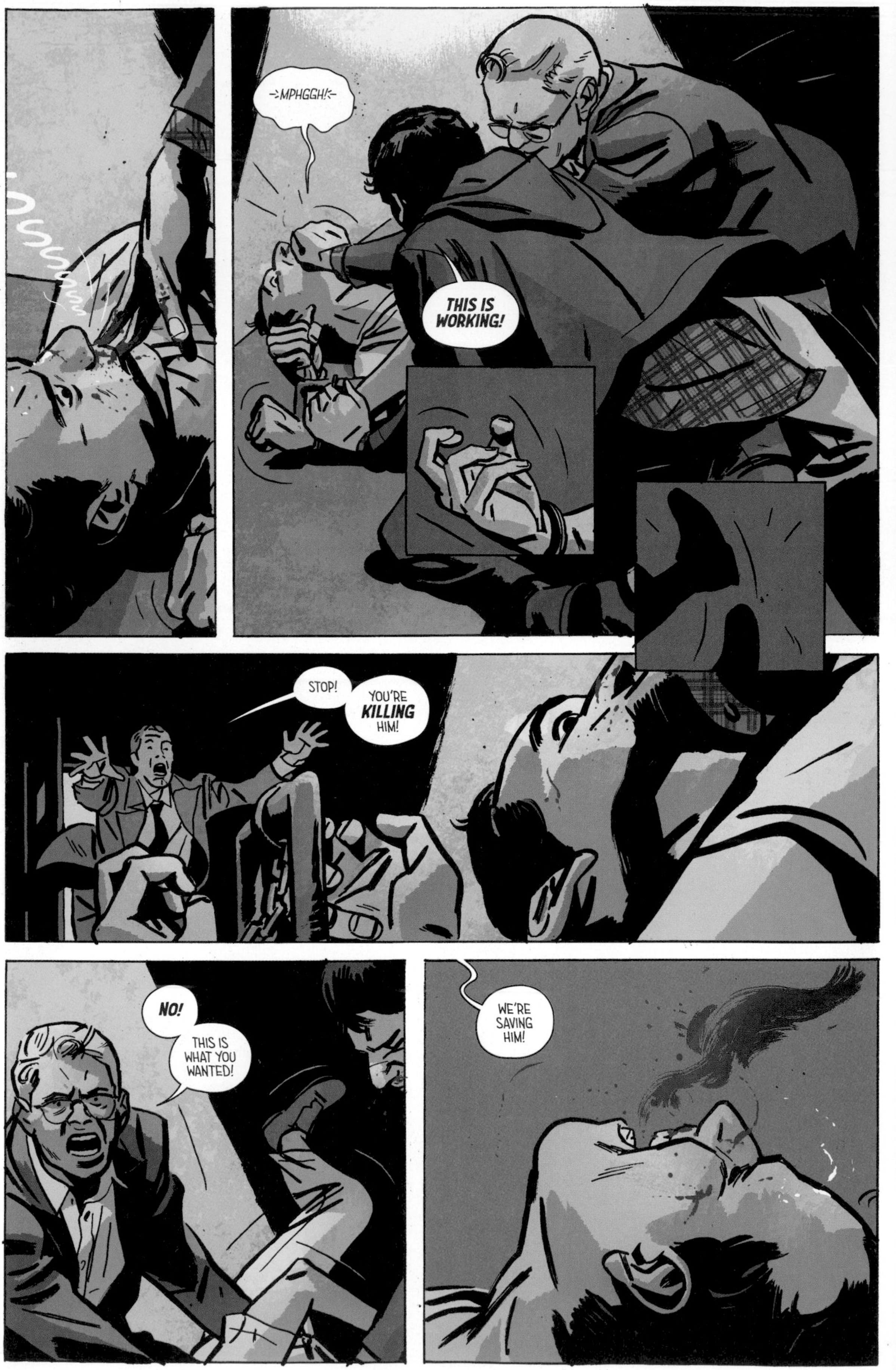
SSSSS
-MPHGGH!-
THIS IS WORKING!
STOP!
YOU'RE KILLING HIM!
NO!
THIS IS WHAT YOU WANTED!
WE'RE SAVING HIM!

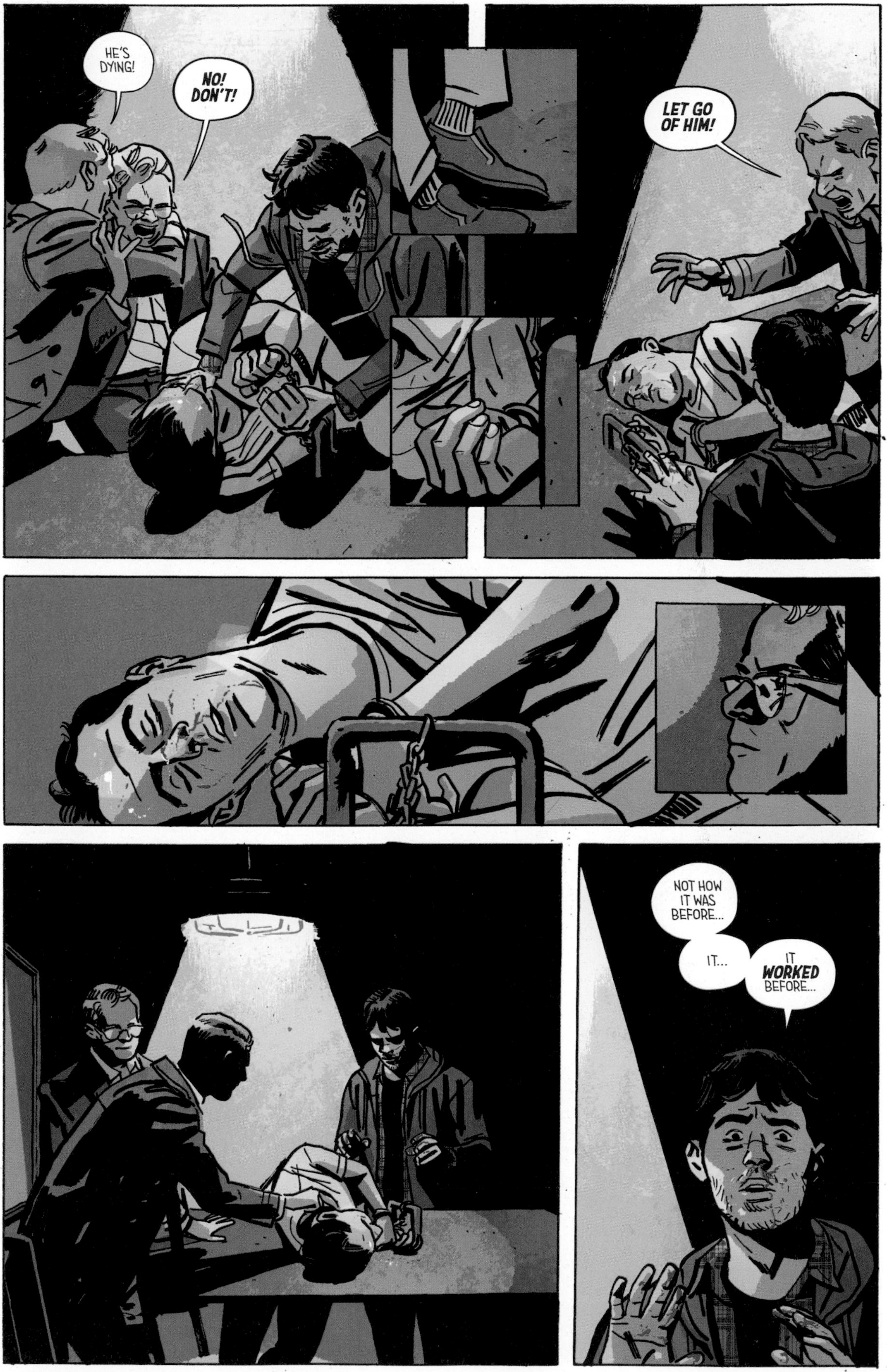
HE'S DYING!
NO! DON'T!
LET GO OF HIM!
NOT HOW IT WAS BEFORE...
IT...
IT WORKED BEFORE...

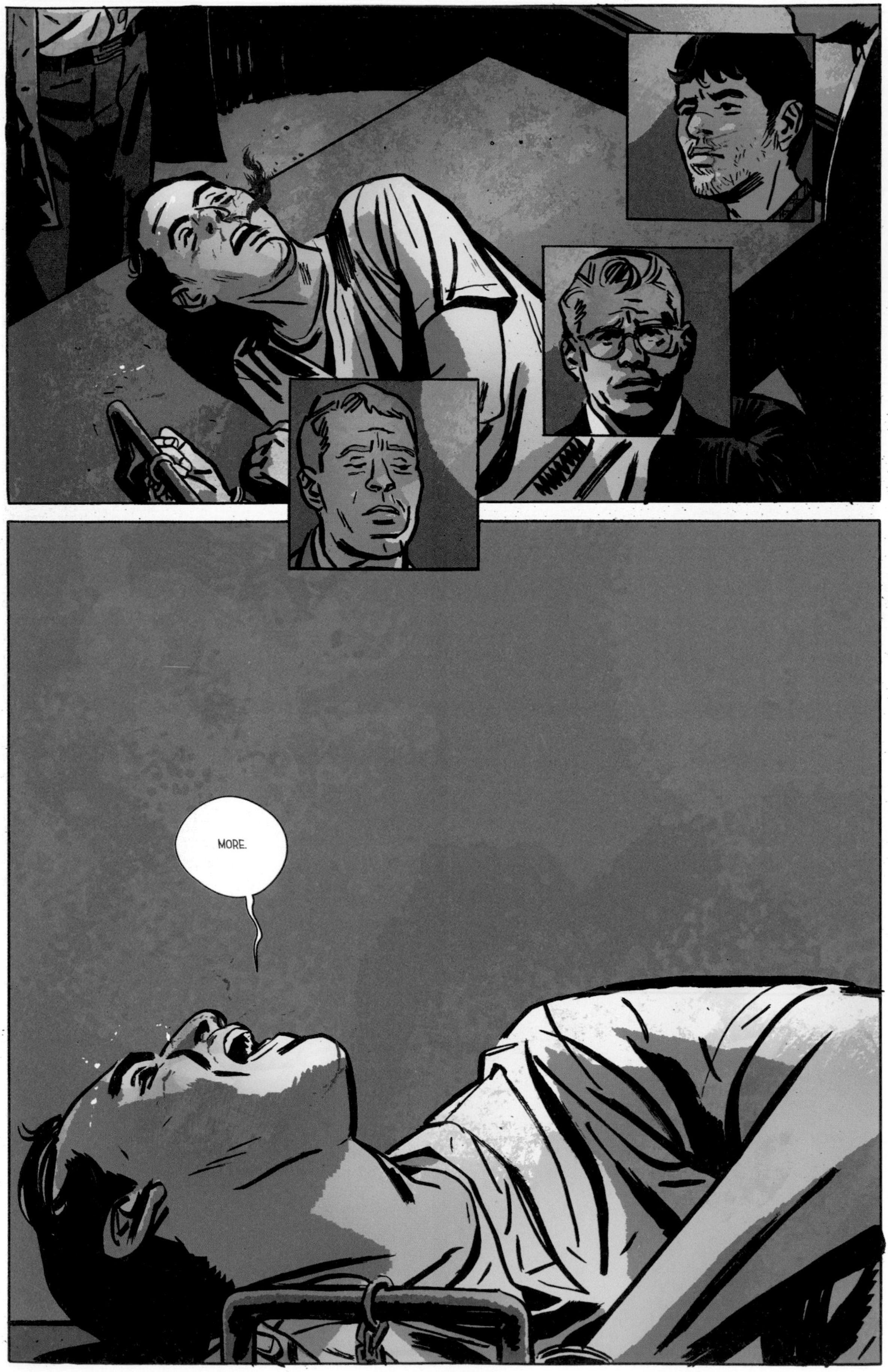
MORE.

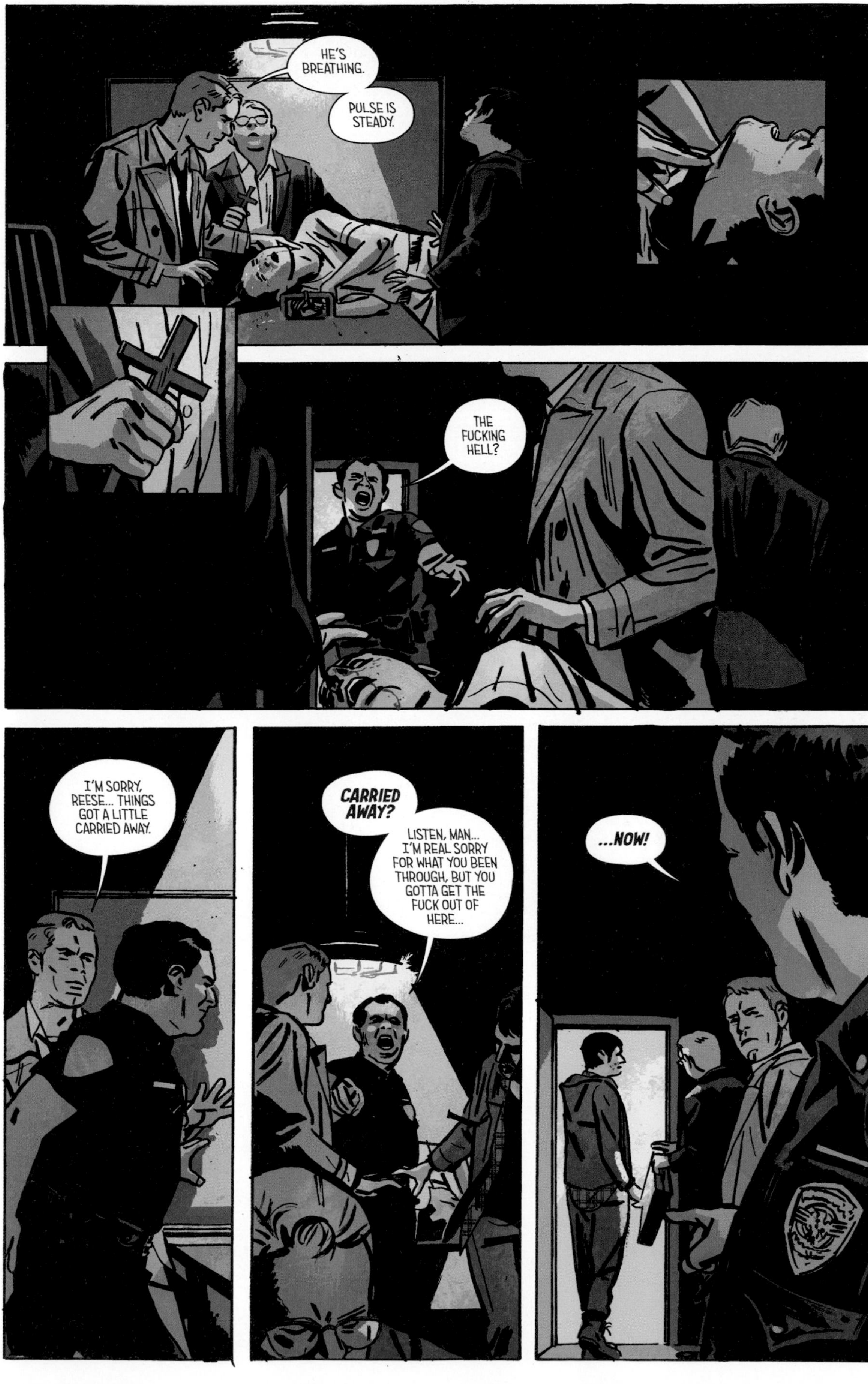
HE'S BREATHING.
PULSE IS STEADY.
THE FUCKING HELL?
I'M SORRY, REESE... THINGS GOT A LITTLE CARRIED AWAY.
CARRIED AWAY?
LISTEN, MAN... I'M REAL SORRY FOR WHAT YOU BEEN THROUGH, BUT YOU GOTTA GET THE FUCK OUT OF HERE...
...NOW!

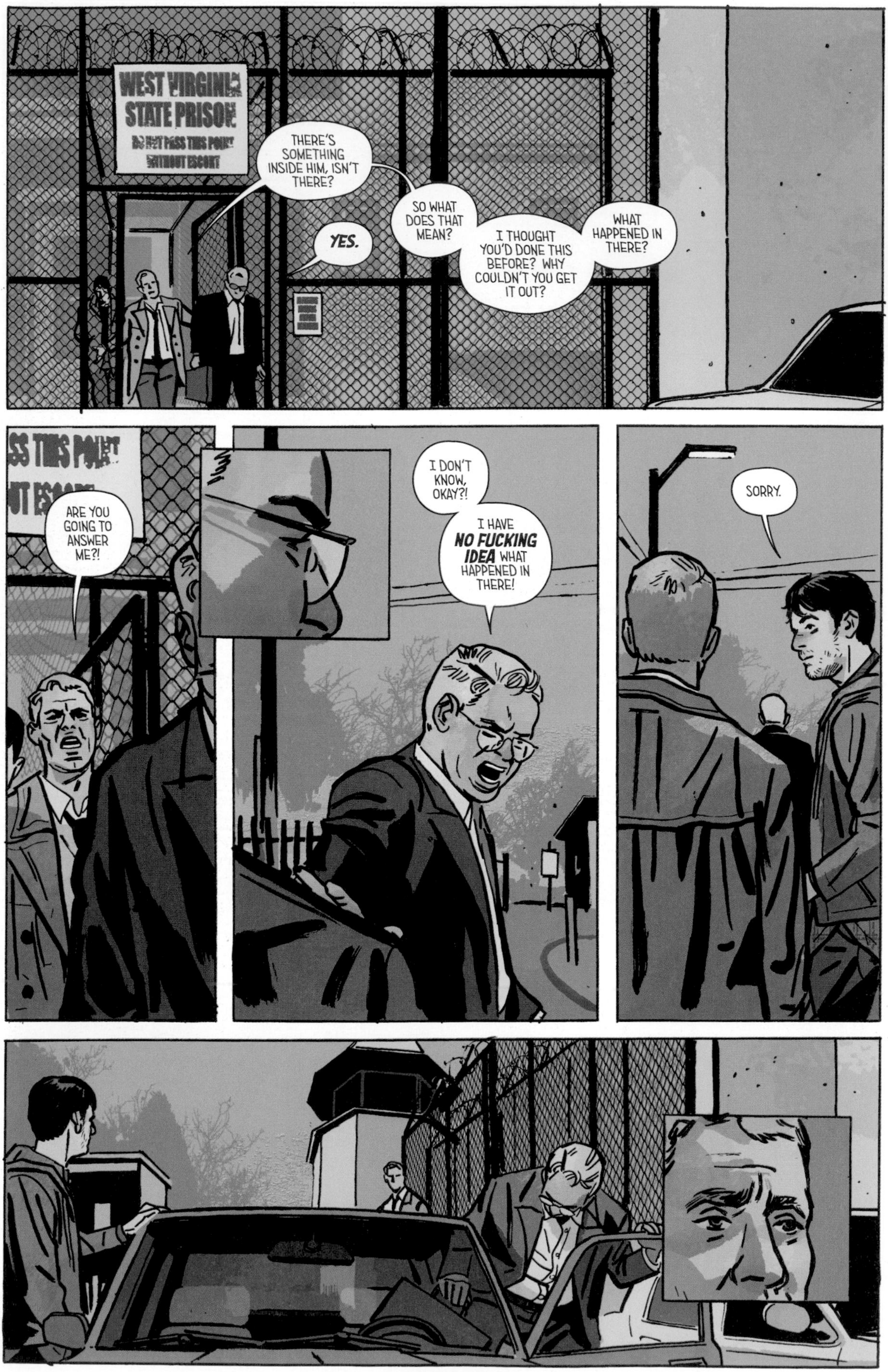

WEST VIRGINIA
STATE PRISON
THERE'S SOMETHING INSIDE HIM, ISN'T THERE?
YES.
SO WHAT DOES THAT MEAN?
I THOUGHT YOU'D DONE THIS BEFORE? WHY COULDN'T YOU GET IT OUT?
WHAT HAPPENED IN THERE?
ARE YOU GOING TO ANSWER ME?!
I DON'T KNOW, OKAY?!
I HAVE **NO FUCKING IDEA** WHAT HAPPENED IN THERE!
SORRY.

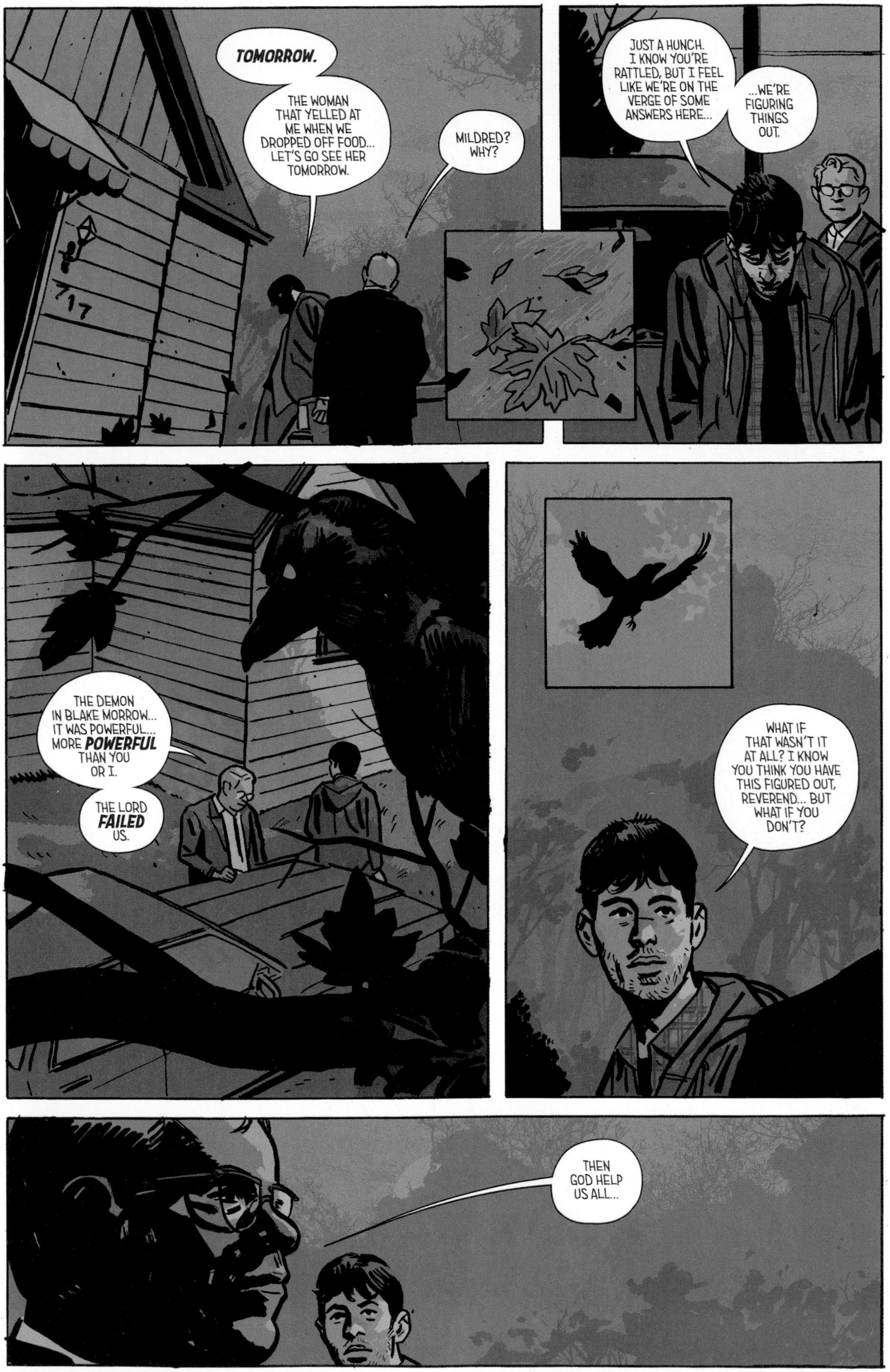
TOMORROW.
THE WOMAN THAT YELLED AT ME WHEN WE DROPPED OFF FOOD... LET'S GO SEE HER TOMORROW.
MILDRED? WHY?
717
JUST A HUNCH. I KNOW YOU'RE RATTLED, BUT I FEEL LIKE WE'RE ON THE VERGE OF SOME ANSWERS HERE...
...WE'RE FIGURING THINGS OUT.
THE DEMON IN BLAKE MORROW... IT WAS POWERFUL... MORE POWERFUL THAN YOU OR I.
THE LORD FAILED US.
WHAT IF THAT WASN'T IT AT ALL? I KNOW YOU THINK YOU HAVE THIS FIGURED OUT, REVEREND... BUT WHAT IF YOU DON'T?
THEN GOD HELP US ALL...

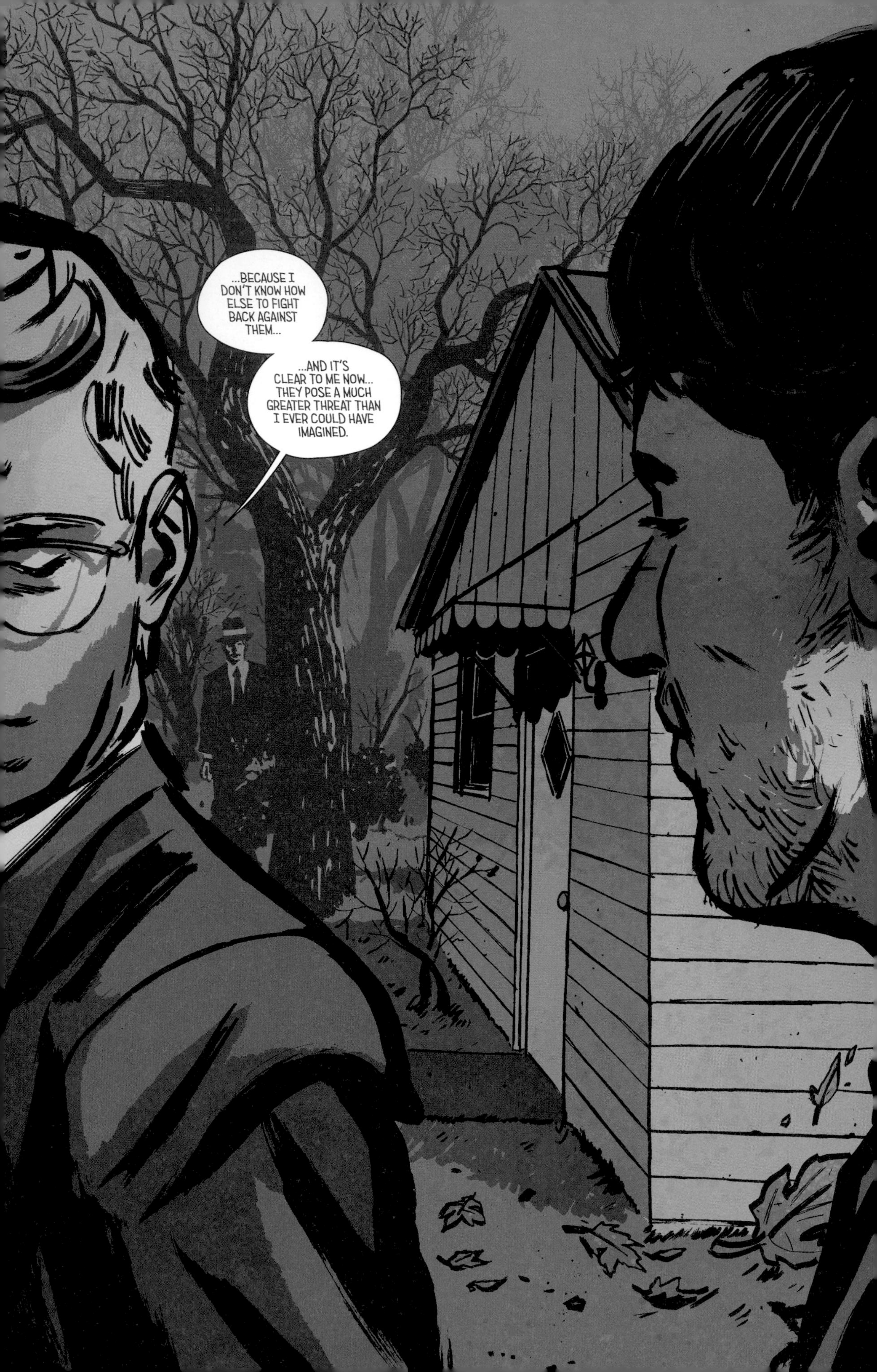
...BECAUSE I DON'T KNOW HOW ELSE TO FIGHT BACK AGAINST THEM...
...AND IT'S CLEAR TO ME NOW... THEY POSE A MUCH GREATER THREAT THAN I EVER COULD HAVE IMAGINED.

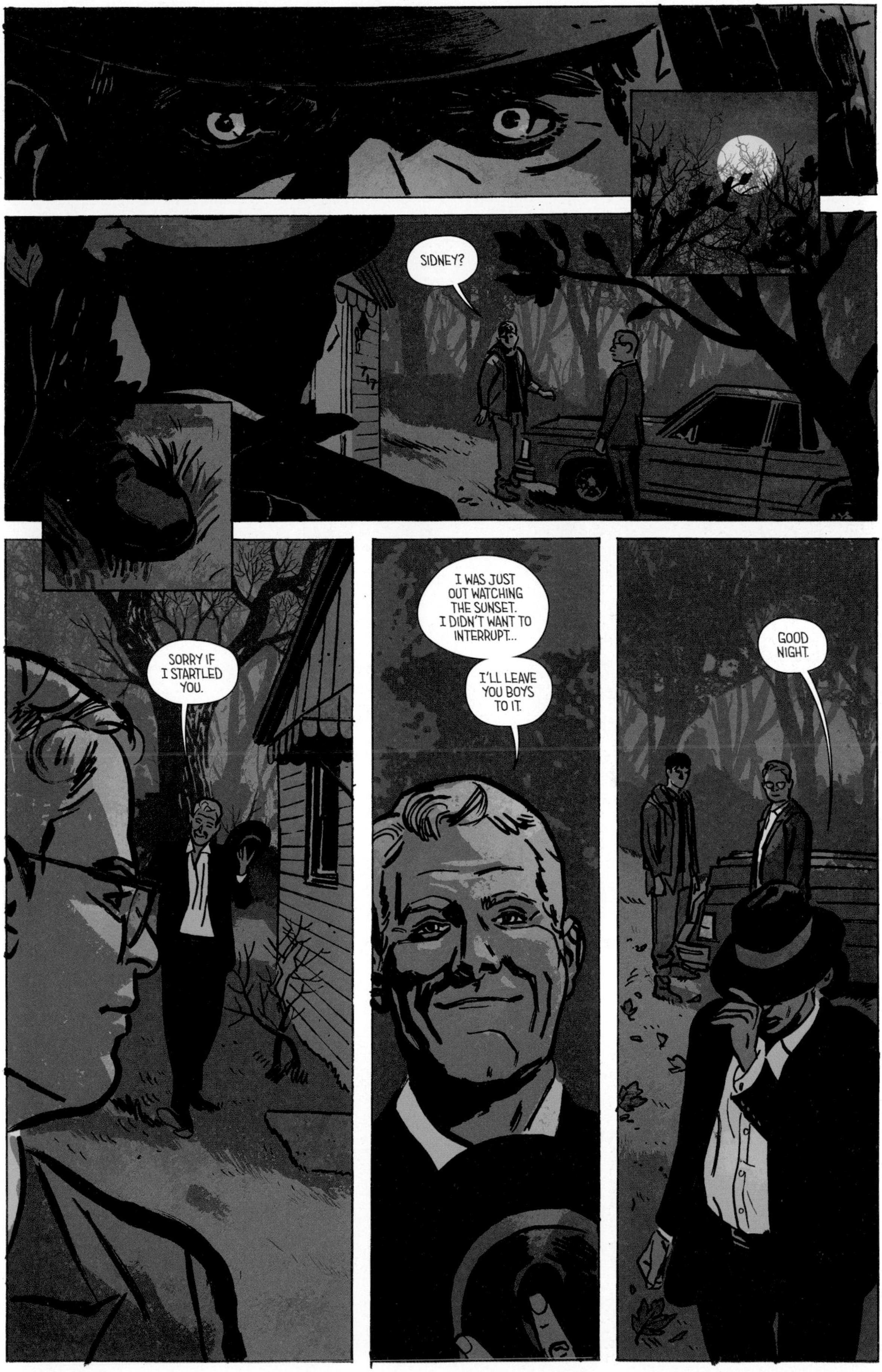
SIDNEY?
SORRY IF I STARTLED YOU.
I WAS JUST OUT WATCHING THE SUNSET. I DIDN'T WANT TO INTERRUPT...
I'LL LEAVE YOU BOYS TO IT.
GOOD NIGHT.

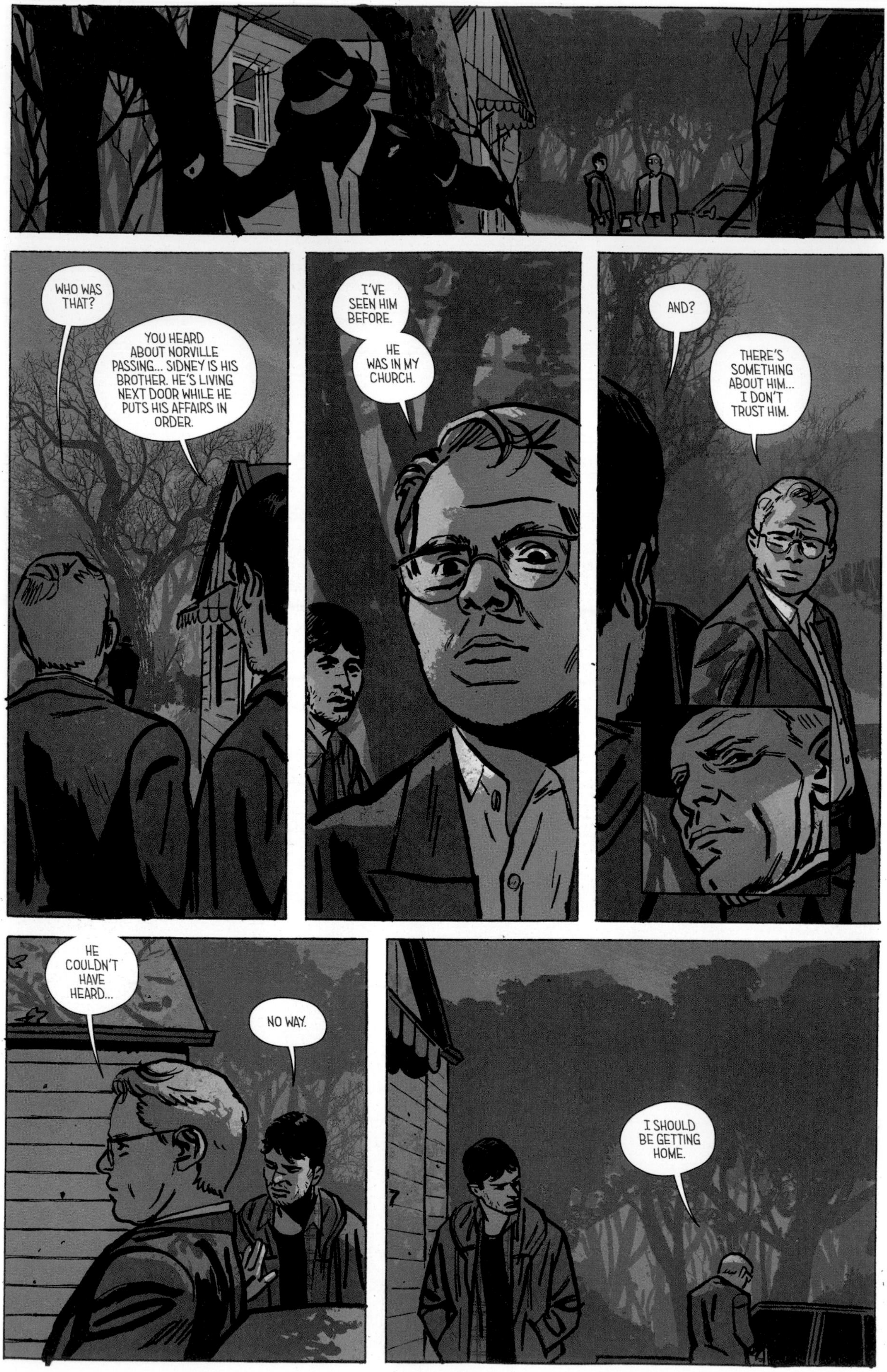
WHO WAS THAT?
YOU HEARD ABOUT NORVILLE PASSING... SIDNEY IS HIS BROTHER. HE'S LIVING NEXT DOOR WHILE HE PUTS HIS AFFAIRS IN ORDER.
I'VE SEEN HIM BEFORE.
HE WAS IN MY CHURCH.
AND?
THERE'S SOMETHING ABOUT HIM... I DON'T TRUST HIM.
HE COULDN'T HAVE HEARD...
NO WAY.
I SHOULD BE GETTING HOME.

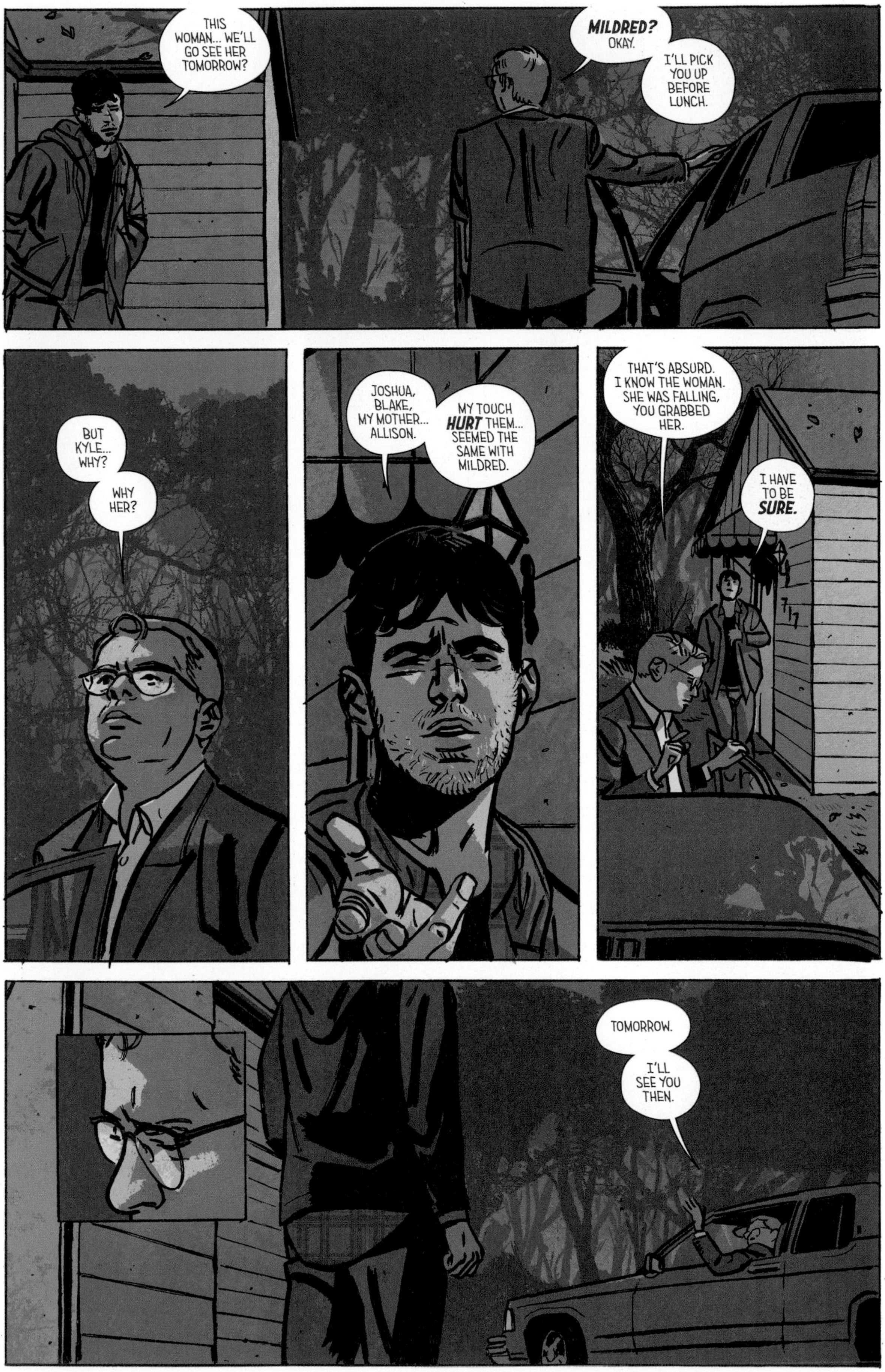
THIS WOMAN... WE'LL GO SEE HER TOMORROW?
MILDRED? OKAY.
I'LL PICK YOU UP BEFORE LUNCH.
BUT KYLE... WHY?
WHY HER?
JOSHUA, BLAKE, MY MOTHER... ALLISON.
MY TOUCH HURT THEM... SEEMED THE SAME WITH MILDRED.
THAT'S ABSURD. I KNOW THE WOMAN. SHE WAS FALLING, YOU GRABBED HER.
I HAVE TO BE SURE.
TOMORROW.
I'LL SEE YOU THEN.

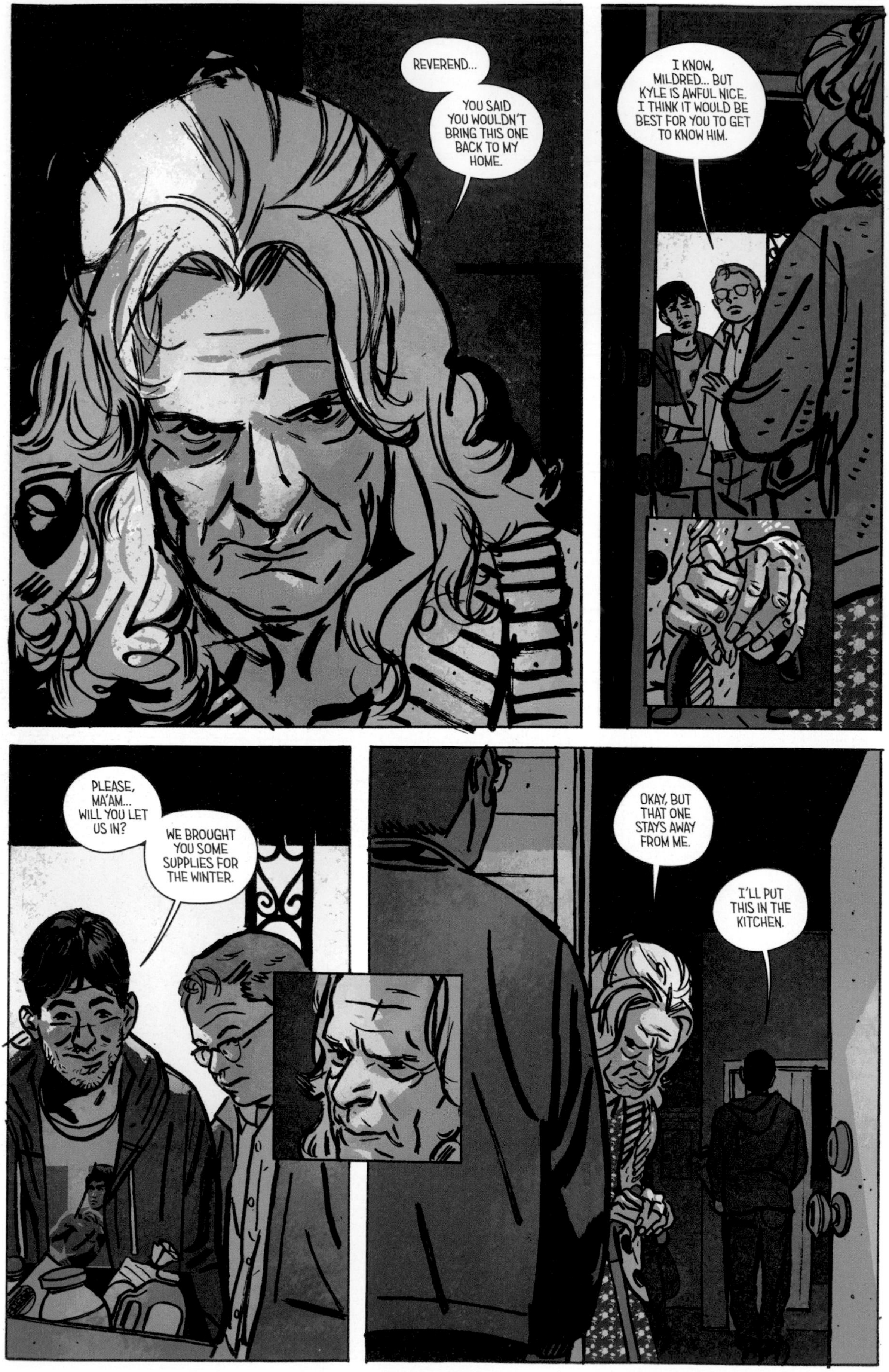
REVEREND...
YOU SAID YOU WOULDN'T BRING THIS ONE BACK TO MY HOME.
I KNOW, MILDRED... BUT KYLE IS AWFUL NICE. I THINK IT WOULD BE BEST FOR YOU TO GET TO KNOW HIM.
PLEASE, MA'AM... WILL YOU LET US IN?
WE BROUGHT YOU SOME SUPPLIES FOR THE WINTER.
OKAY, BUT THAT ONE STAYS AWAY FROM ME.
I'LL PUT THIS IN THE KITCHEN.

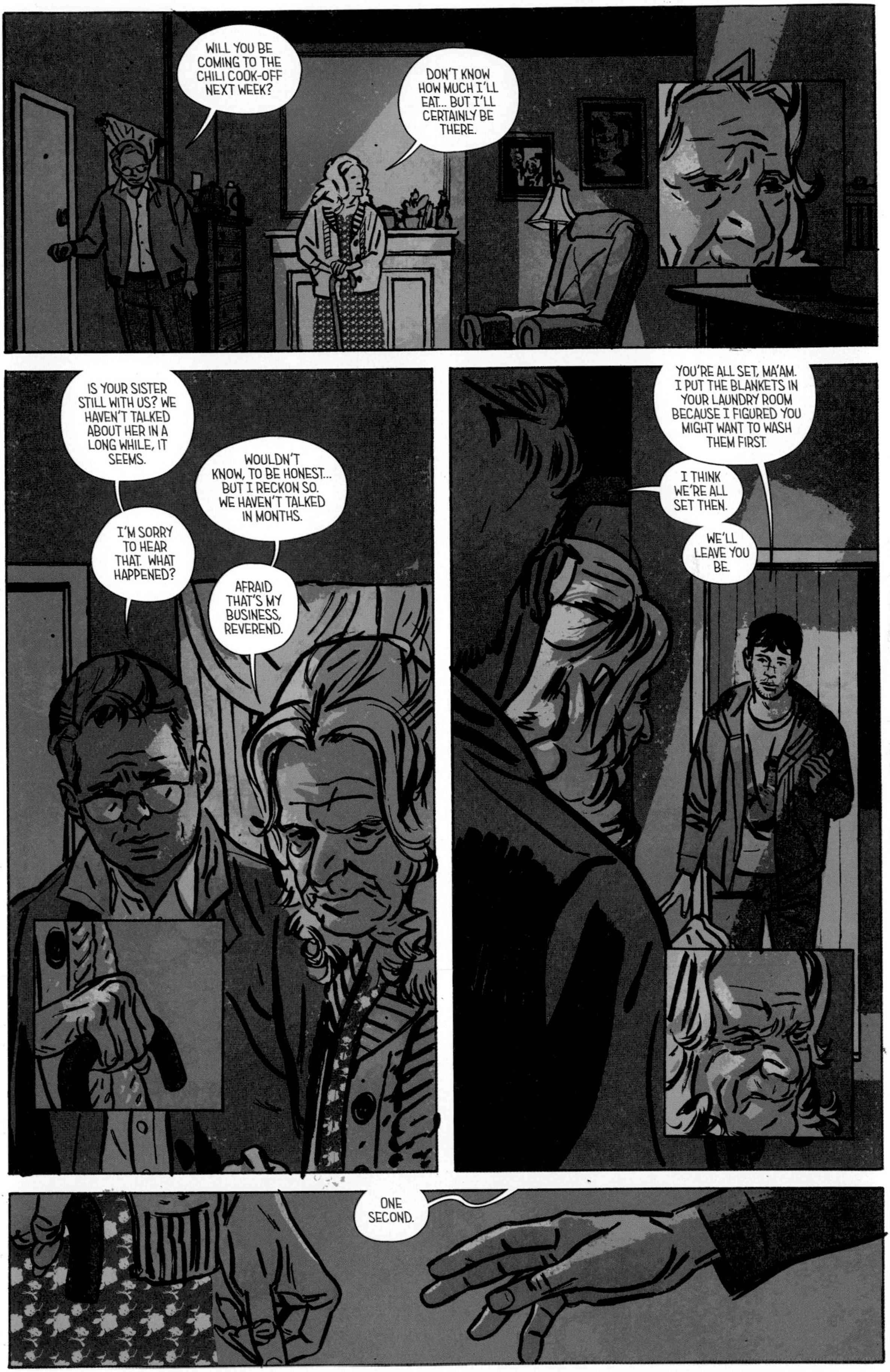
WILL YOU BE COMING TO THE CHILI COOK-OFF NEXT WEEK?
DON'T KNOW HOW MUCH I'LL EAT... BUT I'LL CERTAINLY BE THERE.
IS YOUR SISTER STILL WITH US? WE HAVEN'T TALKED ABOUT HER IN A LONG WHILE, IT SEEMS.
WOULDN'T KNOW, TO BE HONEST... BUT I RECKON SO. WE HAVEN'T TALKED IN MONTHS.
I'M SORRY TO HEAR THAT. WHAT HAPPENED?
AFRAID THAT'S MY BUSINESS, REVEREND.
YOU'RE ALL SET, MA'AM. I PUT THE BLANKETS IN YOUR LAUNDRY ROOM BECAUSE I FIGURED YOU MIGHT WANT TO WASH THEM FIRST.
I THINK WE'RE ALL SET THEN.
WE'LL LEAVE YOU BE.
ONE SECOND.

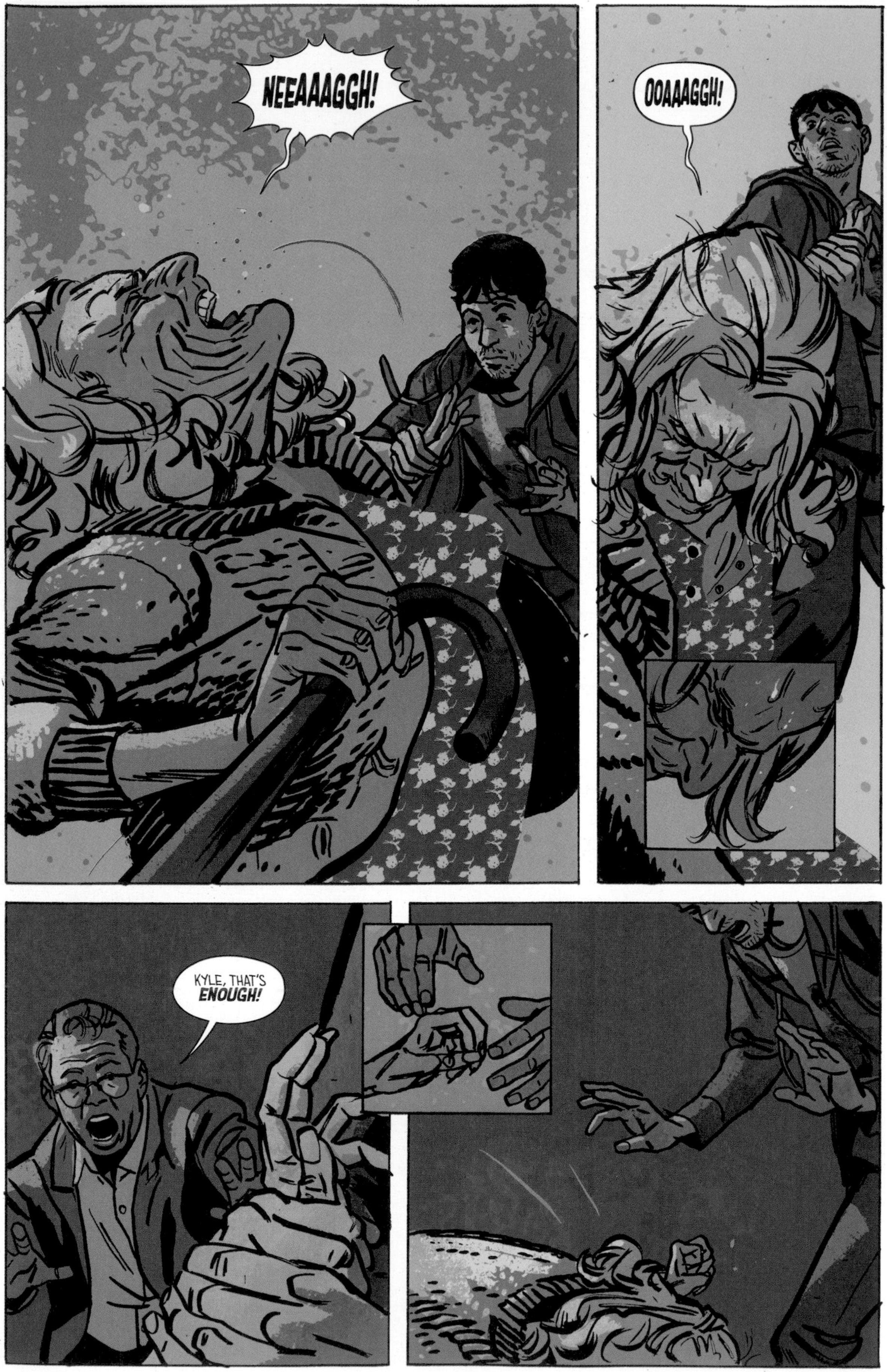
NEEAAAGGH!
OOAAAGGH!
KYLE, THAT'S ENOUGH!

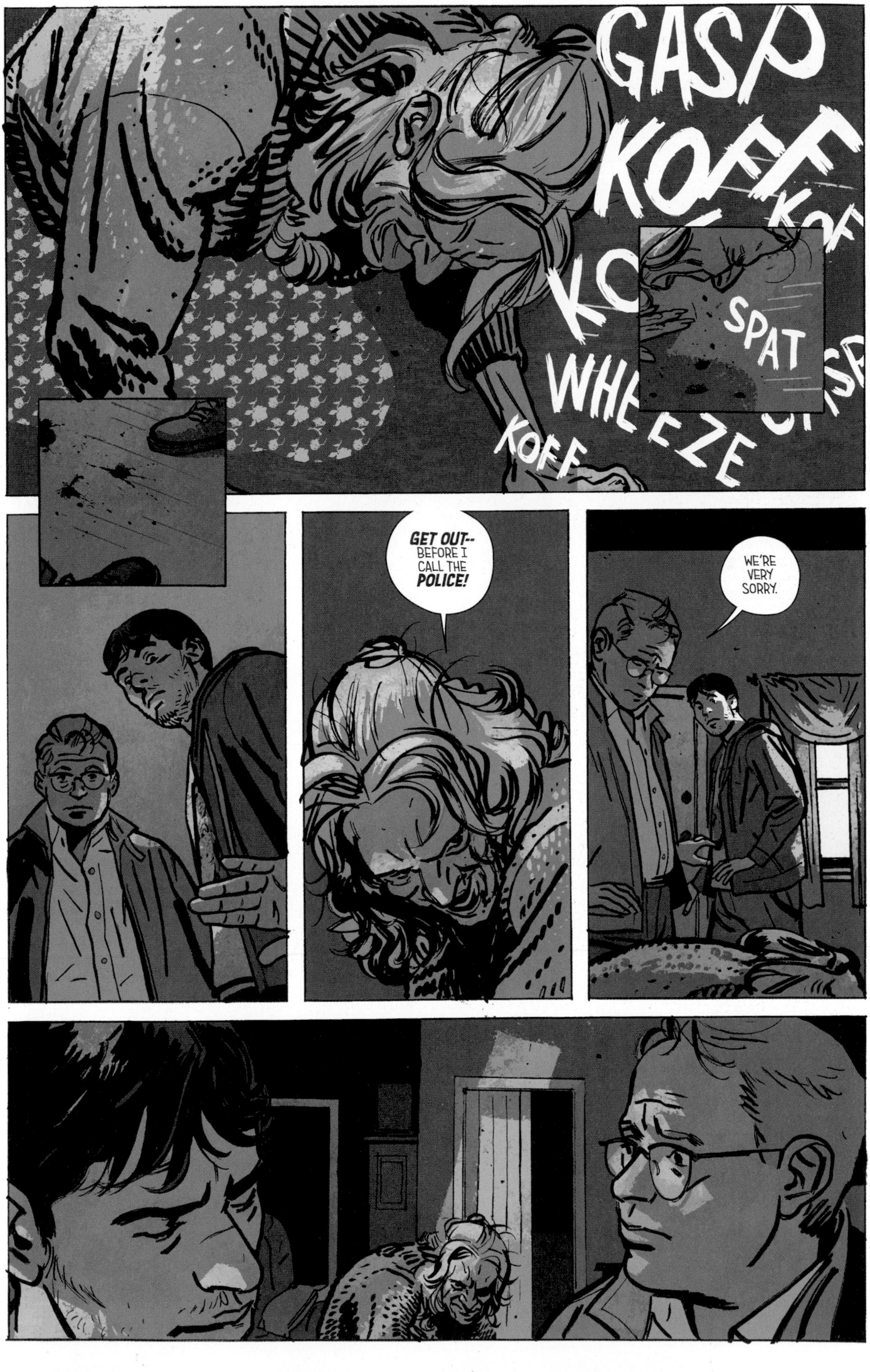
GASP
KOFF
KOF
KOFF
SPAT
WHEEZE
KOFF
GET OUT-- BEFORE I CALL THE POLICE!
WE'RE VERY SORRY.

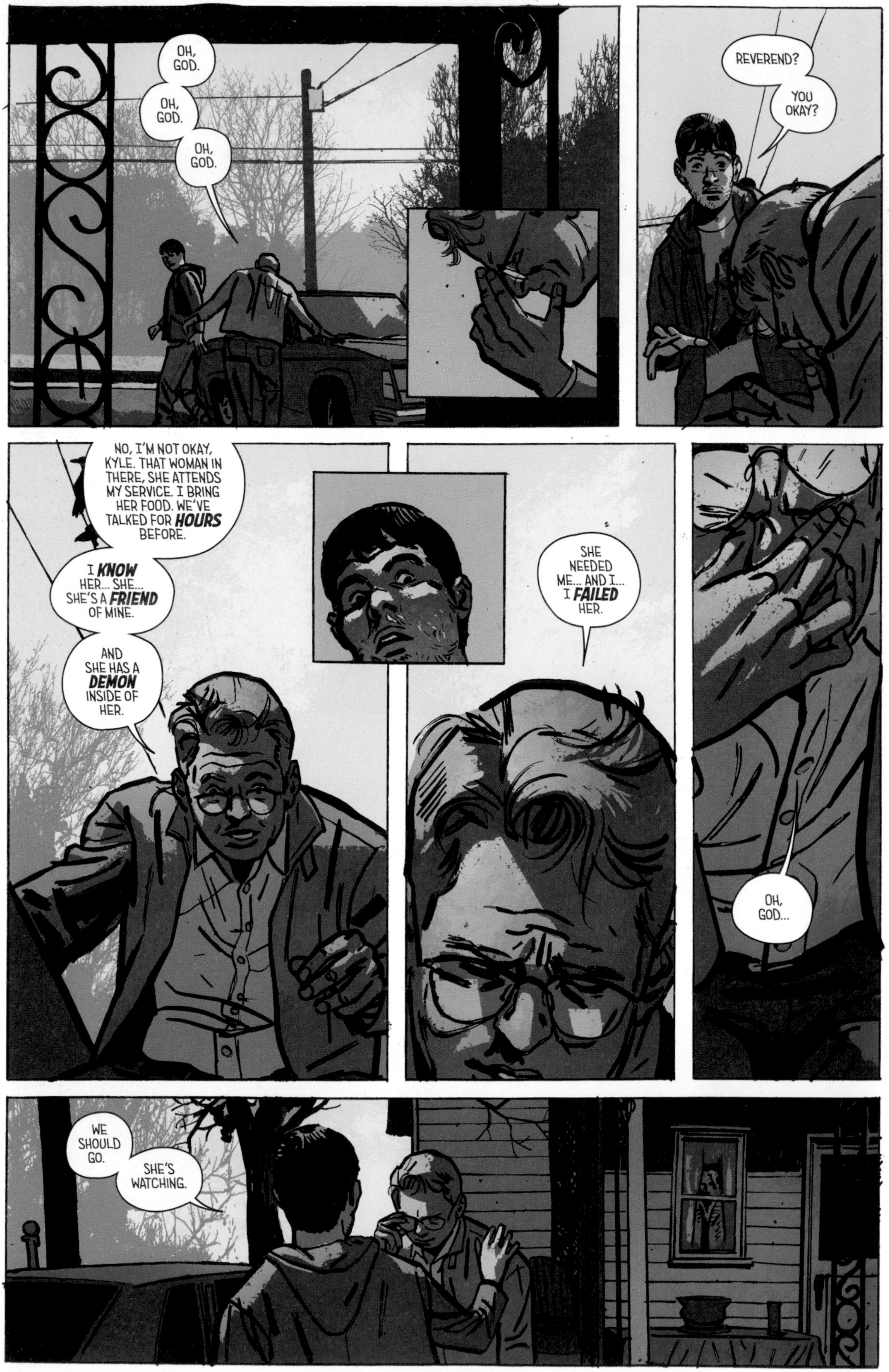
OH, GOD.
OH, GOD.
OH, GOD.
REVEREND?
YOU OKAY?
NO, I'M NOT OKAY, KYLE. THAT WOMAN IN THERE, SHE ATTENDS MY SERVICE. I BRING HER FOOD. WE'VE TALKED FOR HOURS BEFORE.
I KNOW HER... SHE... SHE'S A FRIEND OF MINE.
AND SHE HAS A DEMON INSIDE OF HER.
SHE NEEDED ME... AND I... I FAILED HER.
OH, GOD...
WE SHOULD GO.
SHE'S WATCHING.

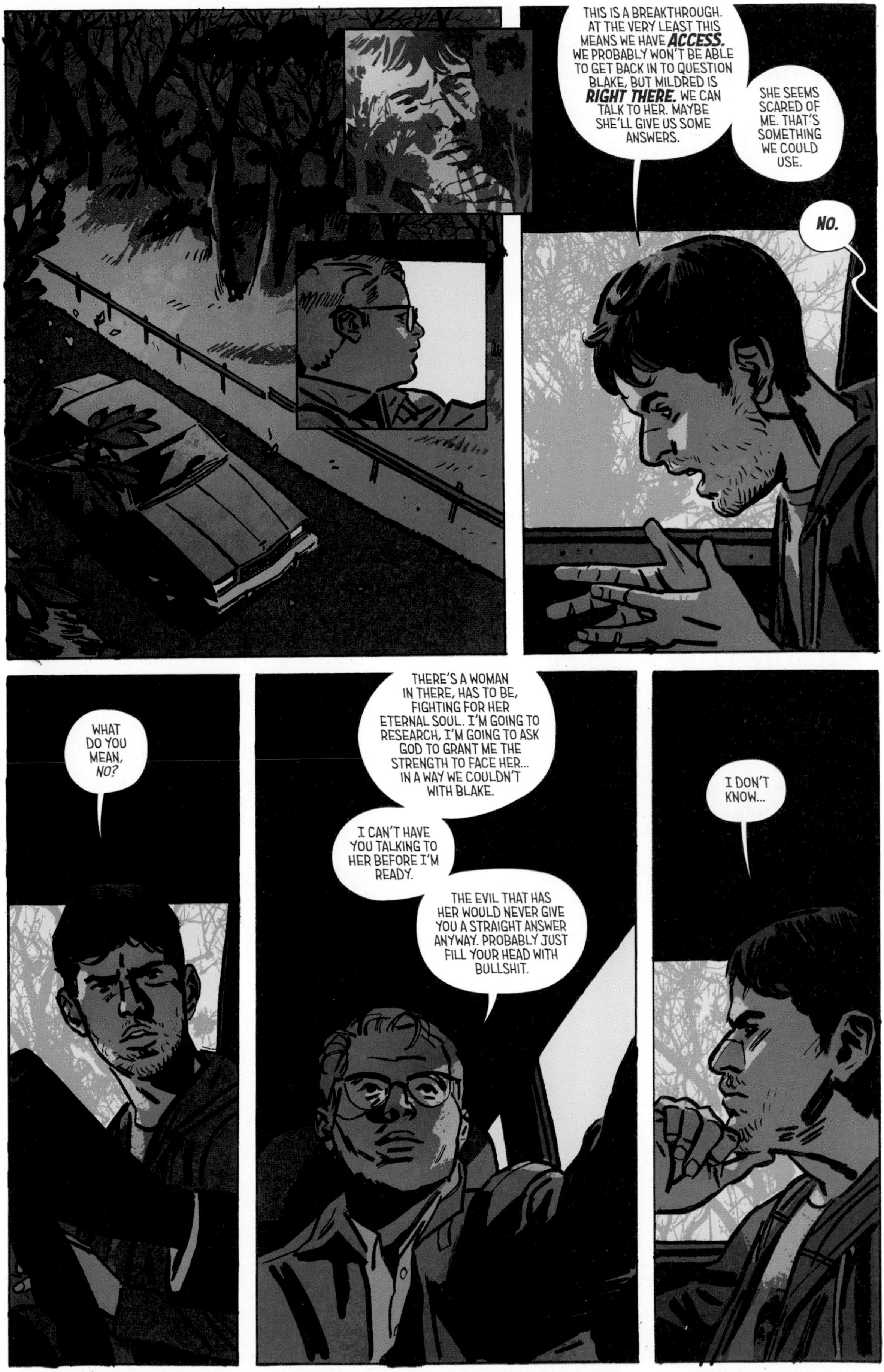
THIS IS A BREAKTHROUGH. AT THE VERY LEAST THIS MEANS WE HAVE **ACCESS.** WE PROBABLY WON'T BE ABLE TO GET BACK IN TO QUESTION BLAKE, BUT MILDRED IS **RIGHT THERE.** WE CAN TALK TO HER. MAYBE SHE'LL GIVE US SOME ANSWERS.
SHE SEEMS SCARED OF ME. THAT'S SOMETHING WE COULD USE.
NO.
WHAT DO YOU MEAN, *NO?*
THERE'S A WOMAN IN THERE, HAS TO BE, FIGHTING FOR HER ETERNAL SOUL. I'M GOING TO RESEARCH, I'M GOING TO ASK GOD TO GRANT ME THE STRENGTH TO FACE HER... IN A WAY WE COULDN'T WITH BLAKE.
I CAN'T HAVE YOU TALKING TO HER BEFORE I'M READY.
THE EVIL THAT HAS HER WOULD NEVER GIVE YOU A STRAIGHT ANSWER ANYWAY. PROBABLY JUST FILL YOUR HEAD WITH BULLSHIT.
I DON'T KNOW...

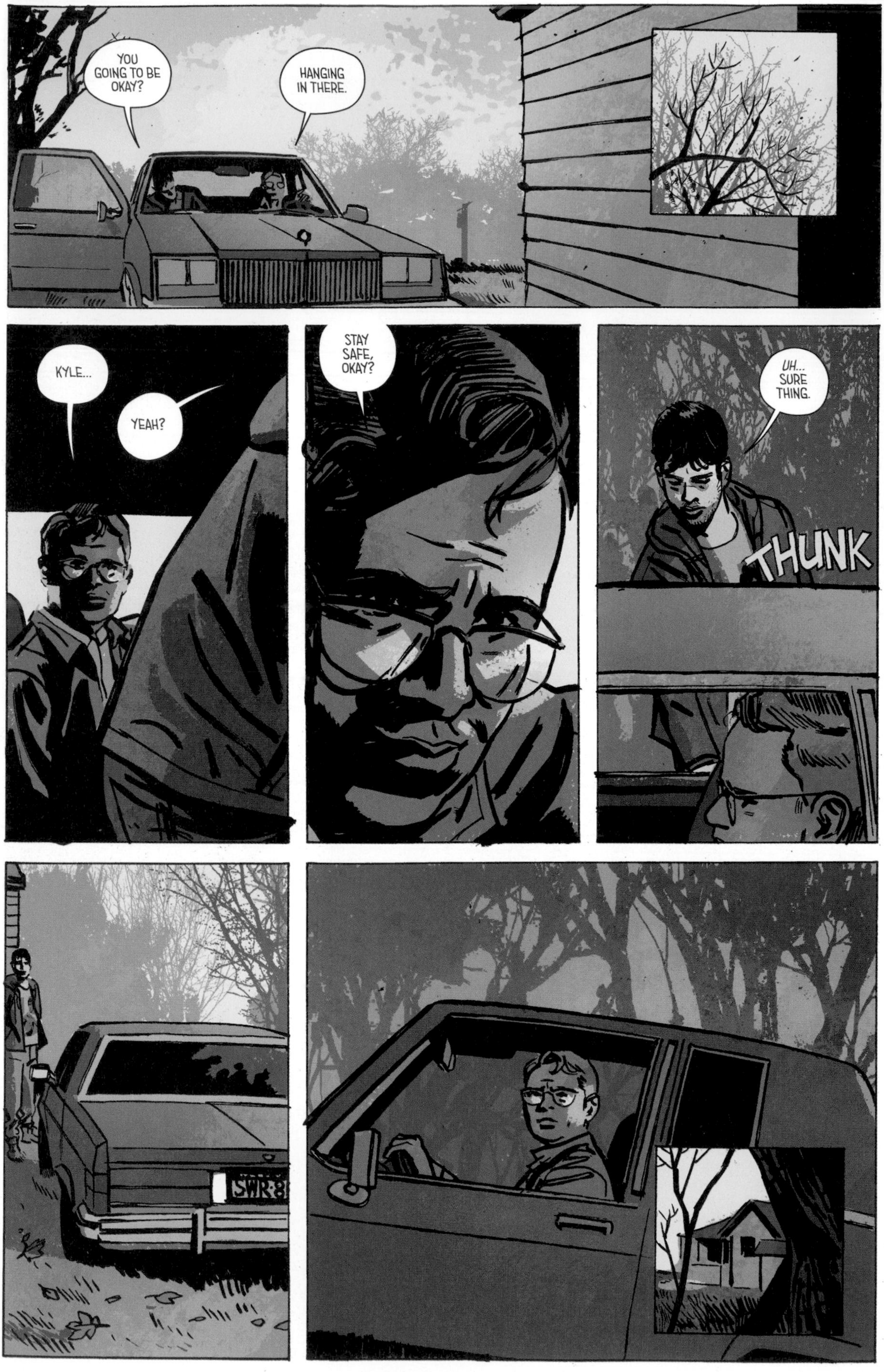
YOU GOING TO BE OKAY?
HANGING IN THERE.
KYLE...
YEAH?
STAY SAFE, OKAY?
UH... SURE THING.
THUNK

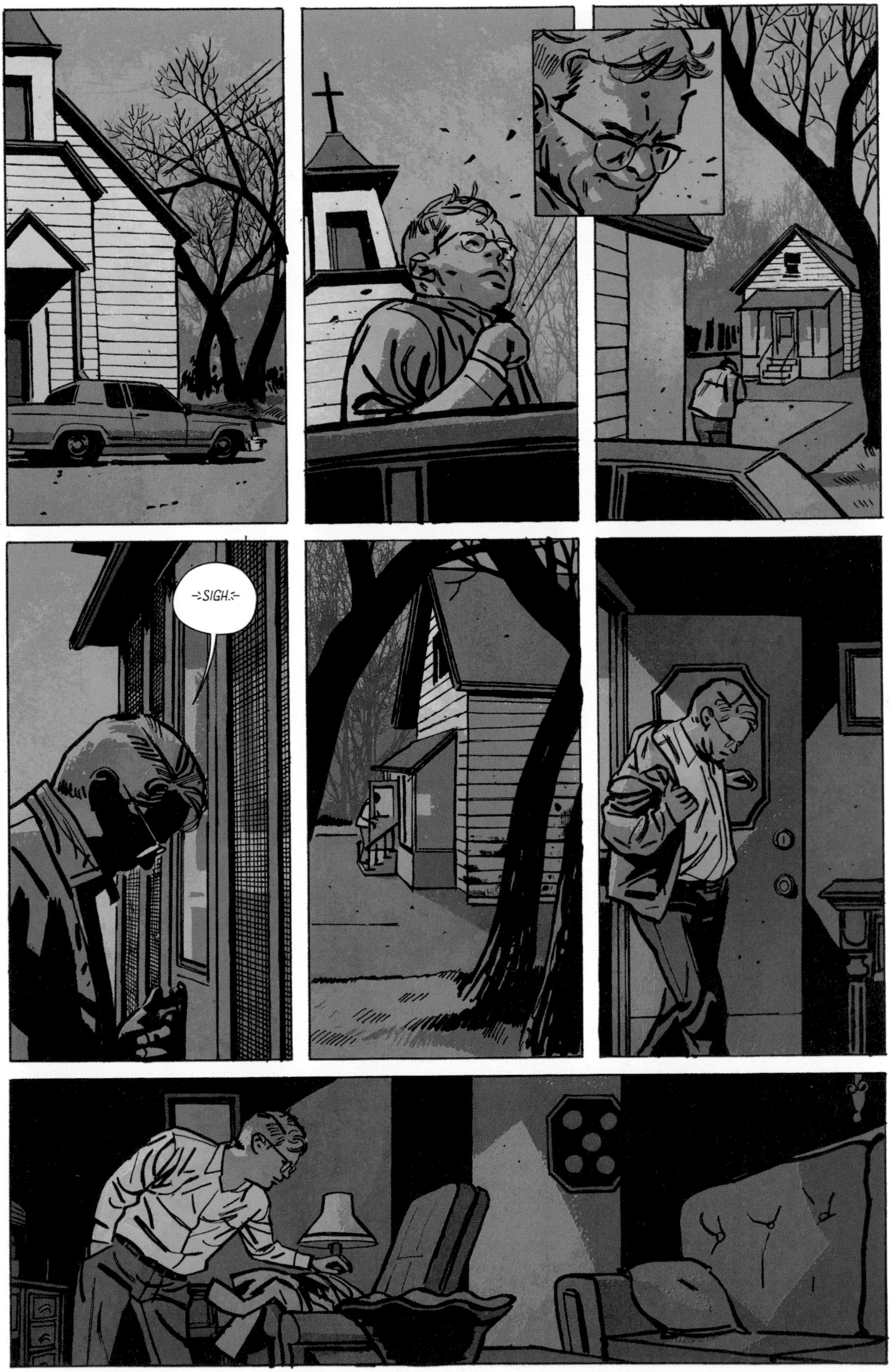
-SIGH.-

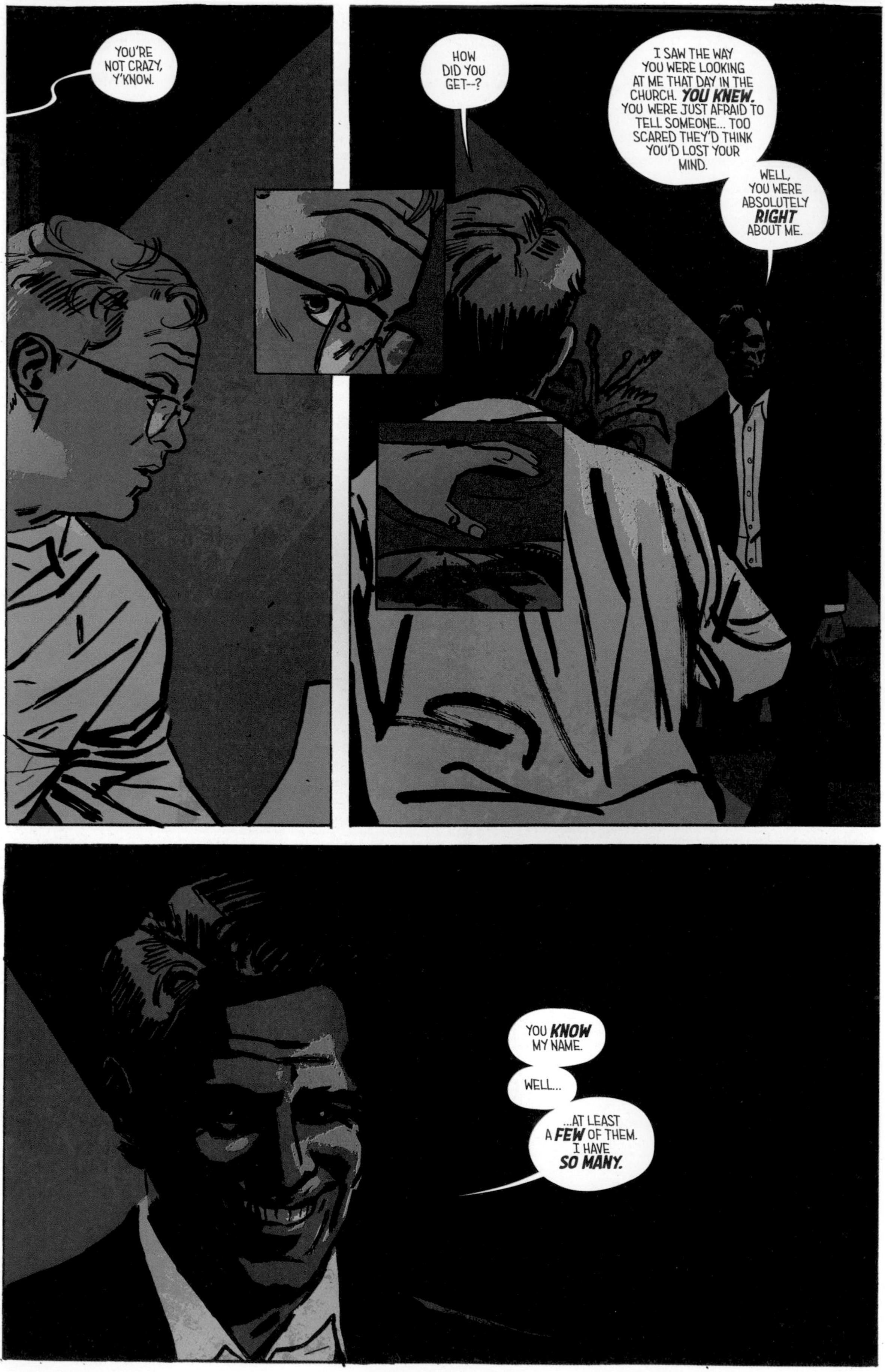
YOU'RE NOT CRAZY, Y'KNOW.
HOW DID YOU GET--?
I SAW THE WAY YOU WERE LOOKING AT ME THAT DAY IN THE CHURCH. YOU KNEW. YOU WERE JUST AFRAID TO TELL SOMEONE... TOO SCARED THEY'D THINK YOU'D LOST YOUR MIND.
WELL, YOU WERE ABSOLUTELY RIGHT ABOUT ME.
YOU KNOW MY NAME.
WELL...
...AT LEAST A FEW OF THEM. I HAVE SO MANY.

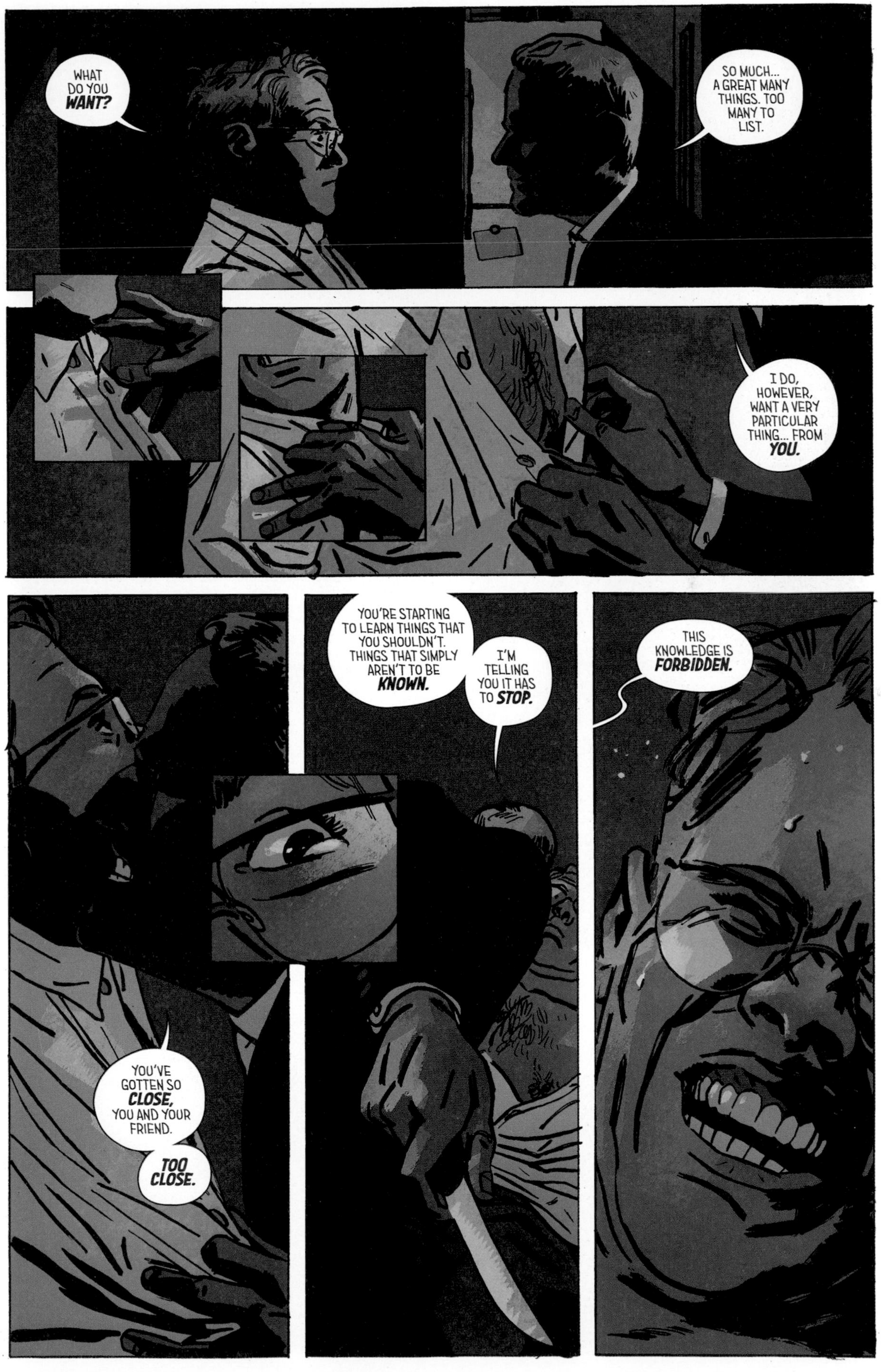
WHAT DO YOU WANT?
SO MUCH... A GREAT MANY THINGS. TOO MANY TO LIST.
I DO, HOWEVER, WANT A VERY PARTICULAR THING... FROM YOU.
YOU'VE GOTTEN SO CLOSE, YOU AND YOUR FRIEND.
TOO CLOSE.
YOU'RE STARTING TO LEARN THINGS THAT YOU SHOULDN'T. THINGS THAT SIMPLY AREN'T TO BE KNOWN.
I'M TELLING YOU IT HAS TO STOP.
THIS KNOWLEDGE IS FORBIDDEN.

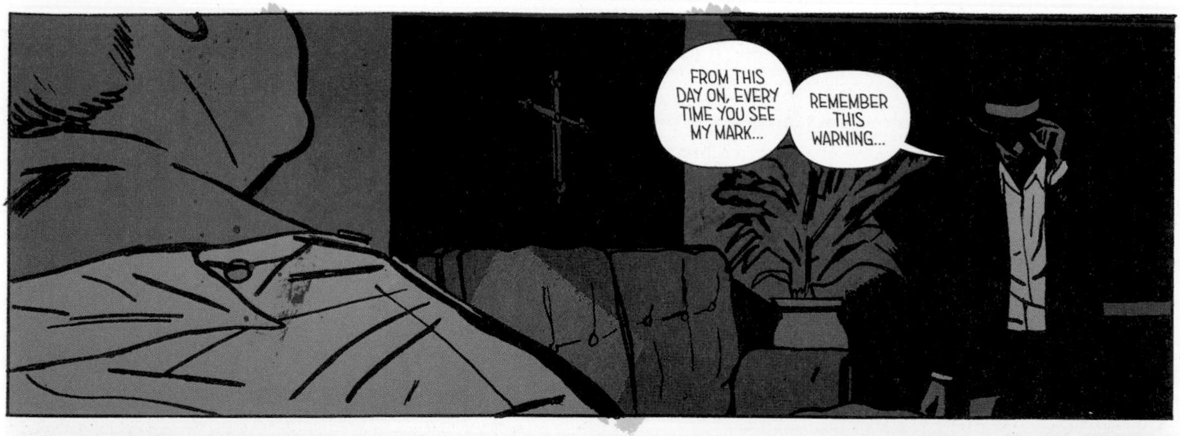
FROM THIS DAY ON, EVERY TIME YOU SEE MY MARK...
REMEMBER THIS WARNING...

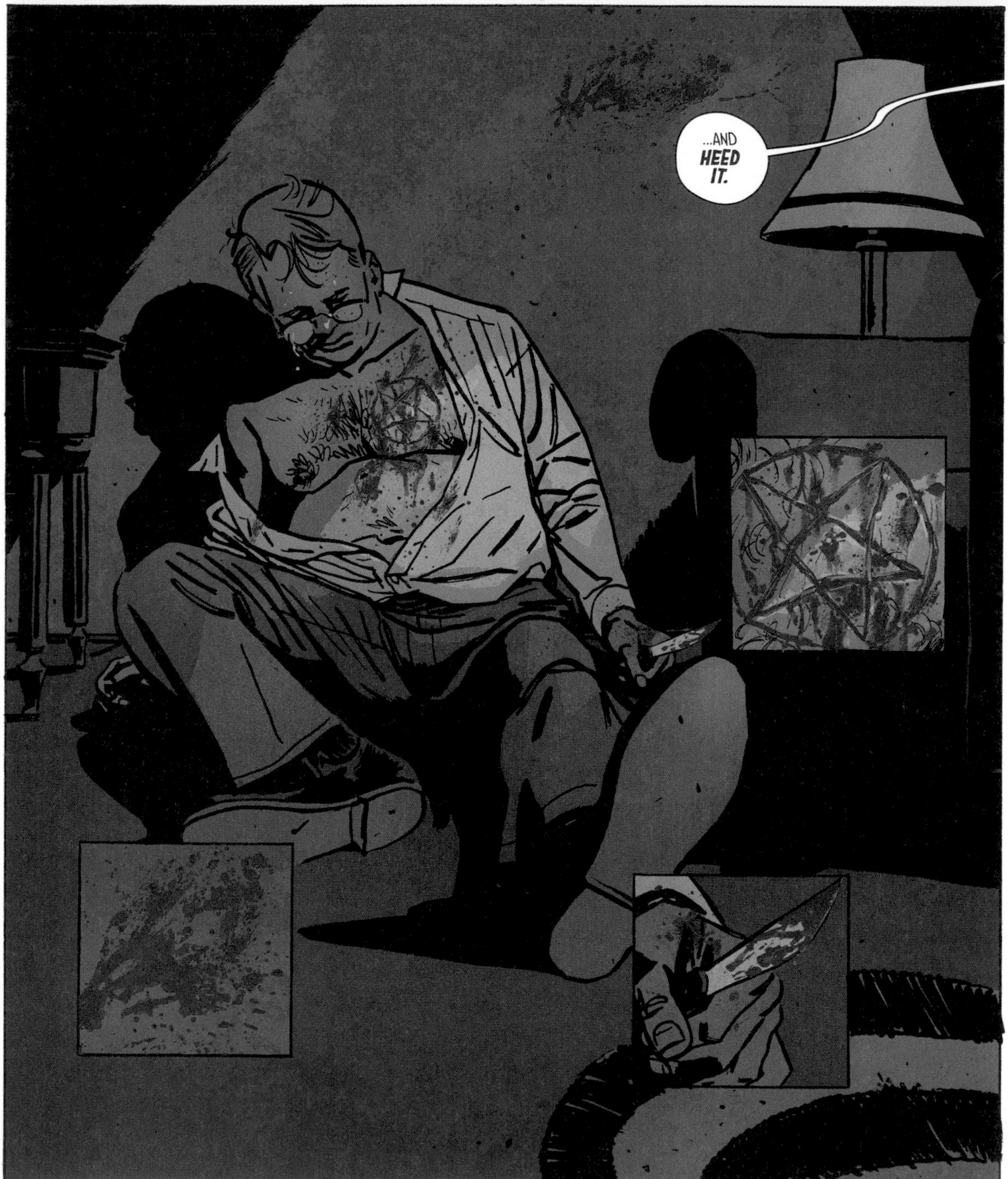
...AND HEED IT.

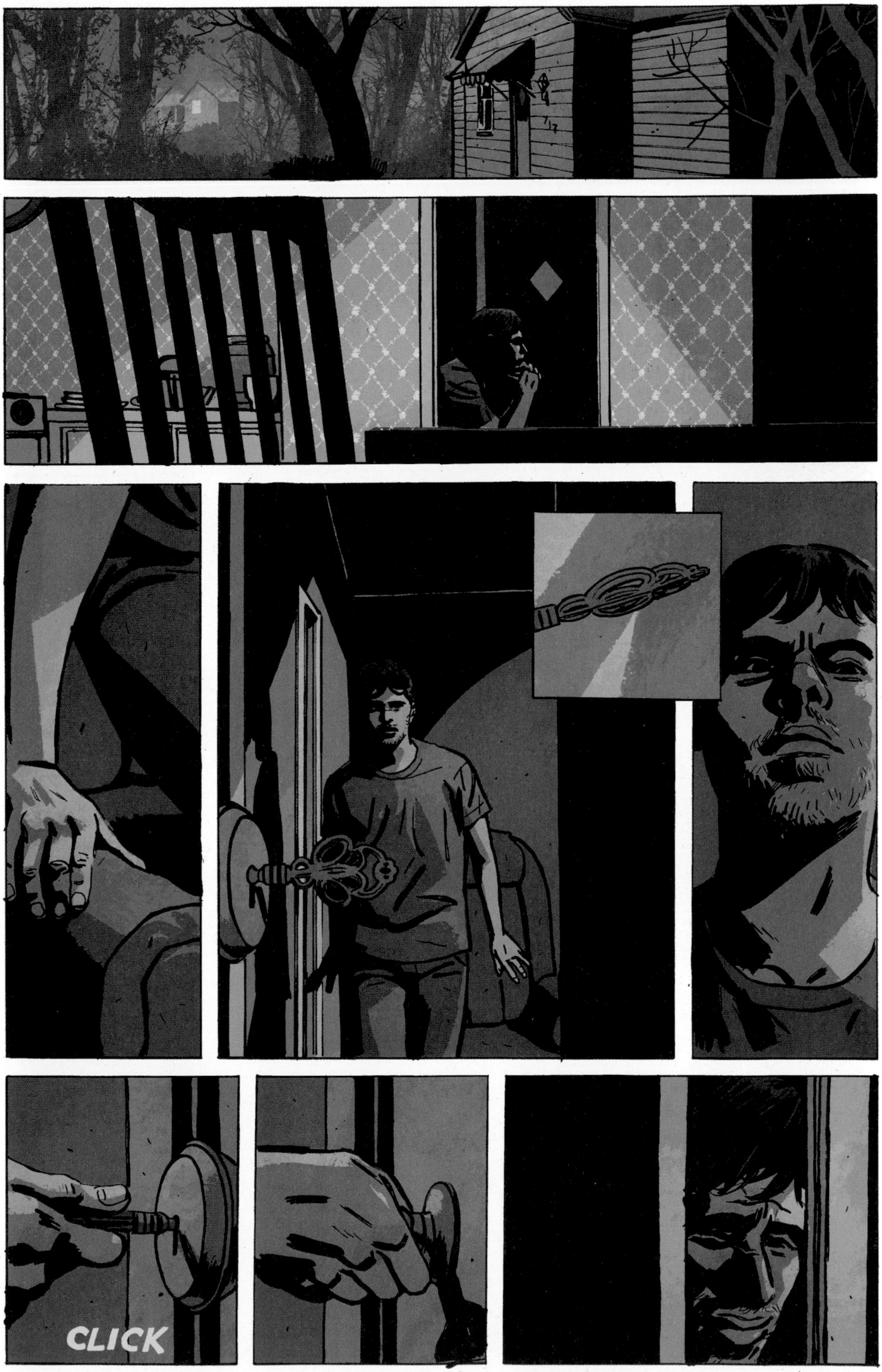
CLICK

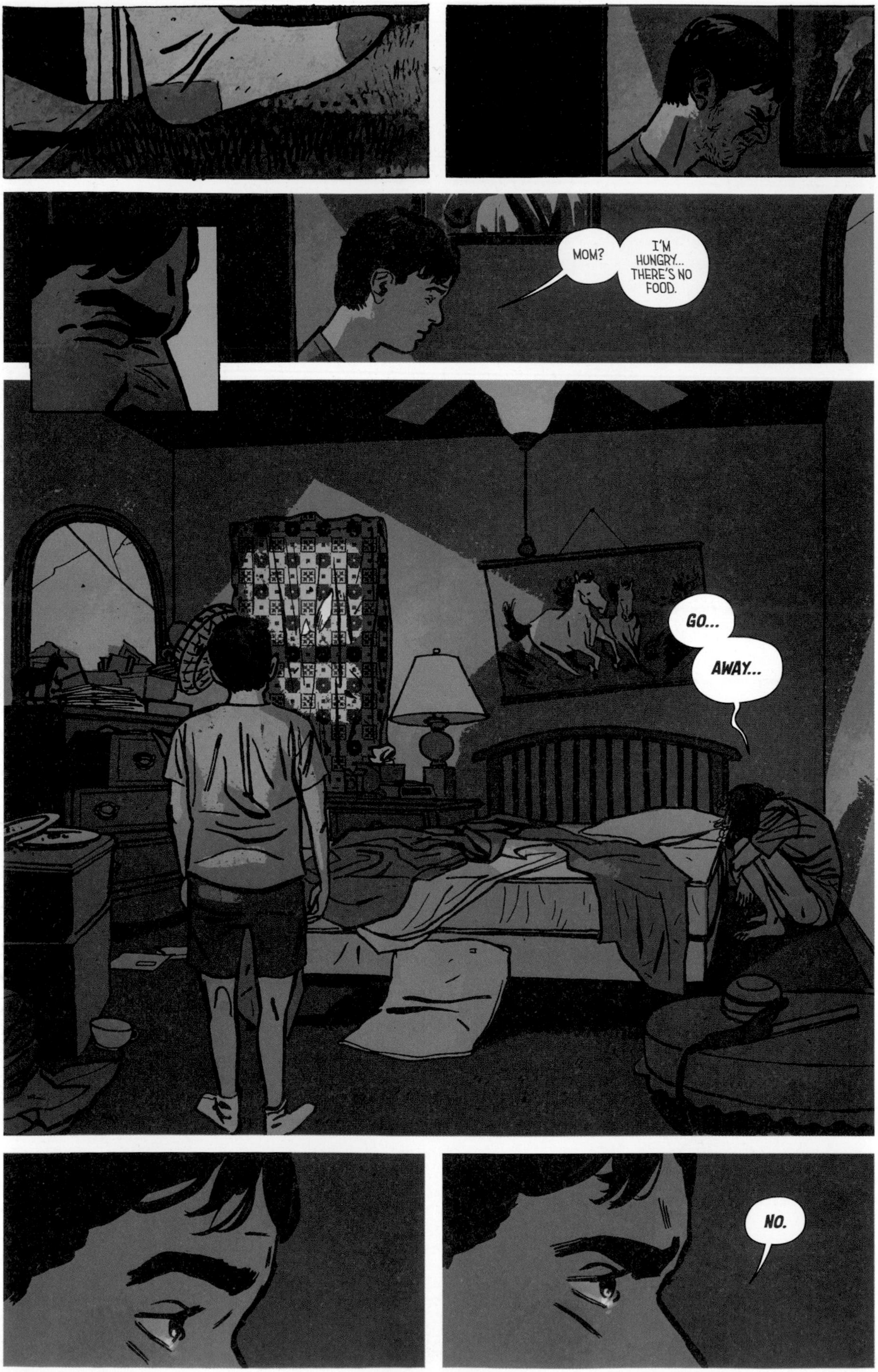
MOM?
I'M HUNGRY... THERE'S NO FOOD.
GO...
AWAY...
NO.

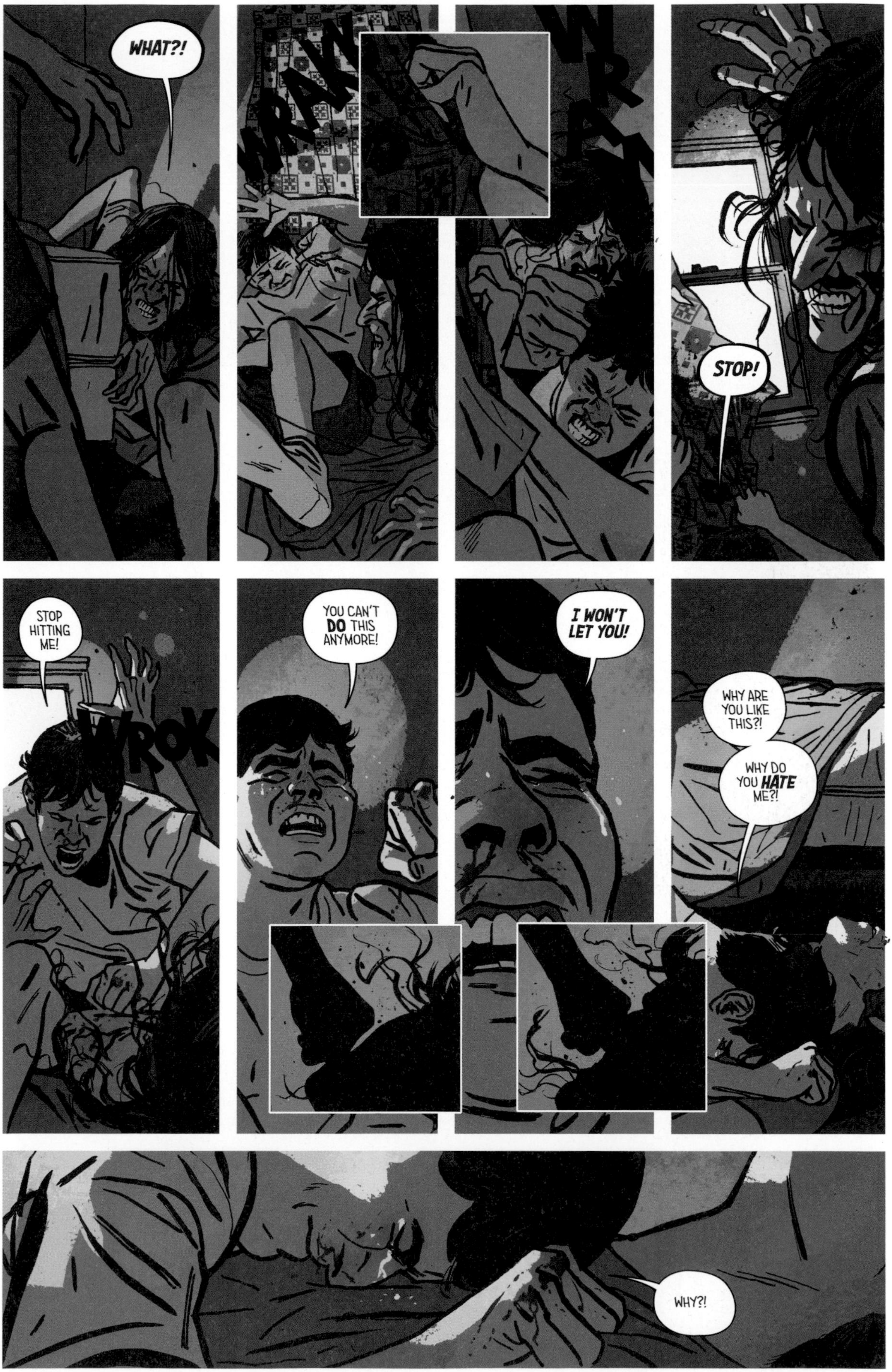
WHAT?!
STOP!
STOP HITTING ME!
WROK
YOU CAN'T DO THIS ANYMORE!
I WON'T LET YOU!
WHY ARE YOU LIKE THIS?!
WHY DO YOU HATE ME?!
WHY?!

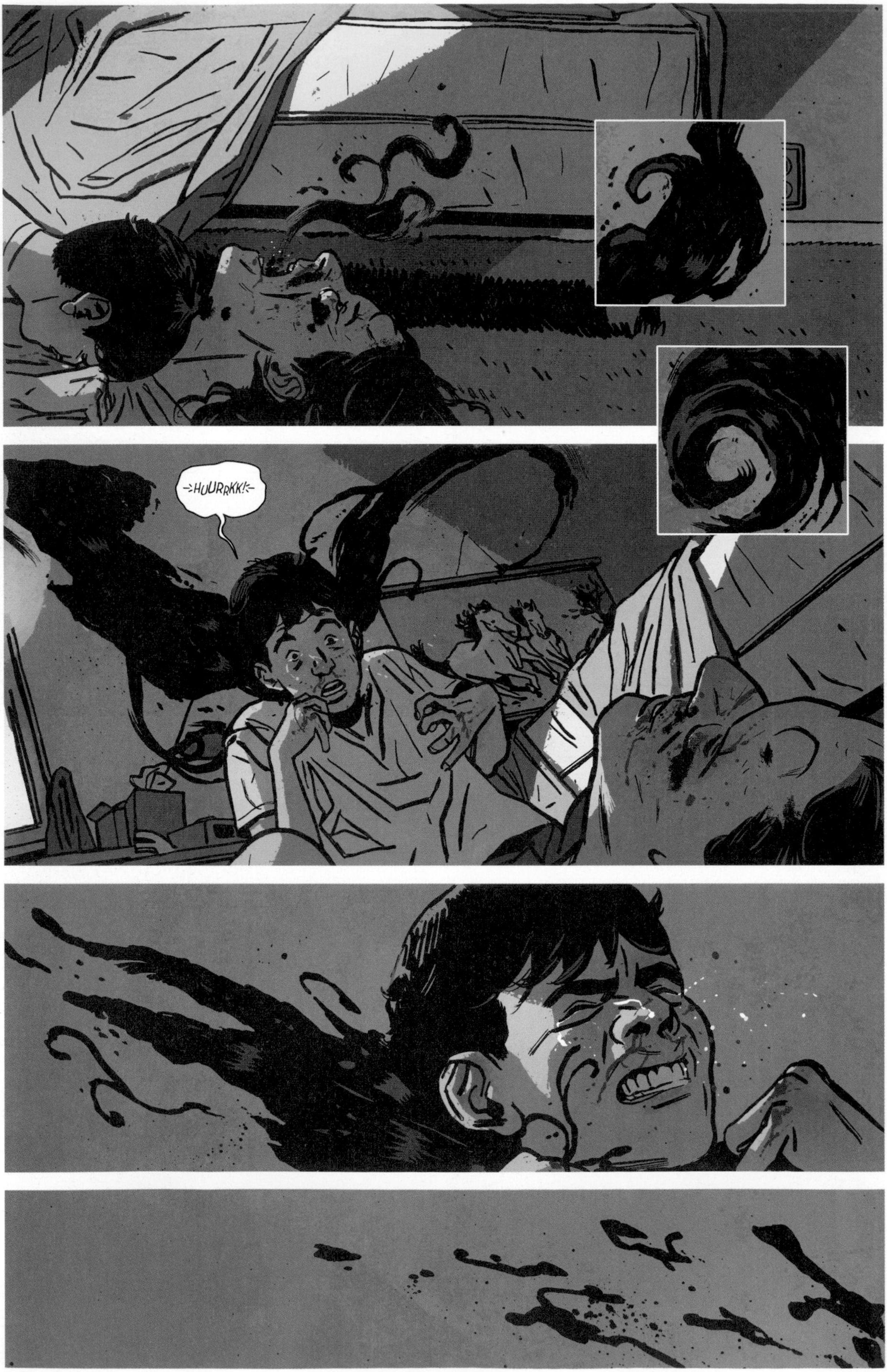
HUURRKK!

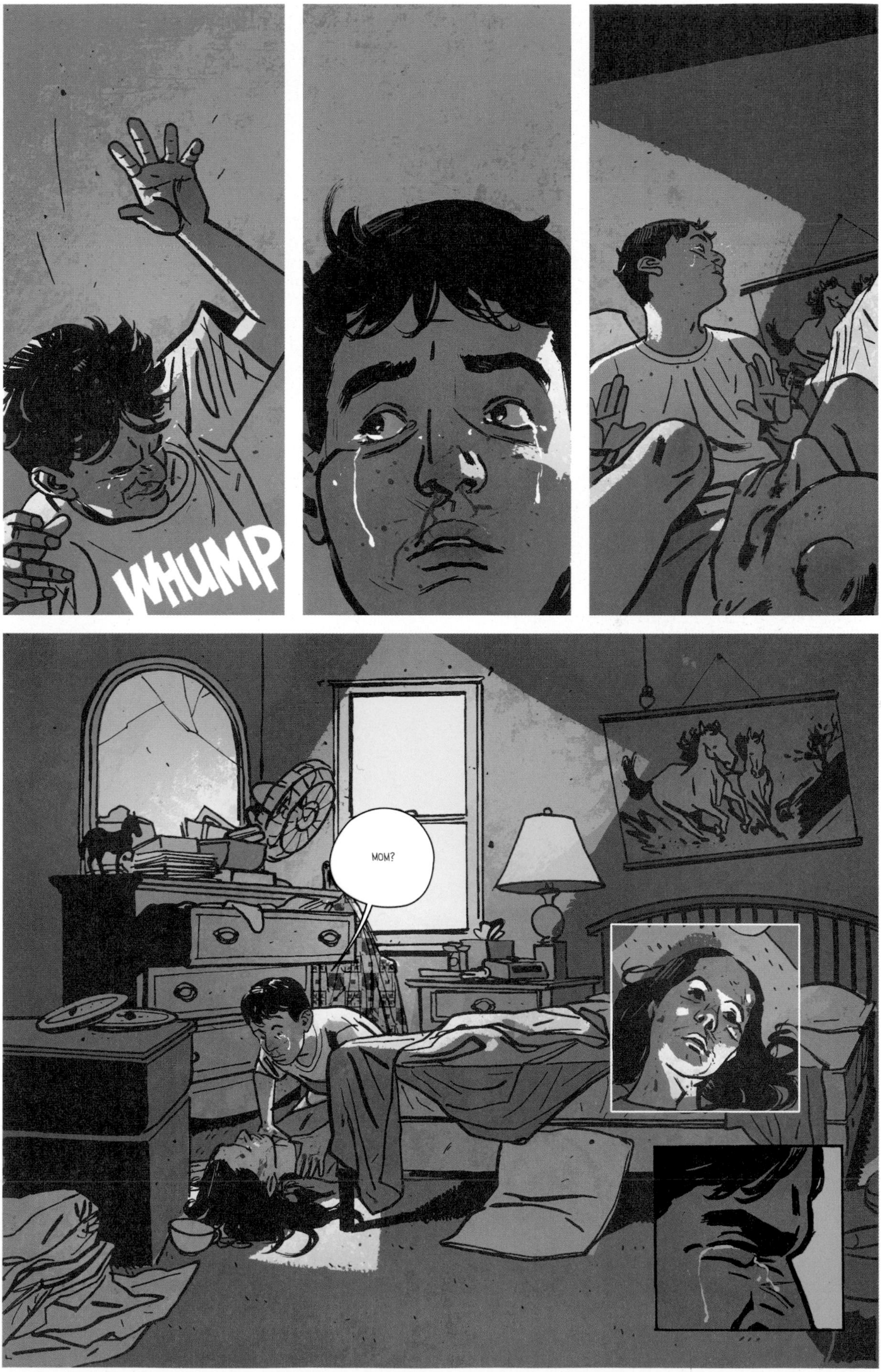
WHUMP
MOM?

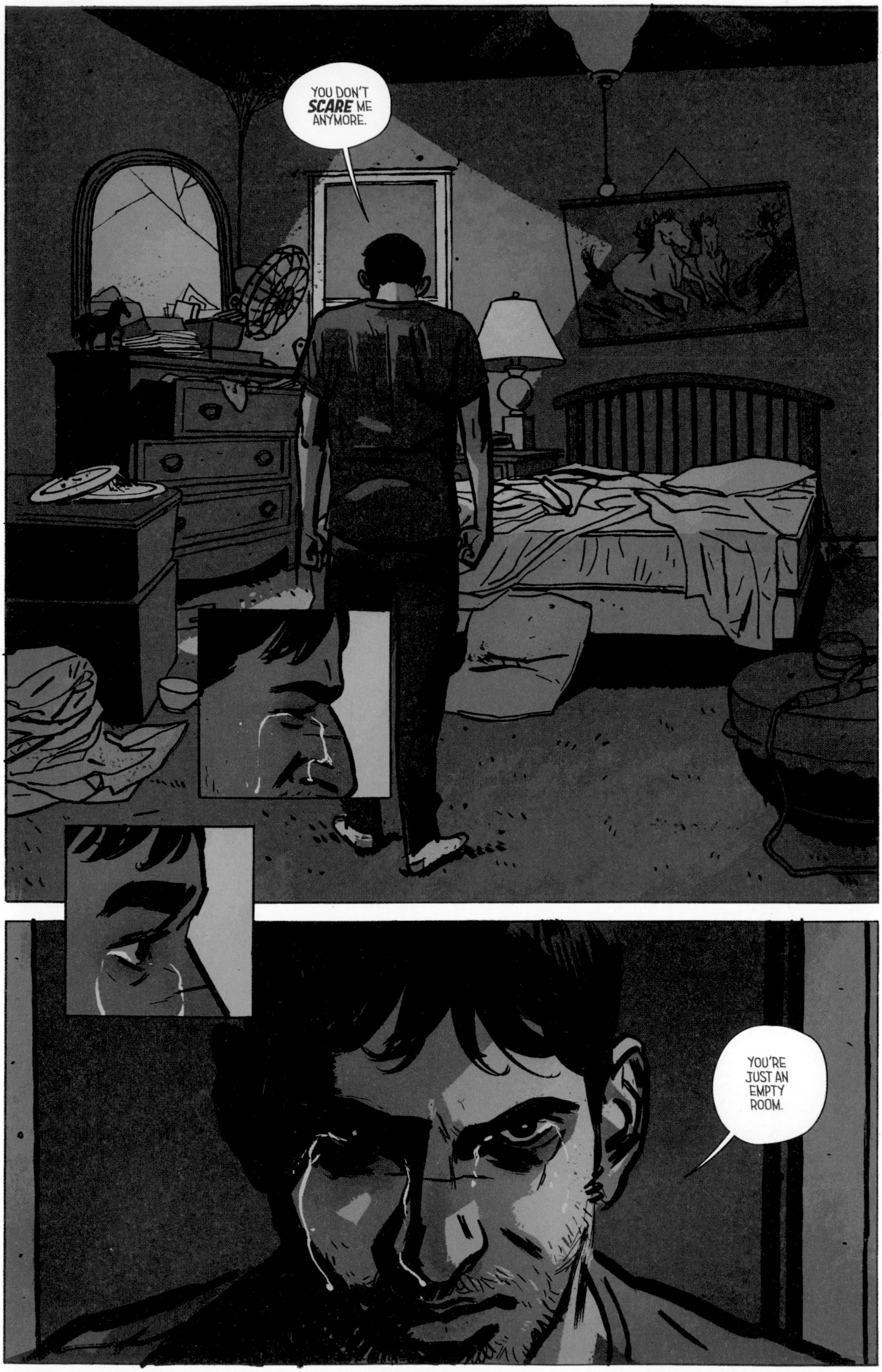
YOU DON'T SCARE ME ANYMORE.
YOU'RE JUST AN EMPTY ROOM.

TO BE CONTINUED

"Seems like they've been trying to hurt me my whole life."

"...I need to find out why."

FOR MORE TALES FROM **ROBERT KIRKMAN** AND **SKYBOUND**

ROBERT KIRKMAN CHARLIE ADLARD STEFANO GAUDIANO CLIFF RATHBURN
THE WALKING DEAD
VOLUME 22
A NEW BEGINNING

VOL. 1: DAYS GONE BYE TP
ISBN: 978-1-58240-672-5
$14.99

VOL. 2: MILES BEHIND US TP
ISBN: 978-1-58240-775-3
$14.99

VOL. 3: SAFETY BEHIND BARS TP
ISBN: 978-1-58240-805-7
$14.99

VOL. 4: THE HEART'S DESIRE TP
ISBN: 978-1-58240-530-8
$14.99

VOL. 5: THE BEST DEFENSE TP
ISBN: 978-1-58240-612-1
$14.99

VOL. 6: THIS SORROWFUL LIFE TP
ISBN: 978-1-58240-684-8
$14.99

VOL. 7: THE CALM BEFORE TP
ISBN: 978-1-58240-828-6
$14.99

VOL. 8: MADE TO SUFFER TP
ISBN: 978-1-58240-883-5
$14.99

VOL. 9: HERE WE REMAIN TP
ISBN: 978-1-60706-022-2
$14.99

VOL. 10: WHAT WE BECOME TP
ISBN: 978-1-60706-075-8
$14.99

VOL. 11: FEAR THE HUNTERS TP
ISBN: 978-1-60706-181-6
$14.99

VOL. 12: LIFE AMONG THEM TP
ISBN: 978-1-60706-254-7
$14.99

VOL. 13: TOO FAR GONE TP
ISBN: 978-1-60706-329-2
$14.99

VOL. 14: NO WAY OUT TP
ISBN: 978-1-60706-392-6
$14.99

VOL. 15: WE FIND OURSELVES TP
ISBN: 978-1-60706-440-4
$14.99

VOL. 16: A LARGER WORLD TP
ISBN: 978-1-60706-559-3
$14.99

VOL. 17: SOMETHING TO FEAR TP
ISBN: 978-1-60706-615-6
$14.99

VOL. 18: WHAT COMES AFTER TP
ISBN: 978-1-60706-687-3
$14.99

VOL. 19: MARCH TO WAR TP
ISBN: 978-1-60706-818-1
$14.99

VOL. 20: ALL OUT WAR PART ONE TP
ISBN: 978-1-60706-882-2
$14.99

VOL. 21: ALL OUT WAR PART TWO TP
ISBN: 978-1-63215-030-1
$14.99

VOL. 22: A NEW BEGINNING TP
ISBN: 978-1-63215-041-7
$14.99

VOL. 1: SPANISH EDITION TP
ISBN: 978-1-60706-797-9
$14.99

VOL. 2: SPANISH EDITION TP
ISBN: 978-1-60706-845-7
$14.99

VOL. 3: SPANISH EDITION TP
ISBN: 978-1-60706-883-9
$14.99

VOL. 4: SPANISH EDITION TP
ISBN: 978-1-63215-035-6
$14.99

COMPENDIUM TP, VOL. 1
ISBN: 978-1-60706-076-5
$59.99

COMPENDIUM TP, VOL. 2
ISBN: 978-1-60706-596-8
$59.99

BOOK ONE HC
ISBN: 978-1-58240-619-0
$34.99

BOOK TWO HC
ISBN: 978-1-58240-698-5
$34.99

BOOK THREE HC
ISBN: 978-1-58240-825-5
$34.99

BOOK FOUR HC
ISBN: 978-1-60706-000-0
$34.99

BOOK FIVE HC
ISBN: 978-1-60706-171-7
$34.99

BOOK SIX HC
ISBN: 978-1-60706-327-8
$34.99

BOOK SEVEN HC
ISBN: 978-1-60706-439-8
$34.99

BOOK EIGHT HC
ISBN: 978-1-60706-593-7
$34.99

BOOK NINE HC
ISBN: 978-1-60706-798-6
$34.99

BOOK TEN HC
ISBN: 978-1-63215-034-9
$34.99

BOOK ELEVEN HC
ISBN: 978-1-63215-271-8
$34.99

CLONE
VOLUME 4
FOURTH GENERATION

VOL. 1: FIRST GENERATION TP
ISBN: 978-1-60706-683-5
$14.99

VOL. 2: SECOND GENERATION TP
ISBN: 978-1-60706-830-3
$14.99

VOL. 3: THIRD GENERATION TP
ISBN: 978-1-60706-939-3
$14.99

VOL. 4: FOURTH GENERATION TP
ISBN: 978-1-63215-036-3
$14.99

GHOSTED
VOLUME THREE · DEATH WISH

VOL. 1: HAUNTED HEIST TP
ISBN: 978-1-60706-836-5
$9.99

VOL. 2: BOOKS OF THE DEAD TP
ISBN: 978-1-63215-046-2
$12.99

VOL. 3: DEATH WISH TP
ISBN: 978-1-63215-051-6
$12.99

MANIFEST DESTINY
VOLUME 2: AMPHIBIA & INSECTA

VOL. 1: FLORA & FAUNA TP
ISBN: 978-1-60706-982-9
$9.99

VOL. 2: AMPHIBIA & INSECTA TP
ISBN: 978-1-63215-052-3
$14.99

THIEF OF THIEVES
VOLUME 4
"THE HIT LIST."

VOL. 1: "I QUIT."
ISBN: 978-1-60706-592-0
$14.99

VOL. 2: "HELP ME."
ISBN: 978-1-60706-676-7
$14.99

VOL. 3: "VENICE."
ISBN: 978-1-60706-844-0
$14.99

VOL. 4: "THE HIT LIST."
ISBN: 978-1-63215-037-0
$14.99

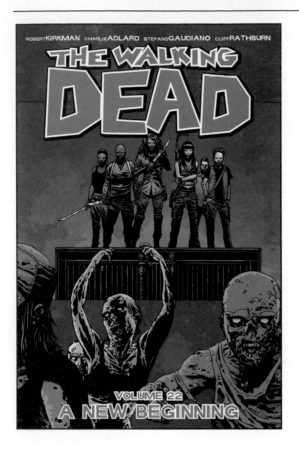

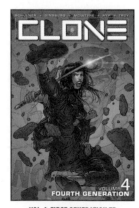

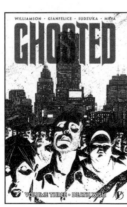

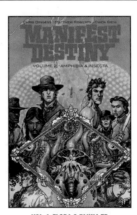

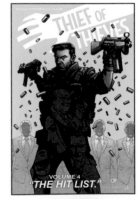